Towards Good Lighting for the Stage

Towards Good Lighting for the Stage: Aesthetic Theory for Theatrical Lighting Design explores the theoretical underpinnings of effective lighting design from conceptualization to live performance.

Through an investigation of the author's own aesthetic point of view—grounded in a broad investigation of art and design that blends pop culture and fine art, theory, and practice—this book documents the author's thinking on the design process to fill the unexplored gap between an aesthetic philosophy and its expression in composition. Redefinitions of the artist, artwork, and spectator link beauty and artistic efficacy to arrive at a set of principles for assessment that demand that contemporary lighting design surpass utilitarian visibility to become a vital part of the total artwork that is a theatrical production. Inspired by the movements of the broader art and design worlds of the mid-19th century through the present day—citing influences as diverse as Jennifer Tipton, Lois Tyson, Dieter Rams, and Dave Hickey—this book charts a course from the artistic team's dramaturgical work to a solo studio concept to the tech table.

Engaging and wide-ranging, *Towards Good Lighting for the Stage* synthesizes years of cross-disciplinary research and case studies of the author's own work into provocative reading for practitioners of lighting design, advanced students, and academics, as well as those interested in connecting theatrical practice, aesthetic theory, and visual art.

Marcus Doshi designs lighting and scenery for opera and theatre. His work has been seen on and off Broadway, extensively at most major regional theatre and opera companies in the USA, and at major venues across five continents. He is a graduate of Wabash College and the Yale School of Drama and is a Professor of Theatre at Northwestern University, Evanston and Chicago, USA.

Towards Good Lighting for the Stage

Aesthetic Theory for Theatrical Lighting Design

Marcus Doshi

NEW YORK AND LONDON

Cover image: Michael Pennington and Jake Horowitz in *King Lear*, Theatre for a New Audience, 2013, photograph by Carol Rosegg

First published 2023
by Routledge
605 Third Avenue, New York, NY 10158

and by Routledge
4 Park Square, Milton Park, Abingdon, Oxon, OX14 4RN

Routledge is an imprint of the Taylor & Francis Group, an informa business

© 2023 Marcus Doshi

The right of Marcus Doshi to be identified as author of this work has been asserted in accordance with sections 77 and 78 of the Copyright, Designs and Patents Act 1988.

All rights reserved. No part of this book may be reprinted or reproduced or utilised in any form or by any electronic, mechanical, or other means, now known or hereafter invented, including photocopying and recording, or in any information storage or retrieval system, without permission in writing from the publishers.

Trademark notice: Product or corporate names may be trademarks or registered trademarks, and are used only for identification and explanation without intent to infringe.

Library of Congress Cataloging-in-Publication Data
Names: Doshi, Marcus, author.
Title: Towards good lighting for the stage / Marcus Doshi.
Description: New York, NY : Routledge, 2023. | Includes bibliographical references and index.
Identifiers: LCCN 2022023966 (print) | LCCN 2022023967 (ebook) | ISBN 9781032073323 (hardback) | ISBN 9781032073316 (paperback) | ISBN 9781003206460 (ebook)
Subjects: LCSH: Stage lighting. | Theaters--Stage-setting and scenery.
Classification: LCC PN2091.E4 D67 2023 (print) | LCC PN2091.E4 (ebook) | DDC 792.02/5--dc23/eng/20220914
LC record available at https://lccn.loc.gov/2022023966
LC ebook record available at https://lccn.loc.gov/2022023967

ISBN: 978-1-032-07332-3 (hbk)
ISBN: 978-1-032-07331-6 (pbk)
ISBN: 978-1-003-20646-0 (ebk)

DOI: 10.4324/9781003206460

Typeset in Times New Roman
by KnowledgeWorks Global Ltd.

For Cole and Lavinia, who are the lights of my life.

Contents

Acknowledgments viii
Foreword x

Introduction 1
1 Beauty 10
2 Artist/Artwork 29
3 The Spectator 58
4 Theatre 72
5 Theatrical Abstraction 93
6 On Design 118
7 The Box 138
8 Praxis 160
Coda: So, Now What? 188

Index 190

Acknowledgments

This book represents the culmination of ideas from nearly three decades of thinking about and making theatre. As such, there are a number of people to acknowledge for helping me along my path. First are my teachers: beginning with Brian Waldron, who introduced me to philosophy in high school, and Cheryl Hughes at Wabash College, who introduced me to aesthetics. Also at Wabash were Doug Calisch and Greg Huber, who welcomed me into the Art Department. They laid the groundwork for my study of craft and opened my eyes to a world of art I had no idea existed. To the faculty of the Theatre Department at Wabash, I owe an unrepayable debt of gratitude for their patience, dedication, and encouragement. They taught me to love the theatre and that design really was a thing I could do: Dwight Watson, Laura Connors, Michael Abbott, Lonna Wilke, and, especially, James Fisher, who also taught me to love writing. My gratitude continues to the faculty of the Yale School of Drama who not only met me with equal patience, dedication, and encouragement but inspired me to become a teacher myself: Ming Cho Lee, Michael Yeargan, Jane Greenwood, Jess Goldstein, David Budries, Ru-Jun Wang and, especially, Stephen Strawbridge and Jennifer Tipton. I also would like to thank a few informal teachers who's early influence in my career taught me much of what I know about professional practice: Roy Hine and Michael Higgins, from the Wagon Wheel Theatre, where I cut my teeth, and Robert Wierzel, whom I assisted for many years.

Thanks to Northwestern University for the research leave on which I wrote a fair share of this text and to the office of the Northwestern Provost for a Provost Grant for Research in Humanities, Social Sciences, and the Arts. Never a more talented group of theatre-makers, scholars, and teachers were assembled, and I thank my colleagues for their patience and cheering, particularly E. Patrick Johnson, Tracy Davis, Rives Collins, Henry Godinez, Dassia Posner, Rámon Rivera-Servera, and my design faculty colleagues Linda Roethke, Todd Rosenthal, Ana Kuzmanić, Andrew Boyce, and Eric Southern. Equal thanks goes to my students, past and present, for teaching me as much as I hope I have taught them. I would also like to thank Northwestern Copyright Librarian Liz Hamilton for her advice and Susanna Caulkins of the Northwestern Searle Center for Advancing Learning and Teaching for unwittingly planting the seed that became this book.

I would like to acknowledge the theatre photographers who's work appears in this book: Alan Alabastro, Joanne Bouknight, Michael Brosilow, Gerry Goodstein, Jenny Graham, Lynn Lane, Liz Lauren, Joan Marcus, Mike Ritter, Carol Rosegg, Richard Termine, and Cory Weaver. For their invaluable assistance in helping source images, I thank Hehn-Chu Ann and Cassandra Peters of the Dieter Rams Archiv im Museum Angewandte Kunst Frankfurt, Richard Beacham, Melanie Broussalian of Los Angeles Opera, Ted DeLong and Freddie Baldonado of Oregon Shakespeare Festival, Sophie Lovell, Brian Mitchell of Houston Grand Opera, and Stian Nybru of Norsk Folkemuseum.

Much gratitude goes to my stewards at Routledge: Editor Stacey Walker, Editorial Assistant Lucia Accorsi, Production Editor Eleonora Kouneni and Project Manager Riya Bhattacharya, all of whom have the patience of saints. Thanks also to Jackie Fox for logistical and organizational support and Liz Laurie for help with citations. Special thanks to Justin Townsend for his generosity of time and thought in responding with deep insight to an early draft. To early reader and editor Skye Strauss, I send boundless gratitude and respect for her provoking questions, thoughtful suggestions, structural advice, and unsparing machete for the extraneous. Her input brought much-needed clarity to the text, structure, and arguments. Her imprint is everywhere, and this book simply would not be what it is without her. We should all be so lucky to see our students become such valuable colleagues.

Finally, thanks to my family: To my parents, Linda and Bipin Doshi, for making a home where growing up to be a lighting designer made perfect sense (if only to me), to my brother, Robert, for setting an example I have always tried to live up to, and, for their unbounded affection, to my children, Cole and Lavinia, who—who knows?—might become lighting designers themselves someday.

Foreword

Welcome to all readers. If ever you doubted the fact that lighting for the stage is an art, this book should convince you that light created to tell a story through composition in space and time onstage is indeed a work of art. You are about to begin a journey that may possibly thrill you. I know of no other book that will so thoroughly lead you to a place that makes it easier to think and talk about the art of lighting the stage; not the nuts and bolts—not the techniques, not the craft—but instead the theories of art and beauty that form thick bonds of comparison between works of art such as paintings, photographs, music, sculpture, poetry AND the lighting of a production put on a stage. Marcus Doshi has a profound need for finding ways to do the impossible—talk about lighting the stage in terms of the art that it makes, not the fixtures and rules that it takes to make that art. I know from my own experience that it is almost impossible to talk about light without falling back on a discussion of the method used to make choices rather than the aesthetics used to shape those choices. In this book, Marcus explores many ideas about and ways of defining art and in doing so makes these ideas available for use in making sense of what one should be thinking about as one approaches the lighting of a new theater production. He quotes many people who use many different methods of defining art in a multitude of ways. His research is deep and fascinating.

Of the many ideas that are explored, I feel that what comes first and foremost for Marcus is a sense of "beauty," as beautifully expressed by Dave Hickey in *Enter the Dragon: On the Vernacular of Beauty*. Beauty can be horrifying, even terrifying, but it is an important element in defining a work of art. It is beauty that engages the audience. It is beauty that holds our attention, our imagination, and our interest. It is the beauty of composition in space and time that shows how light binds together the bits and pieces of structure—architecture and action—that tell the story of the event. When it has all been knitted together in just the right way, it is indeed a thing of beauty—and it is a work of art.

Marcus is a very brainy, intellectual man. He is also a brilliant lighting designer. The most important thing about this book is that it leads to a discussion of many of the productions that he has already lit. His ideas about the art of lighting are informed by what he has already accomplished and, therefore, what he is able to discuss in advance of the next time he begins thinking about the light in a production. His work is dense; his talking about it is rich in detail. He shows the readers connections between one work and the next and subsequently constructs a wonderful tapestry of stage lighting expressed by words that *almost* make the lighting visible to the reader.

Marcus has spent a good amount of time as a lighting designer and as a teacher of lighting for the stage. As a teacher, one strives to find the best word that will stimulate one's student(s) to think more carefully, more fruitfully, and more truthfully about the choice of ideas in lighting a play. The last section of this book is a wonderful display of words used successfully to declare the need for a certain kind of light in a certain situation. It is wide-ranging and covers just about every aspect of the many ways we make theater through lighting. It is Marcus at his best. Enjoy.

Jennifer Tipton

Introduction

Ralph Macchio, *The Karate Kid Part III*, 1989
AA Film Archive/Alamy Stock Photo

DOI: 10.4324/9781003206460-1

Theory

The role of philosophy in society is like that of art: to help us understand the human experience. Philosophy helps us bring order to chaos by posing theories helpful for understanding difficult topics. It also creates taxonomies by setting forth general principles for understanding a particular subject, phenomenon, or field of inquiry.[1] For me, lighting design is a difficult topic and I turn to theory to make sense of—to decode in a way—my own practice. I do not know how to do that without trying to understand lighting design, and theatre writ large, within the context of the broader art world. I must understand what I think an artist is if I am to understand whether a lighting designer is an artist. Likewise, I must understand the same about artwork and the spectator if I am to contemplate their manifestations in theatre. Only then can I really investigate the practice of lighting design. Time and time again, in my own work, the same thing has held true: theoretical insights have led to concrete production choices and a concrete production choices have led to theoretical insights. In this way, to paraphrase D. Soyini Madison, my practice is my theory and my theory is my practice.[2] I often tell my bemused students at Northwestern University, where I teach, that for the same reason the eponymous Karate Kid Daniel LaRusso had to learn to paint the fence and wax the car before he could learn karate, one has to know the theoretical building blocks of lighting—both practical and philosophical—before one can begin to design. As Plato would say, enlightenment makes it hard to go back into the cave.[3] At first glance, this might seem like an awfully circuitous path to get to lekos and cross light, but if one is not interested in aesthetic theory, then I do not know how one can be a good designer for the stage.

Lighting as a component of the art form of theatre—like components of all art forms—is obliged by its very definition to evolve. This is the artistic impulse; there is always further to go and there are always new boundaries to be pushed, pulled, and wrestled with in the unwieldy mire of making a show. But pushing the form forward is not the only thing. Why do we do it? How do we do it? What do we bring to the lighting table in dark rooms for too, too many hours—day after day—that makes the work good? What exactly is good? Beyond the rare mention in newspaper notices, there is very little thoughtful dialog about what makes good lighting for the stage, especially from the point of view of aesthetics. There are tomes upon tomes devoted to the subject of stage lighting—especially the technical aspects—but rare is the one that critically investigates, from a practitioner's position, the work as an applied art form and the myriad influences—cultural, historical, artistic, and philosophical—that find their way into the designer's mind in the heat of tech. This is the motivation for this book. Granted, it is a largely subjective endeavor, but one that should be undertaken in order to push the form forward.

Theatre is a space of collaboration, and an essential component of being an effective collaborative artist is a facility in synthetic thought: the ability to take disparate ideas, make connections between them, and come up with a point of view. It will come as no surprise, then, that the opinions argued in this book are the result of the same process of synthetic thought brought to bear on all the ideas I have encountered over the last quarter-century or so. Likewise, I am shamelessly indebted to every artist, scholar, and student I have encountered as well, as they have all influenced me in one way or another—that is how it works, right? These are the shoulders on which I stand: books and articles read, art seen and made, discussions with students, and many a late-night conversation with collaborators over a drink at the bar long after the rehearsal day is over. In many ways, writing this book has been a revisitation of those influences because, of course, one does not often cry "eureka!" on a barstool, conscious of a moment of profound revelation that causes a permanent aesthetic shift. I find that scrutinizing myself through the lens of my influences has allowed me to say, oh yeah ... that is why I feel this way.

Pedagogy

Wabash College, my small liberal arts college in central Indiana, had a tiny theatre department. If memory serves, I was one of three, total, generalist majors in my class. It was there where I discovered what theatre could be, and, in the classroom, it was primarily through the lens of history and theory. The ideas of the thinkers I studied were little burrs that attached themselves to me, sometimes overtly and sometimes with the sneaky malignancy of a long festering disease, only to reveal themselves as burrs later in life. Then I went to graduate school at the Yale School of Drama and learned how to be a stage designer. After that, I moved to New York as one does, went into practice, and suddenly a decade and a half went by of make, make, make: make shows, make a living, make a career. However, those burrs did not go away, and, at some point, they all started demanding attention. I wanted to investigate them. To pick them off, to identify them, to map them to my aesthetic choices, and carry that insight into the classroom with my students when I began to teach.

This desire to understand my influences was partially a selfish exercise and partially because, in my first years at Northwestern, I noticed what soon became an alarming lack of exposure to and study of dramatic and aesthetic theory—the big ideas that shape, broadly, how we make art and, specifically, how we make theatre—among the graduate design student population. Anecdote suggests this is not specific to Northwestern but to graduate stage design training in general (there was very little in my training). Broadly speaking, the students lacked a sophisticated understanding of key 19th, 20th, and early 21st-century art and design movements and how those movements (eventually) manifest themselves in theatre and impact our current practice. They were, therefore, unable to contextualize their individual points of view as artists within the larger aesthetic world.

This was really scary for three reasons:

The first was pedagogical: in order to critique largely subjective work, we all need a common language that will allow us to at least quasi-objectify what we can. A common language that will do that is a language based on a shared cultural understanding. Without that understanding, the language doesn't exist, and the critique loses efficacy. For instance, if everyone knows what semiotic analysis is, then it becomes a common language that everyone can try to apply to the (self)critique of a work. It does not solve all of the problems we face when evaluating subjective material, but at least if everyone uses the same assessment techniques, the conversation can be more effective.

The second was aesthetic: just as graduate students in physical chemistry rely on theorems that are already accepted to be true, artists stand on the shoulders of those who have pushed the envelope of artistic expression in previous generations. Even though there are few rules beyond the principles of design and composition, there are precedents with established effectiveness and students can either *waste* time rediscovering the precedents or *spend* time informing their own work by studying the precedents. This seemed like a no-brainer to me. But in the world of stage design training, history and theory often take a back seat (if they are let on the bus at all) to practice.

The third was practical: theatre artists are collaborative artists and when we make decisions—when we develop a point of view—we have a responsibility to our collaborators to be articulate about our reasoning. We must be prepared to either to explain or to defend it, even if it instinctually works. "The vocabulary we have developed for our production dictates that the backing should be red" is better than "the backing should be red because that would be cool."[4]

So, I made a class investigating ideas from dramatic and aesthetic theory with a specific bent toward how they have, or could, influence choices in lighting for the stage.

Manifestos

One thing that delights me to no end in the work of the thinkers, the burrs, is the constant occurrence—identified as such, or not—of manifestos. Artists of all ilk saying:

> This. Is. What. I. Believe.

And some of them believed so strongly that they died because of it.

In the class, I asked my students to write their own manifestos. And then I thought that I had better put my money where my mouth is and write one myself.

So, then, this is what I believe:

Good lighting for the stage

Lighting for the stage is an ephemeral and temporal form. It exists in four dimensions, is as much music as it is image, and is made manifest only in the encounter with material objects.

It is an abstract form that exists on the spectrum between pseudo-realistic and purely expressionistic. It is authentic and evocative rather than realistic; it is theatrical.

Lighting for the stage is design. Design implies function. It is obliged to interact in a well-structured way, and it must simultaneously be in dialog with the dramaturgical, the physical, the metatextual, the visual, and the rhythmic—the lighting designer must always and at once make, look, evaluate, and adapt.

Therefore, good lighting for the stage …

> Is collaborative,
> Is constructed with dramatic intent,
> Tells the story,
> Follows compositional principles (both visual and musical),
> Evolves over time,
> Confines itself to that which is essential (precise, minimal, and unobtrusive),
> Is magical,
> Is thorough,
> Is innovative (it pushes the form forward),
> And is beautiful.

Foundations

I wish I could name all of the influences on my aesthetic, but there are five major ones that I wish to acknowledge specifically: Jennifer Tipton, Lighting Designer and my teacher and mentor at Yale; Lois Tyson, literary critical theorist and Professor Emerita of English at Grand Valley State University; Dieter Rams, the former director of design for the Braun Corporation and designer for Vitsoe, whose sensibilities influenced so much of mid-20th-century product design; Arin Arbus, a longtime collaborator who has directed countless productions I have designed; and Dave Hickey, the art critic, former Professor of English at the University of Nevada Las Vegas and Distinguished Professor of Art Criticism at the University of New Mexico, and "art world flame thrower," a title worth aspiring to.[5] Their aesthetics and critical investigations have profoundly influenced mine.

While this book takes a pretty deep dive into other various influences from art movements from the mid-19th century to now, considering it a definitive explanation of modern, postmodern, and contemporary art would be a mistake. I write about these artists and these moments because somehow, at some point, I collided with them and they shifted my trajectory a bit. Sometimes, I hit only a corner of an idea and that corner may not be the entirety of a movement, but it is the corner that is important to me. Likewise, it would be wise to remember that the outcomes of these collisions—when I actually try to put them into practice—are all done through the lens of "what does this mean for my choices when making a lighting design?" So, for example, within the rubric of "realism," there are many kinds of realism, but the salient one for me has to do with the (antiquated) notion of realism in stage design (blergh).

Much of the work cited here is from the Eurocentric canon of performance and aesthetic theory. This is because this is the tradition in which I was taught and in which the industry still does much of its work. However, there are other, more diverse, influences on my work. One is that I am bi-racial and grew up in a household that was a mishmash of two cultural influences (my father is Indian from Gujarat and my mother is of Western European descent and grew up in West-Central Alabama). I remember sitting on the floor next to my parent's record player staring at an Indian miniature mica painting while repeatedly listening to the cast album of Godspell through the earphones, and both have influenced me as an artist. This is but one small example of how my aesthetics are informed by both cultures. I have been lucky that a nontrivial segment of my work has taken me around the world and exposed me to many different geographies and cultures: I have worked all over Europe, the Middle East, North Africa, India, Australia, and South-East Asia. For example, it is impossible to design for traditional Khmer dance without understanding at least some of the aesthetic and cultural history of the form. Taken together, these understandings feed my evolving aesthetic. Putting my multi-cultural and globally informed aesthetic into practice in my lighting designs may only be moving the needle away from a strictly Eurocentric aesthetic in a subtle way, but at least the needle is moving.

Spectrum of aesthetic virtue

This book is predicated on accepting the idea that there is such a thing as good art and that it can be readily distinguished from bad art. This simple notion is essential because, without this concept as a foundation, I think that there is no basis for criticism of art, no ability to identify salient characteristics of art, and no rationale to determine the efficacy of an artwork; for either artist or spectator. The absence of judgment would render all art meaningless for me because for art to have meaning, it must do something. What it is doing need not be complex. For example, the artist wants the spectator to feel a particular emotion or think about a particular thing, and the spectator does. By virtue of doing something, art can either do it well, or poorly, or not at all. If it is possible for it to do something well, it must be possible to do something badly. Thus, there are good versions and bad versions of art. Now, since what the artwork should be doing comes from the artist's vision, so by extension, there must also be good and bad artists; presumably, it takes a good artist to make good artwork. Furthermore, as I will argue, the spectator is responsible for meaning-making upon encountering the artwork, so there must be good and bad spectators too. Phew.

That art can be good or bad is not a novel concept by a long shot. In his 1938 book The Principles of Art, British philosopher R.G. Collingwood writes, "The definition of any given thing is also the definition of a good thing of that kind: for a thing that is good in its kind is only a thing which possesses the attributes of that kind. To call things good and bad is to imply success and failure."[6] To come at successes and failures, I first want to situate the words 'good' and 'bad' on a spectrum. That spectrum, let us say, is bounded on one end by 'not at all' and on the other end by 'perfect.' So, in a line, from left to right, one has 'not at all,' 'bad,' 'good,' and 'perfect.' In the case of an artwork, if it meets the salient characteristics of an artwork (as addressed in "Artist/Artwork") and is determined to have efficacy at doing whatever it is meant to be doing, then that artwork is successful and therefore lands somewhere on the right of the divide between 'bad' and 'good.' (I should note that I think 'not at all' and 'perfect' are concepts and whereas the second is likely unattainable, the first all too often is.) This correctly implies that systems of criteria are necessary for these determinations and that art, if it can be good, can also always be better. Why else would we do previews? Transitively, assessments of the efficacy of the artist, of the spectator, and consequently of a production can be made against this spectrum as well, each with their own systems of criteria.

To complicate this, however, I readily acknowledge that because spectators are involved and because spectators are people with all the attendant histories, backgrounds, and competencies they bring to bear, assessments of works of art involve individual subjectivities and cannot be entirely accounted for by objective standards. De gustibus non est disputandum, as the Roman said; there is no disputing taste. Therefore, any consideration of criteria must necessarily contend with both the objective and the subjective.

Structure

This book is divided into eight chapters. The first three are largely concerned with aesthetic theory in order to provide a scholarly framework for my thinking about lighting design. In "Beauty," I explore beauty, culture, and systems of critique that identify what can be considered beautiful. This discussion is critical because it is not only an entrée into my aesthetic—beauty informs every choice I make—but also because beauty forces us to engage and is, therefore, the most important characteristic of an artwork. In the second and third chapters, "Artist/Artwork" and "The Spectator," I define those terms to scaffold a more specific discussion in chapter four, "Theatre," about how these ideas manifest in live performance. In my experience, these concepts have everything to do with lighting design for the stage. The latter, practice-based chapters are built on these foundational concepts.

As the book continues, I narrow my lens to the stage—making liberal use of case studies of my own work, as well as continued scholarly influences, as I delve into what lies behind my manifesto and work out how I articulate my aesthetic in production. The fifth chapter, "Theatrical Abstraction," addresses style: first airing my gripes with realism/naturalism's grip on much of contemporary Eurocentric stage design and then asserting abstraction as the true language of the stage. The sixth chapter, "On Design," breaks down the components of good design and investigates the dueling influences of modernism and postmodernism on my own work. The last two chapters focus exclusively on lighting design for the stage. The seventh chapter, "The Box," invents a theoretical container for the intent of the design and the choices that delimit its boundaries. Finally, the eighth chapter, "Praxis," is about the time spent in the theatre creating work and addressing the logic behind turning lights on and off. This is followed by a short coda, "So, Now What?" which advances some hopes for the future of theatre. It has been a delightful path of rediscovering myself and a sort of back engineering of my aesthetic point of view. I encourage you to go down the rabbit hole of works cited, to make your own synthetic connections, draw your own conclusions, and feed your own point of view.

The terms theatre, production, show, and performance recur repeatedly in the following pages. I do not mean these to be limiting. When I write 'theatre' it is a convenient stand-in meant to be representational of a broad spectrum of things made for the stage—plays, musicals, operas, dances, and certain pieces of performance art—that are essentially a group of people telling stories in front of another group of people. If I need to narrow a discussion to a particular form, I will do so explicitly. Sometimes I will write 'the theatre,' meaning the place where theatre happens (like the stage) or the broad concept of 'theatre' itself ('the theatre of Ancient Greece,' for example). The term 'creative team' refers to those artists who are generally responsible for conceiving concepts for individual productions—the director and designers. There are others—writers, composers, choreographers, dramaturgs, conductors, and performers—that can also be members of the creative team, situation depending. With these, context will be your guide. When I write of a 'production' or a 'show,' that means an iteration of a piece of work for the stage (a production of *King Lear*, for example), whereas a 'performance' is a single instance of a production. I will use the term 'light plot' to refer to the technical drawings for a lighting design, whereas in other parts of the world, the term 'lighting plan' is used. Likewise, I will use the term 'cueing' to refer to the time in theatre when lighting looks are created, which is sometimes referred to as 'plotting.' Ditto for 'light cue' and 'lighting state.' Lastly, when appropriate, the titles for productions I have designed will be followed by a parenthetical notation of the producer and date, with further details in an endnote.

Finally, if you find the photograph of the Karate Kid at the beginning of this introduction destabilizing, then it is having the intended effect. I want this book to disrupt how you think about lighting design. So, I think approaching this text from a place of foundational uncertainty is a good thing. Here, at the end of this introduction, I also offer an important caveat, which you would be well advised to carry through your reading: This is not meant to be a how-to-light-a-show manual. It is an investigation of what influences me as an artist and storyteller and why I make the choices I make. It is only my voice, one among a multitude of extraordinary and talented designers. I will only offer what I think and why I think it is important, and the rest is up to you.

Notes

1. *Oxford English Dictionary Online*, s.v. "philosophy, n," accessed April 22, 2021, www.oed.com/viewdictionaryentry/Entry/142505.
2. Soyini D. Madison, *Critical Ethnography: Method, Ethics, and Performance* (Thousand Oaks, CA: SAGE Publications, 2012), 18, accessed January 7, 2021, ProQuest Ebook Central.
3. Plato, "The Simile of the Cave," in *Theatre and Performance Design: A Reader in Scenography*, ed. Jane Collins and Andrew Nisbit, trans. H.D.P. Lee (London: Routledge, 2010), 17.
4. Significant parts of this text appeared in my critical account of developing the following class, "Training Artists to Take a Stand: Theatre 450—Dramatic and Aesthetic Theory for Stage Designers," during a Northwestern Searle Center for Advanced Learning and Teaching Fellowship.
5. Jennie Yabroff, "Reenter the Dragon: An Art-World Flamethrower Returns from Exile," *Newsweek* 153, no. 12 (2009): 55.
6. R.G. Collingwood, *The Principles of Art* (Oxford: Clarendon Press, 1938), 280.

1 Beauty

Untitled (*Falling Man*), 2001

Photograph
AP Photo/Richard Drew

DOI: 10.4324/9781003206460-2

A Gordian Knot

Why do I consider beauty the most important characteristic of an artwork? Because beauty is the element that demands attention, demands that the spectator not only look at but engage actively with an artwork. Hickey writes in his essay "Enter the Dragon: On the Vernacular of Beauty"—a work so essential to the formation of my own point of view that I will return to it again and again and again—"In images, beauty is the agency that causes visual pleasure in the beholder, and, since pleasure is the true occasion for looking at anything, any theory of images that is not grounded in the pleasure of the beholder begs the question of art's efficacy and dooms itself to inconsequence!"[1] Without beauty and its attendant pleasure response, there is no compulsion to engage, and without engagement, everything else that might be present in the artwork is meaningless because it doesn't even have the chance to be offered to the spectator. Beauty is, according to Hickey, "the single direct route ... from the image to the individual."[2]

The notion of beauty and the notion of artwork are so tied together that to define one necessarily begs the definition of the other. In an attempt to cleave this Gordian Knot, I will confine myself for now to beauty, as a conceptual conceit, and to the beautiful, as the manifestation of that conceit in an artwork, saving a discussion of the other characteristics of an artwork for "Artist/Artwork." Furthermore, the notion of beauty is so critical to my own aesthetic point of view that it is the foundation on which all the rest of my assertions about art, theatre, and design are built—making it equally critical to understanding this book.

The efficacy of beauty

There are as many different pathways to beauty as there are definitions. On the one hand, Russian director Vsevolod Meyerhold demands that "We must realize that the beauty of Ford's car is a direct outcome of its efficiency and reliability .... we must understand clearly what we mean by beauty and reject all beauty that is not utilitarian."[3] And, on the other hand, Virginia Woolf writes, "The beauty of the world which is so soon to perish, has two edges, one of laughter, one of anguish, cutting the heart asunder."[4] Then there is always Plato: "Beauty is certainly a soft, smooth, slippery thing, and therefore of a nature which easily slips in and permeates our souls."[5] It is an oldie but a goodie—beauty is a gateway drug.

But is pleasure the only desired emotional response to something beautiful? Perhaps not. Fear, too, is an important emotional response solicited by the beautiful. Edmund Burke, in his book *A Philosophical Enquiry into the Origin of Our Ideas of the Sublime and Beautiful*, sets the ideas of the sublime and the beautiful as counterpoints in art. In it, he posits that

> Whatever is fitted in any sort to excite the ideas of pain and danger, that is to say, whatever is in any sort terrible, or is conversant about terrible objects, or operates in a manner analogous to terror, is a source of the *sublime*; that is, it is productive of the strongest emotion with the mind is capable of feeling (italics in original).[6]

He might object to my using his definition of the sublime *within* a definition of the beautiful (instead of using it as a counterpoint), but what is important about this is that the feeling of sublime terror creates an emotional response that has the ability to engage a viewer. Fear is the emotion I feel when I watch Ridley Scott's 1979 movie *Alien*. This movie scared the living daylights out of me when I saw it for the first time at way too tender an age. Even at 47, that feeling comes back and I have to check the closet before I go to bed even though if I looked hard enough I could probably see the zipper in the creature's costume. Yet, I keep going back because the sublime terror demands my attention.

To prove that Burke's 260-year-old treatise on fear still holds true, I cite a 2012 study in the journal *Emotion* in which the authors sought to understand which emotions are responsible for sublime experiences when viewing works of art by testing the effects of fear, happiness, and general psychological arousal when viewing abstract art. They conclude that "Fear was the only factor found to significantly increase sublime feelings."[7] They speculate that it could have to do with fear's relationship to our fight or flight instinct, "Our data suggest that art's allure may instead be a byproduct of one's tendency to be alarmed by such environmental features as novelty, ambiguity, and the fantastic. Artists may be tapping into this natural sense when their work takes people's breath away."[8]

Pleasure and fear are not exclusive. Rather, I think of them as coequal instigators of attention, and while one artwork might be exclusively focused on a pleasure response and another on a fear response, I think they can operate in parallel. For example, the sublime terror it instills in me is one of the reasons I find Richard Drew's photograph of a man falling from the World Trade Center in the aftermath of the 9/11 attacks beautiful. The grotesque, the painful, and the pornographic can all be beautiful to me, but only insofar as it is in service to the intent of the artist and, therefore, the artwork (otherwise, it is not sublime, it is just gratuitous). I also find Drew's photograph beautiful from a formal perspective. My pleasure response to its composition *almost* makes me forget the content. It takes my breath away on many different levels.

Now, some groundwork needs to be laid concerning the relationship between culture and beauty and what methodologies are available to get at the beautiful. This is because analyses making sense of an artwork's aesthetic and non-aesthetic characteristics, broadly speaking, can impact our understanding of what is beautiful as spectators and how to make the beautiful as artists. This requires understanding the components of an artwork and applying multiple methods of critical analysis from the most objective through the most subjective and those viewed through a particular lens. Furthermore, the cultures in which the artist presently operates give their artworks both content and context and provide boundaries against which the artworks can push, leading to innovation in aesthetic and non-aesthetic traits.

Culture and context

Simply put, the beautiful is a collection of preferred aesthetic and non-aesthetic traits. But preferred by whom? And how do we discern those traits? I contend that it all has to do with the culture(s) within which the artwork is created and the culture(s) of its spectators. Cultures can be determined by myriad factors. So, once the bounds of a particular culture are identified, regardless of whether or not art is a defining characteristic of those bounds, one can begin to identify that culture's aesthetic traits and traditions. Thus, by surveying a culture's artwork, commonalities can be discerned and categorized. And the more one knows about a culture, the more acute one's discernment of that culture's aesthetic traits and traditions can be. In this way, by identifying a culture's preferred aesthetic traits, it is possible to identify what that culture typically finds beautiful.

To begin, I must first explain culture as I mean it. To do so, I draw from a number of sources and create a description of something that functions as a tangible group of people, a collection of an individual's experiences, and an evolving abstract concept. The philosopher James O. Young describes a culture as "identifiable groups of people [that] have certain traits (beliefs, customs, achievements, and so on) which distinguish them from other groups."[9] For example, a group might share the same religion, another might share the same coming-of-age rite, and another might share the same architectural philosophy and practice. All of these ideas are examples of what one could call "big ideas." I think that a culture can be defined, or better yet, understood, as the history of a group of people's big ideas, both in terms of abstract thought and concrete achievement. These ideas accumulate and bind people together to form a culture.

In the present tense, culture can be seen as a living breathing organism made up of many different organisms. This asks us to speak in plural: cultures. Tyson clarifies when she states that

> culture is a process, not a product; it is a lived experience, not a fixed definition. More precisely, a culture is a collection of interactive cultures, each of which is growing and changing, each of which is

constituted at any given moment in time by the intersection of gender, race, ethnicity, sexual orientation, socioeconomic class, occupation, and similar factors that contribute to the experience of its members.[10]

Each new idea or experience that is introduced, rebelled against, or subsumed by a particular culture catalyzes a redefinition, expansion, or contraction of some sort, the magnitude and trajectory of which in relation to the thing causing the disruption. A new *Star Wars* movie shifts culture one way and two planes slamming into the World Trade Center in another. In both instances, those are new big ideas that alter certain cultures.

Because a culture is comprised of a group of people, it is reasonable to say that an individual (or yet another group of individuals) can occupy many different cultures at one time. A contemporary example would be a high school kid who likes to skate, plays the sax in the school band, is queer, and is a competitive swimmer. They are part of multiple niche cultures—skate, band, queer, and athletic—and for better or worse for them (if their experience is anything like mine), the broader high school culture. In this regard, their culture is a collection of highly individualized experiences from various different micro-cultures embedded within or coexisting alongside one (or more) larger macro-cultures. A taxonomy of this would read identity (individual), micro-culture (small group), and macro-culture (big group). The aforementioned notion of big ideas still holds water as a defining factor for micro-cultures because "big" is relative. Our exemplary teenager's identities will also, presumably, iterate as they encounter more and different cultures and experiences, and they will likely, because of it, grow up to be a very interesting person. This also points to the need to understand and respect the various cultural identities of cocreators of a production—figuring out the commonalities and tension points, and what that means for communication, is part of the hard work of collaboration. Each artist's context informs their work, and that impacts the final outcome because everyone, regardless of their cultural identities, has to agree, more or less, on production choices.

In literary terms, context is the parts immediately preceding or following a particular unit within a connected passage of text. If that unit is an unknown word, and the rest of the passage is known, then that word can be understood contextually. Similarly, if the passage is a culture, and an artwork is the unit, then its cultural context can be a window into understanding an artwork. Artists, like everyone else, are members of multiple cultures, and their artwork cannot help being influenced by the preferred aesthetic traits and aesthetic traditions of those cultures, and, therefore, the work is in dialogue with those traits and traditions. Context is the sum of these multiple cultures. This is primarily a critical observation, and the takeaway is that an art is, and can be understood to be, in dialogue with its cultures. For example, I designed the lighting for a classical Khmer ballet called *The Lives of Giants* (Tour, 2010), in which the director called for a series of flashing lights in relation to a particular event.[11] I was not keen on this idea and proposed other, more subtle ways to light the moment. However, she explained to me that within the Khmer aesthetic, the flashing lights had a very particular meaning. In other words, in this context, the flashing lights were a preferred aesthetic trait and, therefore, the correct choice.

Art is one of those big ideas that define a culture. Art is also a product of a culture. Like a good sourdough starter, art grows out of a culture and feeds it at the same time, and, because culture is not a static concept, changes in culture beget changes in art. And changes in art beget changes in culture. The space where cultures collide/overlap/synergize in art is embedded with a certain kind of negentropy—a tendency toward creation rather than destruction—the energy of which pushes up against its cultural contexts. This is what makes culture nimble—that it can survive and grow from explosions of big ideas (see the nonrepresentational modernisms of the first half of the 20th century for ample evidence of this). This negentropy in the form of innovation gives rise to new aesthetic and non-aesthetic traits, and by usage, new aesthetic and non-aesthetic preferences, new forms, and, thus, new ideas of beauty.

If a culture is an accumulation of ideas, and art is an expression of those ideas, then art and culture are inexorably tied to one another. As theatrical design visionary Edward Gordon Craig insinuates, artists are explorers.[12] Even a cursory study of history shows that a culture's artistic output is often at the vanguard of that culture's progressive or exploratory thought. In other words, big artistic movements happen when a society has a big philosophical idea to work out. As those ideas are worked out and new ideas pop up, a culture's artistic output (read "art movements") grows along with it. Old forms are discarded, and new forms are discovered in the search for meaningful methods of expression. Art pushes the boundaries of the culture in which it is created. In this regard, an artwork is both a unit of cultural vocabulary and a change agent.

I love Hickey's discussion of this kind of cultural shift, one of which happened when a retrospective exhibition of Robert Mapplethorpe's photographs became the object of an obscenity lawsuit against the Cincinnati Contemporary Arts Center in 1990. As Hickey tells it, "A single artist with a single group of images had somehow managed to overcome the aura of moral isolation, gentrification, and mystification that surrounds the practice of contemporary art in this nation and directly threaten those in actual power with his celebration of marginality."[13] What was the verdict, which was returned after only two hours of deliberation, you might ask? Not guilty on all counts, thus enshrining the right for art celebrating queer culture through the erotic to be exhibited forever as a thing of beauty.[14]

While cultures are living, evolving things, I would argue that a static artwork is a snapshot in time. It becomes a memorial to the moment in which it was made, and it should be viewed as such. That doesn't make it of any less value, indeed, sometimes it makes it of more value, but it is a fact that should be included in critical analysis. A Mapplethorpe in 1990 is different than a Mapplethorpe in 2022. The first is a groundbreaking explosion of expression that is a cultural game changer, and the second (still relevant, no less beautiful) is a foundational part of a whole new cultural moment but no longer so very shocking. Theatre is more complex: it is both a snapshot of the moment of its creation but also a living art form. While the Broadway production of *The Phantom of the Opera* in 2022 is much the same as it was in 1990, the show having been locked, a *new* 2022 production *might* be made to be more culturally relevant.

Finally, cultures, because of how they evolve, are also inclined to entropy. Cultures come and go because people grow beyond them, or because cultures grow beyond themselves, or because cultures are subsumed by other cultures. And as those cultures come and go, so too do their aesthetic preferences. "The history of beauty, like all history, tells the winner's tale," says Hickey.[15] I wonder what I would find beautiful had Aeneas not colonized Latium, had the Romans not colonized Great Britain, had the British not colonized Turtle Island and India ....

Categories

But how do we understand aesthetic and non-aesthetic traits and use them to both understand an artwork and get at the beautiful? Our brains like to categorize things, and this tendency can be useful in understanding the base components of an artwork. Here, I turn to aesthetic philosopher Kendall Walton's pioneering essay, "Categories of Art."[16] His investigation centers on both aesthetic and non-aesthetic properties of an artwork and the notion of correct ways of perceiving. For this discussion, I focus on his non-aesthetic properties of an artwork—which he categorizes as standard, variable, and contra-standard—as a way of analyzing an artwork to make some determinations with regard to beauty. It is important to note that the utility of this idea and the other critical methods discussed herein are not solely in their ability to help a viewer discern whether or not something is beautiful. In fact, they can lead to all sorts of understandings, not the least of which is how an artist might use these methods to analyze the efficacy of their own work.

In brief, a feature of an artwork is "standard" if it is a feature that identifies the artwork as part of a given category, "variable" if it is a feature that does not affect an artwork's qualification within a category, and "contra-standard" if it is a feature that disqualifies an artwork from being a member of a given category.[17] Walton cites as an example, "The flatness of a painting and the motionlessness of its markings are standard, and its particular shapes and colors are variable, relative to the category of painting. A protruding three-dimensional object or an electrically driven twitching of the canvas would be contra-standard relative to this category."[18] For example, a standard feature of a musical or an opera is that the majority of the text is delivered through song. The kind of musical style, however, is variable as it does not affect the piece's categorization as a musical or an opera. If the piece involves no text, that is contra-standard to these forms. From a lighting design perspective, a variable feature is whether a source is a theatrical or non-theatrical fixture. However, the sun is likely to be a contra-standard feature as it is not controllable. Because a lighting design is temporal, I also think this categorization of features can be useful in the development of a design. If the majority of a design creates a standard, then particular variable or contra-standard features can be introduced for a particular effect, a bright daylight source in an otherwise candle-lit opera, for example.

For Walton, an artwork must be classified in order to investigate it aright. Walton identifies four ways of determining how to categorize an artwork, which I here paraphrase:

1   In the way that has the least amount of contra-standard features.
2   In the way in which the artwork comes off best.
3   In the way that the artist's contemporaries perceived the artwork.
4   In the category to which the artist intended the artwork to belong.[19]

Walton claims that there is a right way of investigating an artwork: "… it seems that, at least in some cases, it is *correct* to perceive a work in certain categories, and *incorrect* to perceive in certain others; that is, our judgements of it when we perceive it in the former are likely to be true, and those we make when perceiving in the latter false" (italics in original).[20] For my purpose, when Walton writes 'perceive,' I read 'investigate.' These three types of features are important because they aid the spectator in determining how to investigate an artwork. Once the category of an artwork is known, knowing which features are standard, variable, and contra-standard aids in a critical investigation (one would not critique a concert with the same criteria that one would use to critique a painting). I would even hazard that it allows the spectator to entertain assessments on what is beautiful and what is not because a preferred standard feature—aesthetic *or* non-aesthetic—could be seen as beautiful in a concert, whereas it might be completely non-standard and possibly non-preferred in a painting. So, by investigating the artwork in this way, it will be possible to assess its aesthetic and non-aesthetic properties correctly within a given framework, which is to say that it will be easier to identify that which is beautiful about the artwork.

Methodologies

However, determining the nature of the features of an artwork is not the only way to discern whether it is beautiful. There are myriad critical methodologies with which to speculate about art, and I think many are useful in pursuit of the beautiful, with the caveat that what features or characteristics are found to be beautiful in an artwork will depend on the system of critique used. I have come to think of these methodologies as occupying three broad categories, moving outward from the artwork to encompass the spectator: formal, contextual, and affective. Please note that I do not have an agenda in privileging one methodology over another because a facility with *all of these* methodologies is important to the work of a lighting designer—the better we are able to understand the work at hand, the better the work will be. Indeed, these methodologies overlap so much in practice that they defy linear description.

Formal critique

Formalism, as an initially literary critical methodology, is, in my view, the most objective way to investigate an artwork. It is closely related to new criticism, a school of literary thought from the mid-20th century that asserts the primacy of content over any other aspect of an artwork as a means for criticism. I shall summarize Tyson on the subject as I understand her: new criticism rejects an attempt to understand the artist's intent as a basis of criticism. The artist's intent (especially a dead artist's intent) cannot be known, and, besides, maybe the artwork does not *actually* do what the artist *intended* it to do, so there cannot be a one-to-one correlation between the intent of a creator and the artwork's meaning.[21] That is the crux of the intentional fallacy (the fallacy of knowing the artist's intention).

Furthermore, in this critical framework, a spectator's response to a work cannot be used as a basis of criticism either, it is too subjective. This is the affective fallacy (the fallacy of relying on the spectator's response for meaning). New criticism rejects both the intentional and affective fallacies in favor of "close reading" and focuses exclusively on what is present in the work because what can be read (seen, heard) is the only thing that can be objectively evaluated. A formalist critique wouldn't care if Van Gogh was nuts when he painted *The Starry Night* or if Beethoven was deaf when he composed his Ninth Symphony because neither of those elements is present in the formal elements of the work itself. Rather, a close reading would look at things like the elements of design and composition (line, form, etc.) and the images or sounds being depicted as a way to experience the artwork.

Formalism is useful because, by narrowing our focus to the work itself, it forces us to pay attention to every part of it equally. Hickey states, "The primary virtue of formalism is that it allows you to see and hear patterns that were not put there—that only ended up there as a side effect of some other pattern more urgently desired by the artist."[22] They may be side effects, but that is what the spectator gets. Those side effects are the great equalizer. If they know nothing of either artist, formalism is what can allow the spectator to experience *The Lost Boys* by Kerry James Marshall on the same terms as *A 19* by László Moholy-Nagy. In the purely academic sense, a formal investigation may not be concerned with beauty per se, but within this system we can identify something as beautiful insofar as it adheres to the principles of design and composition, whereas something that does not is not. Likewise, we can identify preferred aesthetic and non-aesthetic traits in the artwork. These are ways a spectator can find those two very different paintings beautiful.

Formally analyzing my own work is a constant part of my design process. I find that if the lighting state does not adhere to the principles of design and composition, or if it deviates from them without reason, it is unlikely to be beautiful, regardless of any other intent it might carry.

Returning to Drew's photograph, a formal, objective critique points to another way that I find the photograph beautiful: the way the strong vertical lines fill the entire frame, the way the contrast of the shadowed ones on the left and the highlighted ones on the right that bisect the image perfectly, the way the figure appears at the line dividing the top third and the middle third of the frame, and the dynamic angle of the seams in the building material push the eye from the top right to lower left, which echo perfectly the diagonal of the falling man's bent leg. And even though it brings back many horrific memories of that day—the image's context—I still find the image itself formally beautiful. Drew did too. He said of it, "That picture just jumped off the screen because of its verticality and symmetry. It just had that look."[23] Formalism is a way to find beauty in images that are otherwise difficult to look at.

Contextual critique

Contextual critique is a methodology that accounts for everything a spectator knows about the context of the artwork, both its history and its current circumstances. Things such as the artist's biography, when the artwork was made, cultural and political influences on the artist, where the artwork is being shown, other external influences (artistic and otherwise) on the artist, etc. Returning to the Ninth Symphony, one might recognize a great work from a formal perspective, and one may be very affected by it, but the impact of the work may be even more acute if the spectator is listening to the Chicago Symphony Orchestra play it and knows that Beethoven never *actually* heard it.

Likewise, knowing that Drew's photograph was one of a sequence of photos of the falling man and that he was one of the countless others that fell from the towers that day brings a broader context to work. The vertical lines fill the frame because Drew was shooting with a telephoto, the contrasted shadows are actually the North and South towers, the seams in the building demarcate floors, and the perfect diagonal of the man's leg was only that way for an instant that morning. Context also shows that Drew was an Associated Press photojournalist at the time, that the photograph was documentation of an event—not premeditated—and that it was almost a fluke that the photo, one of countless many, turned out so compositionally perfect. That it was in *The New York Times* the next day may even lead one to say this photograph is not a work of art at all, just documentation.

If, as Walton claims, the artist's intentions are critical to investigating the artwork, one must find a lens through which to look for those intentions. Furthermore, if one is allowed to investigate a work beyond the primacy of its formal elements, then it may be possible to turn a lens on the work itself. And to milk this metaphor a little more, the lens has to be made. The lens maker's own point of view no doubt influences how the lens does what it does. I also have personal context with Drew's photograph. I was in California lighting a show on the day, but when I came home at the end of the week, I saw the lit destruction from across the river on the way in from the airport. I smelled the acrid smoke from my apartment day after day. I saw the desperate, handmade missing person notices on my way to the subway at Park and 28th for months and months after. At the time, I was a New Yorker—and that is a lens through which I view the image.

I have returned to Walton because he repudiates new criticism, which is important to me because I contend, in later chapters, that much of contemporary American theatre caters to that outmoded critical model. We have a captive relationship to the text that keeps much of our current practice rooted in a mid-century modern aesthetic, which is a sea anchor on the theatre's ability to transcend into newer, better, contemporary forms. In the ultimate burn to formalism, Walton writes, "Thus, since artists' intentions are among the relevant historical considerations, the 'intentional fallacy' is not a fallacy at all."[24] Walton's flamethrower predates Hickey's when he writes that relevant facts surrounding the creation of an artwork "[do] not simply provide hints concerning what might be found in the work. Rather they help to *determine* what aesthetic properties a work has; they, together with the work's non-aesthetic features, *make* it coherent, serene, or whatever" (italics in original).[25] Meaning a choice based on the context of the work rather than the text on the page might be better. Also, from this standpoint, it is not possible to know whether or not an artwork is beautiful without more than just a formal analysis.

Affective critique

Formal and contextual methodologies, as I conceive of them, are primarily, if not exclusively, cognitive methodologies of critique. They are great for describing an artwork, but they are less so for commenting on a spectator's experience of it; how it makes them feel. An affective critique, on the other hand, takes into consideration the spectator's emotion as well. This is borrowed from the field of literary critique called affect theory, which, according to scholar Donovan O. Schaefer, is "an approach to culture, history, and politics that focus on the role of prelinguistic or nonlinguistic forces, or affects. Affects make us what we are, but they are neither under our 'conscious' control nor even necessarily within the register of our awareness—and they can only sometimes be captured in language."[26] A basic definition of "affect" is "A feeling or subjective experience accompanying a thought or action or occurring in response to a stimulus; an emotion, a mood," and also, "the outward display of emotion or mood as manifested by facial expression, posture, gestures, tone of voice, etc."[27] In my understanding, an affective critique prioritizes the spectator's experience. So, mood equals subjective experience plus thought in response to a stimulus. In that regard, any critique based on affect is definitely subjective and will likely yield very different results than a formal or contextual critique on what could be considered beautiful in an artwork.

What is important in my borrowing of this theory is that within it, emotions are the primary motives for human behavior and are, according to the American Psychological Association, "considered to be innate and universal responses that create consciousness and direct cognition. Eight primary affects are postulated: the positive ones of excitement and enjoyment; the negative ones of distress, fear, shame, disgust, and anger; and the relatively neutral one of interest."[28] Primarily what interests me is that there is a universality to these responses. It sounds funky, arguing a subjective response that has some universality, but it gets to how affect can lead to a determination of beauty and further buttresses the idea that some aspects of beauty are universals from a psychological perspective.

But, it is clearly not all psychological. Beauty is also a cultural construct. On the surface, the Enlightenment philosopher David Hume seems to argue on behalf of pure individual subjectivity when he writes, "Beauty is no quality in things themselves: it exists merely in the mind which contemplates them; and each mind perceives a different beauty."[29] Yet, his argument in "On the Standard of Taste" is, I believe, more complex than "beauty is in the eye of the beholder." He argues for a certain standardization of taste when he posits that there are things in nature which are more or less inclined to provoke pleasure in any viewer. Artists have harnessed knowledge of these things in their artworks, and some spectators have learned how to understand them, and, therefore, a "true judge in the finer arts" can identify a "true standard of taste and beauty."[30] Hume does limit this, though, by acknowledging that this standard of taste is bounded by "the particular manners and opinions of our age and country."[31] In other words, if defining a standard of taste is possible, it really is only possible within a cultural framework.

The fact that some aspects of beauty, in my framework, are culturally dependent and others are universal from a psychological perspective is not meant to discount individual subjectivity. In fact, there are many things that interest spectators in very idiosyncratic ways. By way of explanation, I turn to the French philosopher Roland Barthes. In writing his book *Camera Lucida: Reflections on Photography*, Barthes was, among other things, trying to get at why certain photographs interest him, and others do not. He does this by identifying and postulating the relationship between components of a photograph. First, he addresses the pairing of the operator and spectator. The operator makes the photograph, and the spectator views it. For example, Richard Drew and me. Second is the studium: "The *studium* is that very wide field of unconcerned desire, of various interest, of inconsequential taste: *I like/I don't like*" (italics in original).[32] The studium consists of things in the photograph that are interesting to the spectator for many reasons, including cultural context, and might be the cause of the spectator's passing interest. The Twin Towers were my favorite buildings in New York City, they are part of my studium. Third, and most importantly, is the element that "will break (or punctuate) the *studium*" (italics in original).[33] Barthes calls this the punctum, it is a "sting, speck, cut, little hole—and also a cast of the dice. A photograph's *punctum* is that accident which pricks me (but also bruises me, is poignant to me)" (italics in original).[34] The notions of "cast of the dice" and the notion of "accident" are important because, for Barthes, it is not possible to premeditate the presence of the punctum in a photograph. It was certainly chance that Drew was able to catch the photograph that he did. For me, the detail of the falling man's pose is the punctum. It is what draws me in, what I find beautiful. From this perspective, maybe the photograph is art after all.

While Barthes limits the operator and spectator and studium and punctum framework to photographs, I also think it is easily extended to other art forms—including theatre. Given that there are so many elements involved in a production, and, more importantly, so many *people*—spectators,

Peter Tantsits and Jeffrey Tucker in *Der Kaiser Von Atlantis*
Greenwich Music Festival, 2009
Photograph courtesy of Joanne Bouknight

performers, and non-present cocreators—the possibilities for multiplicities of affective responses are almost endless. The work of the theatre is to narrow the possibilities to those that have efficacy for the intentions of the production.

Now, even though an affective critique is spectator-based, I think one must be careful of falling into the "Well, because I like it" trap when articulating an opinion about an artwork. There is always a "why" behind a subjective preference or an emotional response—remember, there is a cognitive component to affective critique—and a good spectator will examine that, as will a good designer when contemplating their own work. Remember from the introduction: designers have a responsibility to their collaborators to be articulate about their reasoning, even subjective or emotional reasoning. After all, we are in the business of making art for others, not necessarily only ourselves.

Rome

Formal, contextual, and affective critique are not mutually exclusive avenues for contemplating beauty, nor should they be. They can all be brought to bear on different aspects of the same artwork. For instance, a formal critique of my set and lighting for a production of *Der Kaiser von Atlantis* (multiple productions, 2009, 2015)[35] might concern itself with the tightly integrated palette, the performative iconography of the lighting (follow spots, festoon lamps, and footlights), and the scrappy nature of the fabric curtain, all as pleasing components of the production vocabulary. A contextual critique, on the other hand, might focus on how those components are stylized evocations of Theresienstadt, where the opera was created and rehearsed (but never allowed to be performed), allowing for a certain sublime response. Finally, an affective critique might consider how a moment in the lighting design functioned as a punctum that kept a spectator engaged, thinking, and feeling.

The methodologies on which I have based my ideas were not specifically developed to identify the beautiful. It could be argued that they are designed to push back against the dominant view of beauty, among other normative aesthetic and non-aesthetic traits, which, from where I sit, are decidedly white, Eurocentric, and male. I am co-opting this triad of methodologies because they are useful ways of articulating other perspectives. In this regard, all manners of critical theories are valid ways of understanding the aesthetic and non-aesthetic traits of an artwork—structuralist, Marxist materialist, feminist, deconstructivist, queer, decolonial, etc. Acknowledging, of course, that what a Marxist materialist and a queer studies scholar might find different things in an artwork coherent, serene, etc.—in other words, might find different things beautiful.

Intentional beauty

There is nothing to be gained in proposing that one critical methodology is better than another. Because as a designer, my job is to use any or all of them to come to a better understanding of what I am doing and what I am making—in analysis, collaboration, and the theatre. These methodologies allow me to dig deeply into the source material *and* think critically about my own work as I make, look, evaluate, and adapt. On one side, there are the (theoretically) objective shared ideas of formal beauty, on the other is the completely subjective, affective personal experience, and, in the middle, there are all sorts of different methodologies that are dependent on one's context or a particular perspective. These methodologies are all valid in the search for beauty because beauty is not the ultimate goal, the ultimate goal is for the artwork to *do* something. This is why intentional beauty is critical and why it is only one of the four characteristics of an artwork that I propose in the next chapter. Back to Hickey to remind us of the stakes: "The task of beauty is to enfranchise the audience and acknowledge its power—to designate a territory of shared values between the image and its beholder and then, in this territory, to advance an argument by valorizing the picture's problematic content."[36] Without beauty, the spectator is not compelled to engage with the artwork and everything else that might be present in the artwork is meaningless. It has zero efficacy and is doomed to inconsequence.[37]

I have started to advance the claim that we can identify aesthetic properties of the beautiful but only within the confines of a fixed system of investigation, for example, a formal, contextual, or affective methodology, and by considering the artwork's cultural context. By nature, a fixed system provides boundaries, and within those boundaries, it is possible to identify the good, the bad, the ugly, *and* the beautiful. Yet, whether we can "make" beauty happen just because we know how to identify the beautiful is more complex because the spectator's perspective, according to the same principles outlined above, will inevitably vary.

For example, had I grown up on the Cornish coast, I might find via an affective analysis, a certain sublime (fear-affect) beauty in the stormy seas and imposing sky of Théodore Géricault's *The Raft of the Medusa*. That attraction might pull me into the painting, which then makes possible any other consequence of the work. In fact, I like sailing ships (interest-affect), so this subjective facet of myself already makes me predisposed to find nautical paintings beautiful; if there is a ship or a boat, I already want to look. So, the studium of *The Raft of the Medusa* pulls me in because of my past subjective excitement, but then the faces intensely interest me. They are the prick that draws me in, and a formal analysis of the painting will show that that is where Géricault wants the spectator's eye to go. In particular, the

The Raft of the Medusa, 1819

By Jean Louis Théodore Géricault
Oil on canvas
193 × 282 in. (490 × 716 cm)
Musée du Louvre, Paris
Public domain, via Wikimedia Commons

grey-haired figure in the lower left quarter of the image. For me, he is the idiosyncratic punctum that engages my own rabid curiosity. Why is he the only one with gray hair? Why does the artist frame his head so? Who is the nude figure he is holding? Is he bored? (He looks bored to me.)

On the second question from above, is it possible to overtly make things that other people will find beautiful? The answer is maybe.

This is an annoying answer.

Maybe the answer is yes, depending on the fixed system in which one is trying to attain the beautiful. If a system of critique allows one to declare, "because of x, y, and z, this is beautiful." Then one can. Think about it this way: if spelling the word "beauty" is beautiful, then b-e-a-u-t-y only works within the fixed system of the English language. But I am wary of that because it presupposes that only one system of critique is valid, and as I have shown, that is not the case.

I think the best we can do, especially in the context of the theatre, is to *create the circumstances* for intentional beauty to be present and for the spectator to find something beautiful. Thankfully art is not science; it is impossible to hyper-accurately predict the outcome when there are people (spectators) involved. Experience can teach us what particular spectators will respond to based on certain aesthetic and non-aesthetic properties that, as composer and painter Arnold Schoenberg would say, are in common usage and have established effectiveness.[38] We can create the studium and, given our experience and analyses, *create the circumstances* for puncta to exist. The best we can do is to provide sufficient catalyst because the only thing we can really control is the stimulus. We cannot control how people respond.[39]

Whether or not we succeed, we still have to try. After all, beauty is necessary to living, right? In her essay "Why Tyrants are Afraid of Art and Beauty" A.L. Kennedy posits that in the face of all that is wrong or difficult in the world, art is unnecessary beauty. She's just setting up her sucker punch. She goes on to say that "those unnecessary beauties are perhaps especially necessary. Mankind's imagination can create ugliness and destruction so it would seem an act of self-defense to create the opposite in response. We are small and solitary beings and frail and short-lived—we deserve the opposite as consolation."[40] I am not sure I can say it better. We do need beauty. We do need it to survive. In Maslow's hierarchy of needs, it ought to be right there at the base of the pyramid alongside food, clothing, and shelter.

Notes

1 Dave Hickey, "Enter the Dragon: On the Vernacular of Beauty," in *The Invisible Dragon: Essays on Beauty, Revised and Expanded* (Chicago: University of Chicago Press, 2009), 2.
2 Hickey, "Enter the Dragon," 12.
3 Vsevolod Meyerhold, "From the Reconstruction of the Theatre," in *Twentieth Century Theatre: A Sourcebook*, ed. Richard Drain, trans. Edward Braun (London: Routledge, 1995), 100.
4 Virginia Woolf, *A Room of One's Own,* annotated and with an introduction by Susan Gubar (New York: Harcourt, 2005), 16–17.
5 Plato, "Lysis, or Friendship," The Internet Classics Archive, trans. Benjamin Jowett, accessed December 17, 2020, classics.mit.edu/Plato/lysis.html.
6 Edmund Burke, *A Philosophical Enquiry into the Origin of Our Ideas of the Sublime and Beautiful* (1757; repr., Whithorn, GB: Anodos Books, 2017), 22.
7 Kendall J. Eskine, Natalie A. Kacinik, and Jessie J. Prinz, "Stirring Images: Fear, Not Happiness or Arousal, Makes Art More Sublime," *Emotion* 12, no. 5 (2012): 1072, doi: 10.1037/a0027200.
8 Eskine, Kacinik, and Prinz, "Stirring Images," 1073.
9 James O. Young, *Cultural Appropriation and the Arts* (Chichester, UK: Wiley-Blackwell, 2010), 10.
10 Lois Tyson, *Critical Theory Today: A User-Friendly Guide*, 3rd ed. (London: Routledge, 2015), 281. Here, Tyson is defining culture as it relates to new historical and cultural criticism.
11 *The Lives of Giants*, conceived of, dir., and chor. by Sophiline Cheam Shapiro, set and lighting design by the author, costume design by Merrily Murray-Walsh for Khmer Arts Ensemble, with on Stage Series, New London, US, Hopkins Center for the Arts, Hanover, US, Flynn Center for the Performing Arts, Burlington, US, Goodhart Hall, Bryn Mawr, US, Cal Performances, Berkeley, US, Arts & Lectures, Santa Barbara, US, and Khmer Arts Theatre, Takhmao, KH, 2010.
12 See Ch. 2, "Artist/Artwork."

13 Hickey, "Enter the Dragon," 14.
14 Alex Palmer, "When Art Fought the Law and Art Won," *Smithsonian Magazine*, October 2, 2015, accessed December 17, 2020, https://www.smithsonianmag.com/history/when-art-fought-law-and-art-won-180956810/.
15 Hickey, "Enter the Dragon," 12.
16 Kendall L. Walton, "Categories of Art," *The Philosophical Review* 79, no. 3 (1970): 334–367.
17 Walton, "Categories of Art," 339–340.
18 Walton, 340.
19 Walton, 357.
20 Walton, 356.
21 Tyson, *Critical Theory*, see Ch. 5, 281. Here, Tyson is defining culture as it relates to new historical and cultural criticism.
22 Dave Hickey, "Formalism," in *Pirates and Farmers* (London: Ridinghouse, 2013), 87.
23 Tom Junod, "The Falling Man," *Esquire Magazine* 140, no. 3 (September 2003): 177.
24 Walton, "Categories of Art," 364.
25 Walton, 364.
26 Donovan O. Schaefer. "It's Not What You Think: Affect Theory and Power to Take the Stage." *News from Duke University Press* (blog). February 15, 2016. https://dukeupress.wordpress.com/2016/02/15/its-not-what-you-think-affect-theory-and-power-take-to-the-stage/.
27 *Oxford English Dictionary Online*, s.v. "affect, n," accessed November 16, 2021, www.oed.com/viewdictionaryentry/Entry/3321.
28 *American Psychological Association Dictionary*, s.v. "affect theory," accessed November 16, 2021, https://dictionary.apa.org/affect-theory.
29 David Hume, "Of the Standard of Taste," in *Art and Its Significance: An Anthology of Aesthetic Theory*, ed. Stephen David Ross, 2nd ed. (Albany, NY: State University of New York Press, 1987), 84.
30 Hume, "Standard of Taste," 92.
31 Hume, 94.
32 Roland Barthes, *Camera Lucida: Reflections on Photography*, trans. Richard Howard (New York: Hill and Wang, 1980), 27.
33 Barthes, *Camera Lucida*, 26.
34 Barthes, 27.
35 *Der Kaiser von Atlantis*, composed by Viktor Ullmann, libretto by Petr Kien, dir. Ted Huffman, chor. and co-dir. Zack Winokur, set design by the author and costume design by Paul Carry, Greenwich Music Festival, Greenwich, US, 2009 and Julliard Opera, New York, US, 2015.
36 Hickey, "Enter the Dragon," 9.
37 Hickey, 2.
38 Arnold Schoenberg, *Theory of Harmony, 100th Anniversary Edition*, trans. Roy E. Carter, with a new foreword by Walter Frisch, 2nd ed. (Berkeley, CA: University of California, 2010), 11.
39 Thanks to my former student Sara Gosses for the precise articulation of this point.
40 A.L. Kennedy, "A Point of View: Why Tyrants Are Afraid of Art and Beauty," *BBC News*, January 23, 2015, www.bbc.com/news/magazine-30939668.

2 Artist/Artwork

David Shrigley, *Untitled (In his studio the artist has no social responsibility)*, 2014
Synthetic polymer paint on paper
60 1/4 × 43 3/4 in. (153 × 111 cm)
© 2021 Artists Rights Society (ARS), New York/DACS, London

(Re)definitions

To understand the other characteristics of an artwork (besides beauty) and to understand the nature of the artist, I find I have to investigate the two together. The concepts are rather like a chicken and an egg: the cause of one is the effect of the other. To try to pry the two concepts apart somehow, for me, and put them in their own chapters does not do justice to my understanding of their intractable interrelatedness. Here, I will lay out some distinct characteristics of both artist and artwork before I put them back together again.

Artist

I believe that the artist, the maker of the artwork:

1 Is a kind of mystic who has a way of seeing both the world as it is and a world beyond rational objective understanding, with a novel, singular point of view.
2 Is possessed of a need to express that vision as a communicative act.
3 Does so by making artwork utilizing an accomplished craft.

The artist sees something only they can see. The artist has a need to express their point of view on what they have seen, so they make a thing (object or idea) utilizing an accomplished craft, which is more than a craft object. The thing is also beautiful, moves the spectator beyond some threshold of understanding, and, because what the artist is expressing is by nature novel, it is innovative.

Mystic

The word "mystic" is admittedly problematic. It feels secretive, incomprehensible, and of some mythic religious priestly realm that rubs hard against my innate desire to understand the world from a rational, objective, egalitarian, atheistic perspective. However, human beings are irrational, subjective, biased creatures, and our subject here—the artist—works very hard at being undefinable. No less than Carl Jung wrote, "the creative aspect of life which finds its clearest expression in art baffles all attempts at rational formulation."[1] So, I think that embracing this troublesome word, mystic, with the ensuing messiness, has some utility, especially given that sometimes I do not even understand *my own* motivations, even when the outcome has efficacy. I use the verb embrace specifically because it is not my word. I borrow "mystic" from Conceptual Artist Sol LeWitt, who wrote in his "Sentences on Conceptual Art," "Conceptual Artists are mystics rather than rationalists. They leap to conclusions that logic cannot reach."[2] And from mythologist Joseph Campbell, whose essay *The Way of Art* has helped me clarify my thinking. As much as I rebel against it, venturing into the world beyond rational objective understanding *is* a leap of faith.

For Campbell, the mystic and the artist are separate entities and it is necessary for me to explain his distinction because it bears directly on why I have plucked the word and embedded it within my definition of the artist. For him, the artist has a craft, whereas the mystic does not, but they are otherwise similar.[3] Therefore, understanding the function of the mystic is equally foundational to understanding the artist. Campbell then winds his way to Jung's position that "the function of religion is to protect us from an experience of God."[4] In other words, God and Godly things are too mighty to be understood by us mere mortals, so we need the intercession of the priesthood to protect us.[5] I do not believe in God, so when I read Campbell, I replace the idea of God with what I call the world beyond rational objective understanding. Putting two and two together, this presents an idea that the world beyond rational objective understanding is pretty thorny and we need help—from the priest, the mystic, and the artist—to understand it.

As for priests, it is convenient for me to assign to them the same definition that Campbell does, more or less, in that they are intercessors, using "a vocabulary already coined"—a set of religious rites—to sell us whatever religion's bill of goods happens to be.[6] The mystic—and by extension the artist—leapfrogs the priest, boldly going into the breach, come what may. As Campbell puts it, "the mystic deliberately offers himself to the blast and may go to pieces."[7] That the mystic and the artist, in Campbell, find "their own inmost truth brought to consciousness: by the mystic, in direct confrontation, and by the artist, through reflection in the masterwork of his art," ergo the artist is a kind of mystic.[8]

I also think the artist does not always understand what they experience, or, as Craig maintained, even how much they experience, "For that is what the title of artist means: one who perceives more than his fellows, and one who records more than he has seen."[9] Sometimes figuring something out— what one has seen or what one needs to express—comes from blind stabbing in the dark and sometimes it comes from intuitive understanding, but no matter the method, the leap of faith is risky business and it is never easy.

Point of view and need

But seeing is nothing without expressing, so a point of view is essential; it is a way of seeing in general and an approach to an idea in specific. An artist deals in ideas and the perspective they bring to those ideas is their point of view. It defines every choice and is the answer to every question they ask.

Study of Study of Perspective, 2015

National Gallery of Victoria
Photograph by the author

To be clear, point of view is about a take on *how* to express something, not *whether* to express something. The artist has a unique way of seeing, of experiencing, and a unique way of translating that into a thing. Often the characteristics of the material outcomes of this unique way of translating, over time, accumulate into an artists' style. Examining the work of Emory Douglas, Pina Bausch, Robert Wilson, and John Cage, for example, will yield identifiable styles honed over years of work.

Anyone can take a photograph of themselves flipping the bird at a building, but only Ai Weiwei could have made the photographs that constitute *Study of Perspective*. His photographs, as presented, coalesce around a point of view challenging a spectrum of authority in his choice of political and cultural targets. But what is the point of him taking those photos if no one sees them? The vision must be communicated in order for it to have any ability to express an idea (more about that soon). Ai has a point of view about these targets and I can sense his need to communicate that. I, too, have a point of view about the challenge of authority being presented in a place of art world authority and used my photo to express it, if only ironically.

Not only must an artist have a point of view, they must also have what early 20th-century Polish artist Stanisław Witkiewicz calls "a *genuine creative necessity*" to express their vision (italics in original).[10] The need to express something is a primal urge of the artist, a thing tied into their fundamental nature, to their very identity. "[I]dentity is sought through expression; the media of expression are what I find to texture and realize my expressive needs ..." said composer Benjamin Boretz in his seminal talk, "If I am a Musical Thinker," continuing, "and the effectiveness of a medium, of my media, in drawing out from me an adequate depth and breadth of expression will determine, ultimately, what—and how much—I can be for myself."[11] Meaning, without expression an artist's identity is incomplete. Leo Tolstoy, too, cites need in his essay *What Is Art?* When he says, "the artist should be impelled by an inner need to express his feeling."[12] Finally, the German opera composer Richard Wagner, in *The Art-Work of the Future*, cites need as a central component of art making. However, it should be noted that he speaks of it in terms of Necessity: a common and collective want of a particular group, who he calls "The Folk."[13] Here, I am using this charged word specifically as an analog for any given culture. (Wagner, of course, also has a deeply problematic history that will be discussed further in "Theatre," where I have space to weigh the pros and cons of acknowledging him as an influence.) I am hammering this point home because thinkers across the philosophical spectrum agree that *need* is such a powerful force that the artist has no other recourse than to act upon it.

In other words, expression alone might be a pile of garbage if there is not a point of view driving the expression. The rationale for invoking Wagner above is to be able to nod to "Luxury," what he calls an unwanted need, product for the sake of product and output for the sake of output.[14] If the expression is not driven by a need, it will become, returning to Witkiewicz, "... a kind of *schematic nonsense*, devised in cold blood, artificially, without real need, it would probably arouse nothing but laughter" (italics in original).[15] In other words, also a pile of garbage. Without a point of view, the work is either meaningless or utilitarian and, in both instances, *not artwork*. There have been many shows I will not name that fit in this category where the need, if any, was purely commercial (both for the producers and for me). Whereas there have been other shows in my life where the urgent need to get the artwork onstage has been palpable—*Where Elephants Weep* (Chenla Theatre, 2008),[16] *Party People* (multiple productions, 2012–2016),[17] and *Pass Over* (multiple productions, 2017–2021)[18] to name a few.

Need is tricky though, because how can a spectator really know what the specific need of the artist is, without the artist there to say it? I am not sure it is always possible, especially when the spectator is viewing an object from a different culture or a different time, for example. Whether the artist would articulate it in words instead of saying "why don't you look at the work?" is also a question in and of itself. This is maybe why I tend not to read program notes—I want to experience the work on its own terms without someone telling me how to engage with it. So, my point is not that the spectator explicitly understands the need, per se, but that they can at least sense it. Tolstoy sums it up neatly: *"To evoke in oneself a feeling one has experienced, and having evoked it in oneself, then by means of movements, lines, colors, sounds, or forms expressed in words, so to transmit that feeling that others experience the same feeling—that is the activity of art"* (italics in original).[19] Experiencing something beyond rational objective understanding and then transmitting that feeling is a communicative act.

I think one could also cut to the chase and ask any working artist—they would confirm that the need to express is central to an artist's being. An artist is possessed by a need to express their vision as a communicative act. But how?

Accomplished craft

With the exception of the rare Henry Dargers of the world, artists need to train with more experienced practitioners to become accomplished in their craft. Mystic vision, singular point of view, need, and innovative thought are all unable to combine to achieve their full potential in an artwork without the artist's ability to express them. That ability lies in an expertise of craft, of special skills and knowledge required to produce work in a particular medium that is most effectively acquired through formal education.

Young, in his book, *Cultural Appropriation and the Arts*, provides a particularly useful framework around which to discuss artist training. He outlines four components necessary in the training of artists: first, the study of successful works in their medium; second, train in the techniques and materials in their medium; third, learn the significance of certain conventions and symbols; and fourth, repeatedly practice their craft.[20] Young's precisely crafted arguments appeal to me because they are closely aligned with my pedagogical approach.

Studying successful examples allows one to learn about precedents: all training in the arts must be built on its historical foundations. As I wrote in the introduction, artists stand on the shoulders of those who have pushed the envelope of artistic expression in previous generations. Training obviates the need to waste energy doing what has already been done. If for no other reason than to break from them, one must learn the precedents of the past (history being doomed to repeat itself and whatnot). The idea of precedent, as I employ it relating to art, bears explanation. It should not be understood in this context to be something that exists *only* because it is, or was, common practice; rather, a precedent is *something of value* that alters, or altered, common practice. In the legal sense, a precedent is a decision made by a court after contemplating an idea of law, which is binding on courts of equal or lower stature. This definition is the appropriate simile because it proposes that an idea at hand has been tested by the community in which the idea exists and has been found to be worthy (community being a handy word that can be defined narrowly or broadly as needed).

Shin busters, for example, are a precedent in designing for ballet: they can light a dancer's entire leg without a shadow from a tutu. Learning that precedent in my early training helped me not waste time learning how to light the leg appropriately and, more importantly, impressed upon me how critical it is to the form as a whole that we actually *see* the entire leg. Another is that cross light works well because actors face each other to talk, and thus the dominant source lights their faces well while not shadowing each other. Others include that sometimes it is better to treat the chorus as a mass rather than individuals, a bump in light on a button at the end of the number makes sense because it propels energy into the audience which they will want to return, and programming with relational data (palettes and presets) will always save time in the long run.

A thorough understanding of the techniques and materials of a medium is the only way to master the craft of that medium. For instance, I believe the fundamental tool of any visual artist is the point where a pencil meets a piece of paper, which is to say, drawing. A grasp of that form of expression is the gateway to all other visual media, which is why I think it is important for lighting designers to know how to draw, especially the figure. In theatre, a near-constant is the presence of human beings, therefore, the dominant unit of measure on the stage is the height of a human. These two points describe a line along which one can then identify other medium-specific needs.

I am all for iconoclasm, but one has to know the conventions one is destroying before one breaks them. All art forms have specific conventions that govern their crafts and an artist needs to learn the significance of those conventions. The theatre is full of them. For example, big things like different working styles in opera, theatre, and dance; pseudo-realistic production choices vs. expressionistic ones; and the differences in staging practices between proscenium, thrust, and in-the-round. I will expand, casting a wider net, and say that aspiring artists also need to understand the sign systems that are available in their form (both historically and in contemporary use). As he discusses the training of an artist, Young points to conventions and symbols, which, essentially, are sign systems of a given medium.

The study of sign systems is called semiotics. Tyson succinctly defines sign systems as "a linguistic or nonlinguistic object or behavior (or collection of objects or behaviors) that can be analyzed as if it were a specialized language."[21] Signs, as summarized by Tyson, consist of the thing that is signified and the signifier of that thing. There are three recognized classes of signs in semiotics: index, where there is a causal relationship between signifier and signified, for example, the light on an actor's face is indexed by the lamp they are standing next to (even if the light is coming from a different source); icon, where the signifier physically resembles the signified, for example, a sphere held in a hand in a particular way is an icon of a crystal ball; and symbol, which is where the signifier is seemingly arbitrary, but based on cultural conventions, such as a crystal ball as a symbol for mysticism.[22] A practical example of this is how we used a hanging lamp in a production of *Les Mamelles de Tirésias* (multiple producers, 2012–2019)[23] to evoke a crystal ball in support of lyrics about the enchantress Morgan le Fay. Learning the significance of conventions and symbols will make aspirating artists better.

Finally, artists in training must practice, practice, and practice their craft. This word—practice—is important in two senses. The first in the sense of a verb: practice as the repeated doing of a thing to get better at it. The second sense is of a noun: practice as the application of an established procedure or system.

Artwork

Now that I have explained what I think defines an artist, I turn my attention to the expression of their point of view: artwork—an object or idea imbued with special qualities. While beauty is the single most important characteristic, I believe an artwork must also possess three other characteristics. To provide a complete taxonomy:

1. It is beautiful because beauty demands engagement from a spectator.
2. It is more than a craft object.
3. It confronts the spectator with troublesome knowledge.
4. It is innovative in that moves the form forward.

These characteristics are slightly vague to encompass the vast array of media in which contemporary artists work. It is important to think about these four characteristics, not as a simple, linear list of boxes that must be checked for something to qualify as an artwork. Rather, they define a multi-dimensional spectrum on which the work can be mapped (insofar as such a definitively objective critique is possible, which it very well may not be).

Beyond objectness

While an artist must be an accomplished craftsperson, an accomplished craftsperson is not necessarily an artist. This might be accurately described by a large circle encompassing craftspersons and a smaller circle within it distinguishing artists. One might think, therefore, that it would follow that if the work of craftspersons falls within that circle, then the artwork must necessarily then be a craft object as well. This is not true because

Mathieu Gardon, Nathalie Morazin, Romain Pascal, Eva Ganizate, and company in *Les Mamelles de Tirésias*

Festival d'Aix-en-Provence, 2013
Photograph by the author

while craft objects and artworks may share characteristics, there are also features of each that are separate from the other. Picture a Venn diagram rather than concentric circles.

This section is concerned with such characteristics:

1. Those of a craft object.
2. Those that overlap between craft object and artwork.
3. Those that distinguish an artwork from a craft object.

Craft object

A craft object is an object whose form is dictated by its function. In this regard, a light plot is a craft object. A light plot needs to be designed to fulfill its function for a production, for example, to light the scenes in such and such a way. Fixtures are chosen and the light plot is designed. At this stage of the process, the lighting designer functions as a craftsperson. A craft object is a means to an end, and the end is predictable, and because its form is dictated by its function, any aesthetic considerations—beauty, for example—are secondary to the function. We do not care if the light plot itself is beautiful, as long as it works.

Collingwood shapes my thinking on craft. He writes that craft is "the power to produce a preconceived result by means of consciously controlled and directed action."[24] He outlines six characteristics of craft, using the terms 'means' for process, and 'ends' for product:

1. Craft involves a distinction between the means and the ends.
2. Craft involves a distinction between planning and execution; the result is planned before it is made.
3. Means and ends have an inverse relationship when moving between planning and execution: in planning, the end is determined first, then the means; in execution, the means come first, through which the ends are reached.
4. There is a distinction between raw material and finished product.
5. There is a distinction between matter and form; matter is raw material and form is a product of means.
6. There is a hierarchical relationship between various crafts; one craft's ends are another craft's means.[25]

In the instance of a lighting design:

1. One uses the light plot (means) to make a lighting design (ends).
2. The specifications of the light plot are meticulously designed before it is hung.

3 In planning, the use of the lighting design is determined (ends), then the light plot is made (means). In execution, the light plot (means) is used to make the lighting design (ends).
4 The light plot is distinct from the materials from which it was made.
5 Lights on a plot and a random group of lights are the same fixtures, but the light plot is a product of the (planned) process of design.
6 The fixtures used in the light plot are the end of the fixture maker's means.

Overlap between craft object and artwork

I do have a dispute with Collingwood. His definition of craft is a useful one, but his distinction between art and craft, his "fallacy of precarious margins" wherein "the only things that are allowed to be works of art are those marginal examples which lie outside the overlap of art and craft," is antiquated.[26] Rather, I posit that it is possible for each of his criteria for a craft object to be *also true* of an artwork, that they can be shared characteristics. The shared characteristics can be summarized as follows:

1 The requirement of physical means is true of both craft objects and artwork. In the creation of an artwork, there are multiple means to the end. Yes, the genesis of the artwork stems from an intention to express a point of view, which is essentially an idea whose development uses the means of the mind. But, without physical expression, it cannot be an artwork (this argument requires acceptance of the requirement that art is material, which I do not necessarily believe. Please bear with me). Therefore, the artist must also have a physical means to the end.
2 Meticulous planning of an artwork in the manner employed for a craft object does not disqualify it from being an artwork.
3 It is possible for the relationship between ends and means in planning and execution for an artwork to be the same as they are for a craft object. It is possible to determine the shape of an installation and the precise means to make it and then employ those precise means to create the installation.
4 The raw material of art is both physical matter *and* intent.
5 There is a distinction between what is expressed in an artwork (intent) and that which expresses it (material), but not only is the material critical to the identity of the artwork, it is the entrée to understanding the expression. Language is the material of a poem and understanding the language in which a poem is written is critical to understanding the expressive intent of the poem.
6 There are plenty of hierarchical relationships in the arts. A play is written, and a production is wrought. A song is produced, then it is sampled. Sturtevant's copies of the work of Warhol, Lichtenstein, etc.[27]

Boundaries between the two

The careful distinction is that each of the above elements does not *have to be* true for an object to be an artwork, only that it *can be* true; that there is inevitably some overlap between craft objects and artworks, but the extent to which they overlap need not be prescribed. This might be accurately described by a Venn diagram whose overlap is selectively elastic; determined on a case-by-case basis. The elasticity of the shape representing the artwork allows it to fully absorb the craft object, but the reverse is never true. So, in addition to the list above, these things are *true* of an artwork and *not true* of a craft object:

1 There is no distinction between the means and the ends of an artwork. A lighting design is inseparable from that which it lights (the production).
2 An artwork is its means and its end, but the end is not completely predictable because it requires the engagement of a spectator—in the theatre, the audience.
3 An artist's intentions may not be clear at the outset of art-making, with happenings, devised theatre, and improvisational forms being prime examples.
4 Because its form is dictated by its intention, expressing a point of view, an artwork's aesthetic properties are primary to its function.

Is it possible to elevate a craft object to the status of an artwork by virtue of the perspective of the spectator? No, because an artwork relies on the intention of an artist (whether or not we actually know it). Conversely, is it possible to elevate a craft object to the status of artwork by virtue of the intervention of an artist? Yes, because intention would be involved.

A craft object is an object made to accomplish a utilitarian need, it is a means to a predictable end whose form follows function and whose aesthetic features are secondary to that function. An artwork can also possess those characteristics or not. It is an object that may not have a utilitarian function, whose form is dictated by its intent to express, where the end-result is not predictable, and whose means—including its aesthetic properties—are its ends, which is to express the point of view of an artist. It is beyond objectness.

Troublesome knowledge

Continuing the metaphor of artist as explorer, the artist shows the spectator something new in their artwork. Because that something new is from beyond the realm of rational understanding, it is often troublesome. Equally, something completely rational but culturally foreign can be troublesome. In their seminal paper, education researchers Jan Meyer and Ray Land set forth the notion of the threshold concept: "A threshold concept can be considered as akin to a portal, opening up a new and previously inaccessible way of thinking about something. It represents a transformed way of understanding, or interpreting, or viewing something without which the learner cannot progress."[28] Meyer and Land's focus is on students in the classroom, but I believe their research is also portable and directly translatable to the experience a spectator has with an artwork. They continue, "As a consequence of comprehending a threshold concept there may thus be a transformed internal view of subject matter, subject landscape, or even world view. This transformation may be sudden or it may be protracted over a considerable period of time, with the transition to understanding proving troublesome."[29] They also point out that the time the transformation takes can place the learner in a liminal state, a place between levels of understanding.[30] One can read subject matter as an artwork, subject landscape as an art form, and world view as, well ... world view.

A scientific example is useful as a descriptor because, of course, science is meant to be objective. The fact that gas density in a given volume is determined by depth is a threshold concept in scuba diving. The deeper one dives, the greater the ambient pressure; the greater the ambient pressure, the more pressure is exerted on breathing gas and the tighter the molecules get. This idea can challenge pre-existing notions that air is air no matter what, and it is one of the most important principles to understand in diving because not understanding this is a very, very easy way to die. This principle informs the foundation from which most diving practices stem. It is not so easy with art. Threshold concepts embedded in artworks are likely to be variable because they are dependent on what the spectator brings to the table, which, inevitably, is subjective.

Returning to the Mapplethorpe exhibition, his images challenged boundaries by valorizing a controversial culture of queer eroticism that had hitherto been largely seen as marginal or not seen at all. The ideas embedded in his photographs constitute threshold concepts. Imagine if an open-minded someone in power would have looked at them and said to themselves, "his culture is valid and worth preserving," and then done something—*anything*—about the AIDS crisis. While troublesome knowledge is destabilizing, once it is understood, it becomes a threshold concept; an idea that once learned, cannot be unlearned.

To understand how one might posit the existence of a threshold concept, it is necessary to identify some key characteristics. Meyer and Land, along with their colleague Glynis Cousin, identify five, which are paraphrased here. A threshold concept is likely to be:

1 Transformative, in that understanding it involves both an ontological as well as a conceptual shift.

2 Irreversible, in that once it is understood, it is unlikely to be forgotten.
3 Integrative, in that it exposes previously hidden interrelatedness of phenomena.
4 Bounded in that it has edges that push up against other ideas.
5 Troublesome in that it involves forms of troublesome knowledge.[31]

Transformative

Ontology has to do with the nature of being, so an ontological shift resulting from grasping a threshold concept embedded in an artwork would involve shifting the spectator's own sense of being in response to a new understanding. A conceptual shift involves how new knowledge informs existing knowledge and what that means for the spectator moving forward. For example, the song "You've Got to be Taught" from Rogers and Hammerstein's musical *South Pacific*:

CABLE: You've got to be taught to hate and fear,
You've got to be taught from year to year,
It's got to be drummed in your dear little ear—
You've got to be carefully taught![32]

Embedded in the lyrics of this song is the notion that racism is not a product of nature but of nurture. For me, as I listened to this song a child, this was a threshold concept. It involved a conceptual shift around the notion of racism. And because the song concerns a white man not marrying a Polynesian woman because of her race, it engendered a shift in my own sense of being as the child of white mother and brown father. Suddenly, I understood why people might perceive me as different and what that might mean for their behavior.

Irreversible

The sort of conceptual shift that happens as the result of understanding a threshold concept is unlikely to be forgotten. In that sense, it is irreversible. This is not to say that a threshold concept cannot be challenged by what researcher Glynis Cousin refers to as "more refined or rival" understandings.[33] In the instance above, a more refined conceptual understanding would contemplate Joe Cable's socio-economic status and what that might for how trapped he might feel in his circumstances at the moment of that song. It doesn't make the embedded racism any more bearable, but it does make it understandable, which aids in a spectator's ability to empathize with the lieutenant.

Integrative

Threshold concepts allow for "a-ha!" moments where the hidden connection between things are revealed. Take, for example, Tony Kushner's *Angels in America* plays, which weave together a great many fictions and truths to expose connections the spectator may not have been aware of. Among which was the systematic refusal of the American government to recognize the ravages of the AIDS crisis, the Mormon religion's relationship to homosexuality, how the weeds planted by McCarthyism continued to choke our political system, and what those things mean at a very human level. The integrative nature of threshold concepts, as I apply them as a characteristic of an artwork, is not restricted to existing within the closed ecosystem of the individual artworks themselves. Not only are they integrative in the way that those concepts can inform how a spectator engages with another artwork—for example, a spectator can take their understanding of cubism via engagement with a painting by Georges Braque and apply it to a painting by Pablo Picasso or Aleksandra Exter—but, more importantly, they are integrative with how a spectator then takes what they have learned away from the artwork and into other interactions.

Bounded

Threshold concepts are likely bounded as well, "in that any conceptual space will have terminal frontiers, bordering with thresholds into new conceptual areas."[34] One such bounded threshold concept is embedded in act two, scene one of *Othello*.[35] During a 2009 production directed by Arin Arbus, and my first at Theatre for a New Audience (TFANA), I had a conversation with Artistic Director Jeffrey Horowitz that I remember distinctly: it was in the back of the house during a break from technical rehearsals. The scene begins with a storm so intense that when Montano asks the First Gentleman what he can see, Montano responds. "Nothing at all. It is a high-wrought flood./I cannot, 'twixt the heaven and the main,/Descry a sail."[36] He describes a storm so strong that it has completely wrecked the Turkish fleet. Yet, somehow, within 75 lines the storm has abated itself enough for Desdemona to pass, unharmed, and make landfall:

CASSIO: Tempests themselves, high seas, and howling winds,
   The gutter'd rocks and congregated sands—
   Traitors ensteep'd to clog the guiltless keel—
   As having sense of beauty, do omit
   Their mortal natures, letting go safely by
   The divine Desdemona.[37]

In his description of the storm, Horowitz helped me understand that Shakespeare has it "sense" Desdemona's "beauty" and react, all within a very short span of time. In so doing, Shakespeare calls into question what the spectator might assume to be true about nature (that it is not sentient) and time (that it is constant), advancing pathetic fallacy, a theory of relativity, and the importance of beauty at the same time.[38] The threshold concept that in Shakespeare, nature and time do not play by the rules pushes hard against the terminal frontiers of what one might be tempted to call "reality."

Troublesome

The characteristics outlined above can all be very destabilizing for a spectator, adding up to knowledge that is very troublesome indeed. Knowledge, in this sense, meaning familiarity with something gained by experience; an idea understood through engagement with an artwork. Troublesome because it is counter-intuitive, alien, or seemingly incoherent.[39] Such knowledge could be counter-intuitive by virtue of it going against knowledge that is tacitly thought to be true. E.g., that time does not always function as we expect it to in Shakespeare. It could be alien because it is knowledge that comes from another culture or form of investigation. When I find Mapplethorpe's *Jim and Tom, Sausalito, 1977* to be beautiful, it destabilizes my pre-existing sense of beauty and requires that I rethink my concept of what I find beautiful. Finally, knowledge embedded in an artwork can be incoherent in that it seems to follow no known principles or structure. Dada and its decedents being my favorite examples. Threshold concepts take many forms, but they all alter an engaged spectator's perceptions by challenging a set way of thinking. Because they are dependent on the spectator, they are also subjective and, perhaps, the most slippery of the characteristics of an artwork.

Urge to innovate

As I wrote in "Beauty," art is embedded with a certain kind of negentropy, which, in the form of innovation, gives rise to new forms. Of new forms, choreographer Pina Bausch, speaking of her early move into choreography, said: "I didn't feel fulfilled. I was hungry to dance a lot and had the urge to express myself ... So I started to choreograph my own pieces ... To express what really lay in my heart, it was impossible for me to use other people's material and forms of movement."[40] In order to express herself, she had to move beyond the forms she knew—the forms in which she trained and that she was dancing—and create her own. As artist Wassily Kandinsky writes in *On the Question of Form*, "Form is always temporal,

Ned Eisenberg, Robert Langdon Lloyd, Lucas Hall, Elizabeth Meadows Rouse, Alexander Sovronsky, and John Douglas Thompson in *Othello*

Theatre for a New Audience, 2009
Photograph courtesy of Gerry Goodstein

i.e., relative, for it is nothing more than the means necessary today through which the present revelation makes itself heard."[41] Constant negentropy. So, like Kandinsky, "we should not look for salvation in *one* form only" (italics in original).[42] To reiterate: innovation in form leads to innovation in what is considered beautiful.

The need to express an internal need is not the only motivator for innovation. Often, the urge to innovate comes from discontent with current forms as they relate to current society, cultures, and/or political systems. This is eloquently evidenced in playwright August Wilson's "The Ground on Which I Stand" speech about how the Black Power Movement (a movement subsumed into the Civil Rights Movement in some histories) shaped his art.

> I find it curious but no small accident that I seldom hear those words 'Black Power' spoken, and when mention is made of that part of black history in America, whether in the press or in conversation, reference is made to the Civil Rights Movement as though the Black Power Movement—an important social movement by America's ex-slaves—had in fact never happened. But the Black Power Movement of the '60s was [in fact] a reality; it was the kiln in which I was fired, and has much to do with the person I am today and the ideas and attitudes that I carry as part of my consciousness.[43]

For Wilson, that experience was critical to his art: "I have strived to live it all seamless—art and life together, inseparable and indistinguishable"[44] and must have been, at least in part, the motivation for his exceptionally innovative American Century Cycle plays.

Violent political revolutions have also been a major motivating factor in artistic innovation. Russian actor and director Evgeny Vakhtangov wrote of the Russian Great October Socialist Revolution (1917) that it divided the world into the old and the new.[45] In 1922, he said, "When the revolution came, we all felt that things in art cannot remain the same. We did not yet know the form–the real, appropriate form ... The next stage of our work will be dedicated to the search for the eternal form."[46] For Vakhtangov, the cultural change dictated a change of aesthetic. Meyerhold, just a few years later, concurred, "Today's aesthetic must take account for the new standards which have been created by new social conditions."[47] The Russian revolution is not the only political revolution to spawn new forms by a long shot, but its theatre is a particularly fertile and resilient ground from which to pull rationales of my point that revolutionary movements are catalysts for artistic change precisely because social revolutions are big ideas, big ideas lead to cultural change, and cultural change leads to innovation. When the world changes, its art must change too or risk irrelevance.

To wit, as I write this, theatre in the United States is grappling with two social revolutions. The first has to do with the call for equity, representation, and anti-racism across all facets of theatre making—from the content onstage to those who are making the work to those who are in the audience—as an outgrowth of Black Lives Matter and other similar movements. The second has to do with what we have been able to understand about the impact of our problematic labor conditions—from spans of day to the obscenely perilous healthcare situation for freelancers to the difficulties of simply having a family—as the COVID-19 pandemic roils our industry. Both have illustrated that changes are long overdue and many producing organizations are making some changes. It is hard to see the horizon from the center of the storm, but I am cautiously optimistic that these changes will be long-lasting. Only time will tell.

Finally, innovation can come as a byproduct of other drives. This takes us to the art critic Clement Greenberg who said, in his influential lecture "Modern and Postmodern," of the modernists and their motivation to innovate:

> And yet all the great and lasting Modernists creators were reluctant innovators at bottom, innovators only because they had to be—for the sake of quality, and for the sake of self-expression if you will. It's not only that some measure of innovation has always been essential to aesthetic quality above a certain level; it's also that Modernist innovation has been compelled to be, or look, more radical and abrupt than innovation used to be or look: compelled by an ongoing crisis of standards.[48]

His perspective is that the modernists were reluctantly forced to innovate as a reaction to bad art. These are a lot of differing rationales for innovation, yet they all point to an active need.

True innovation involves risk-taking because it moves beyond the "known" into the "unknown." Just like a scientist, an artist asks questions. "Creativity and 'questioning'," graphic designer, curator, and writer Kenya Hara writes, "are made of the same stuff. A creative question is a form of expression."[49] It is easy to do what one knows works, especially in an art form that is often dominantly driven by the market, like theatre. If the goal is to sell tickets, then maybe too much risk is not worth it. Disney took a chance on what was at the time a very risky production: *The Lion King*. That show was as innovative a piece of theatre as I was likely to see in a good long time. But how many subsequent Disney produced movies-to-stage have been as innovative? It depends on one's metric. Theatre is not the only art form subject to this sort of economic decision, overt or not. In the eyes of the bean counters, the benefits of innovative work are often outweighed by the potential cost of not selling. If it were possible (and I am not sure it *is* possible) to remove money from the equation, then what would be the point of mitigating risky aesthetic decisions? I am not sure there is one.[50]

Form forward

The urge to innovate must be put into practice. This involves the introduction of the new: new elements, new forms, and new ways of doing things. Breaking with the established and introducing new methods. However, novelty alone does not equal innovation. As Young concludes, "Newness is not a good in itself, but without new things there are no *good* new things" (italics mine).[51] Any new attribute must make the thing of which it is an attribute *better* for it to be a true innovation. Lewitt's sentence number 20 is: "Successful art changes our understanding of the conventions by altering our perceptions."[52] When the form is pushed forward successfully, it changes the basis of criticism for all other similar artworks. This is how the contra-standard becomes standard and how room is made for innovation. "If we are exposed frequently to works containing a certain kind of feature which is contra-standard for us," according to Walton, "we ordinarily adjust our categories to accommodate it, making it contra-standard for us no longer."[53] Today's revolution is also tomorrow's status quo, and much artistic innovation is also reactionary, imagining a future different from the present moment.

Mind you, artworks that are no longer innovative survive in our estimation. All one has to do is look at the walls and halls of the great institutions. They survive for myriad reasons. That they are held to be beautiful is one—many forms of beauty are timeless. Another is that they are recognized to have been remarkably innovative *for their time*. I have no problem with an artwork ceasing to be innovative for whatever reason (cultural shifts, evolution of form, etc.), but I maintain that for an object to be an artwork, it must have, at the moment of its creation, been *somehow* innovative.

The history of art shows that the cycle of innovation is constant and overlapping. This section is concerned with three such forms of innovation:

1 Applied
2 Conceptual
3 Cultural Borrowing

Applied innovation

Applied innovation has to do with the way the artwork is made, specifically innovations regarding process and tool. A famous example of applied innovation is the particular varnish developed by Antonio Stradivari, whose instruments are still highly sought after circa 300 years later. This varnish, I am told, contributes particular character to his instruments which, in the hands of virtuosic musicians, cannot be beaten. Another processual innovator was Eva Hesse, who's use of latex and fiberglass in her work was groundbreaking and who's work blew my mind when I was introduced to it in college. In a similar vein, some applied innovations are innovations that are co-opted from other domains and used in the creation of artwork. Infamously, Vantablack, the darkest black paint ever invented, was licensed for the exclusive use of Anish Kapoor. Regardless of on what side of the art-world spat that that engendered one happens to land on, one would have to agree that Kapoor's use of that color has contributed to some stunning contemplations of void.

Other easy examples closer to home include multi-attribute (moving) lights and projection design. Multi-attribute lights allow the lighting designer to, for example, introduce more expansive movement possibilities and a near infinite color palette to their work, thus expanding the vocabulary possible when iterating design ideas, for better or worse. Likewise, advances in projection technology allow endless possibilities for the use of projected image as a design tool, for better or worse. Both innovations are "for better or worse" because, like all other strictly technical innovations one chooses to name, just because it is *possible* to do a thing does not mean it is *aesthetically efficacious* to do that thing; just because one is holding a Stradivarius does not mean one can play it. In other words, applied innovation alone does not automatically create innovative artwork.

Process-based, applied innovations need not be strictly limited to the physical realization of a specific artwork. They can also include the frameworks within which artists work. Arguably, one of the most critical process innovations was the development of true linear perspective by Filippo Brunelleschi and Leon Battista in 15th century Florence.[54] This discovery almost immediately appeared in work by the painter Masaccio, notably in his church of Santa Maria Novella *Holy Trinity*, circa 1427, and onwards from there. Another example is the twelve-tone technique pioneered by Arnold Schoenberg. This innovation was then put to practice by composers Alban Berg, Anton Webern, and Igor Stravinsky to name a few. In both instances, the process innovations then influenced a new style of art making.

Conceptual innovation

Conceptual innovation has to do with two things: First, the vision that the artist is expressing in their artwork. The ideas, concepts, discussions, etc. that underlie or govern the artwork's manifestation. This term is somewhat vaguely borrowed from conceptualism—an art movement where the idea of the art is more important than the actual manifestation of the artwork—in that these sorts of innovations are idea-based and also contemplate aesthetic characteristics (like beauty). Second, because the term "manifestation" implies something that is tangible to the senses, conceptual innovation is also concerned with the surface phenomena of artwork. Surface phenomena can be shape, sound, appearance, material, and so on; outward facing things. These phenomena are subject to endless iteration (think brush strokes or musical notes) and are typically, though not exclusively, non-aesthetic properties.

In "Beauty," I proposed three broad categories of critical methodologies with which to speculate about art (formal, contextual, and affective). Each of these methodologies is equally valid for determining if an artwork has characteristics that one can categorize as conceptually innovative. For example, a psychoanalytic approach (contextual) to investigating August Strindberg's *The Father* might help determine whether or not its novelty foreshadowed ideas he was more explicit about investigating via *A Dream Play*. Likewise, one might glean whether or not *Miss Julie* was novel in the sense that it accomplished what he wanted it to do; to "modernize the form"[55] with "a complicated way of looking at things [that] is in tune with the times," where "the times" references the prevalence of psychoanalysis.[56]

Likewise, one might apply a structuralist lens (also a contextual approach) to investigate an artwork in the search for conceptual innovation. Structuralist criticism, broadly, examines the world at two levels: visible surface phenomena and invisible organizational structures. The organizational structures give a framework with which to make sense of surface phenomena.[57] Surface phenomena alone do not form an idea, they need to be interpreted within a framework to be understood. As Tyson puts it, "Without a structural system to govern communication, we would have no language at all. Analogously, without the structuring principles that allow us to organize and understand the natural world, the data provided by our fives sense would be overwhelming and meaningless."[58] Words are just words, but when one puts words together in a sentence, using the organizational structure of a language, then meaning can be derived.

The organizational structure for an artwork exists in two planes, macro and micro. The macro-structure is the type of art it is, the form of art, and the micro-structure is the artwork itself; paintings and *Un Dimanche après-midi à l'île de la Grande Jatte* or skyscrapers and The Seagram Building. Identifying the macro-structural framework of an artwork and then using that as the basis for criticism is essential to determining whether an artwork is conceptually innovative. It is the way one interprets the micro-structure of little dots of paint instead of brush strokes for George Seurat and glass and the use of steel instead of concrete for architect Mies van der Rohe in order to understand the macro-structure of their artworks.

Cultural borrowing

Most, if not all, artists engage in a form of cultural borrowing; it is mostly not morally wrong and quite often a good thing. In the instance of theatre makers, it is almost exclusively true. I have never once designed an opera about a lighting designer and professor of mixed parentage, who grew up in Connecticut and Indiana and who now lives in Chicago and who has two children who live in Paris. It does not exist. If all of those things I have just named are markers of my cultural background, then it is possible that for every single show I have designed, I have, in one way or another, been complicit in acts of borrowing from cultures to which I do not belong. I have borrowed from early 17th-century British culture when I designed *King Lear* (Theatre for a New Audience, 2014),[59] I have borrowed from mid-19th century Italian culture when I designed the *La Traviata* (multiple productions, 2013–present),[60] I have borrowed from 20th-century Khmer culture when I designed *Where Elephants Weep,* I have borrowed from late 20th and early 21st century African American and Latinx cultures when I designed *Party People*, and I have borrowed from contemporary American white cis male culture when I designed *Linda Vista* (multiple productions, 2017–2019).[61] The list is endless.

My thinking here is shaped by arguments put forth by Young and director Daniel Banks. Young's central impact on my thinking revolves around his concept of content appropriation, aesthetic traits appropriated from the "artistic commons" of a particular culture; styles, motifs, subjects, and the like.[62] For artists operating within their own cultures, those aesthetic traits are the foundations of their work; what artwork is built from. This is true if the aesthetic traits are used directly, inform cross-cultural work, or are rebelled against. These traits may be directly identified, or like foundational pillars to a building, below the surface. For example, the art culture in fin de siècle Paris, with all its history and energy, informed Picasso and Braque as they developed a style that would be come to known as cubism. In effect, they rebelled against extant aesthetic traits and created new ones. And when Exter began painting in the cubist style, she could not help but bring her Ukrainian culture to bear in her use of color.[63] Her work borrows from the artistic commons of cubism and the artistic commons of Ukrainian culture to create its own set of aesthetic traits, creating new iterations of beauty. And so it goes.

Respectful cultural borrowing aids in aesthetic and non-aesthetic negentropy. Young explains: "A work can have aesthetic virtues precisely because it is not the work of an insider. The perspective of an outsider on a culture can be an advantage when it comes to producing works of art that provide insight into the culture. The best biography is not always autobiography," explains Young; all cultures have an interest in the exchange of free ideas engendered by this form of borrowing.[64] Ideas that when appropriated do no harm to the culture from which they come and can contribute to artworks with "considerable aesthetic merit."[65] A classic example is George Lucas's borrowing of plots, characters, and forms from the films of Japanese filmmaker Akira Kurosawa. Kurosawa's Samurai film *The Hidden Fortress* led directly to *Star Wars*. Arguably, *Star Wars* neither does harm to Japanese culture nor does it render *The Hidden Fortress* any less relevant to both Japanese and world culture.

A specific example of respectful, productive inter-cultural borrowing is my set design for *Party People*. Part of the set was an abstracted billboard covered in graffiti. The source material for the graffiti included period graphic design elements from The Young Lords and the Black Panthers as well as contemporary Puerto Rican nationalist imagery, the #blacklivesmatter slogan, an Arab Spring graffito, graffiti I found during a research trip around then present-day Oakland, a poster from Melbourne, and a hint of Banksy. Another example is my set design for *Where Elephants Weep*, which made ample use of contemporary and historical Khmer materials, religious iconography, and shadow puppetry techniques. None of these are cultures to which I belong, but brought together in a postmodern way, they did no harm to their source cultures and contributed meaningfully to the innovative wholeness of the productions. The history of art is the history of cultural cross-pollination.

Throughout his book, Young is careful to point out that there are some forms of borrowing that cause harm, especially including object appropriation—the stealing of tangible artworks from one culture by another—and forms of appropriation that lead to assimilation or perpetuates a negative stereotype. Where borrowing from Khmer iconography for *Where Elephants Weep* was a positive contribution that did no harm, to loot Khmer temples for props in order to make claims to "authenticity" would do great harm. Another form of harmful appropriation is misrepresentation, the wrong, incorrect, inadequate, unfaithful, or misleading representation of a person. This issue is relevant to a discussion about culture as it relates to artworks precisely because the body is the central point of focus and the densest medium for expression within the theatre. Embodied

Christopher Livingston, Ramona Keller, Horace V. Rogers, Jesse J. Perez, Oberon K.A. Adjepong, Mildren Ruiz-Sapp, Gizel Jiménez, Steven Sapp, Sophia Ramos, Michael Elich, Robynn Rodriguez, William Ruiz aka Ninja in *Party People*

The Public Theatre, 2016
Photograph by the author

aesthetics are a critical part of the performative experience and we must guard against the pitfalls of stereotypical representation.

Utility

The utility of this theoretical understanding of both artist and artwork is twofold: This definition of the artist makes from for creativity and defining an art in this way helps me continually assess my work. As I wrote in the introduction, I must understand what I think an artist is if I am to understand whether a designer is an artist. The definition I have proposed here helps me understand that being an artist has more to do with how one thinks than what one makes. For my analytical self, the word "mystic" is an act of compassion in that I do not feel obligated to be able to rationally justify every artistic impulse as long as I maintain my point of view and effective practice of craft when creating a design.

Furthermore, the necessary characteristics of an artwork that I have advanced provide a metric for my own work, against which I judge its efficacy, both as a standalone design and as a component of the artwork that is the production. As I light a show, I quite literally interrogate my design and its relationship to the production by asking myself: Is it beautiful and does it help make the production beautiful? Is it more than just illumination (a craft object)? Does it help the production advance its content (thresholds)? Is it innovative and does it help make the production innovative? Drilling deeper into each definition is needed to find the answers. Answers which inform how I make, look, evaluate, and adapt.

But the artwork and the artist are only one part of the equation, the proverbial tree falling in a forest. Someone has to witness it, right? That final part of the equation, hitherto mentioned but not defined, is a spectator. Without a spectator, the tree may as well not fall.

Notes

1. Carl Gustav Jung, "Psychology and Literature," in *Art and Its Significance: An Anthology of Aesthetic Theory*, ed. Stephen David Ross, trans. W.S. Dell and Cary F. Baynes, 2nd ed. (Albany, NY: State University of New York Press, 1987), 508.
2. Sol Lewitt, "Sentences on Conceptual Art," in *Art and Its Significance: An Anthology of Aesthetic Theory*, ed. Stephen David Ross, 2nd ed. (Albany, NY: State University of New York Press, 1987), 636.
3. Joseph Campbell, *The Inner Reaches of Outer Space: Metaphor as Myth and as Religion* (Novato, CA: New World Library, 2002), 89.
4. Campbell, *Inner Reaches*, 91.
5. Dave Hickey, "Enter the Dragon: On the Vernacular of Beauty," in *The Invisible Dragon: Essays on Beauty, Revised and Expanded* (Chicago: University of Chicago Press, 2009), 11. Here, I am poaching the metaphor from Hickey's discussion of the intercession of the priesthood in Caravaggio's painting *The Madonna of the Rosary*.

6 Campbell, *Inner Reaches*, 91.
7 Campbell, 91.
8 Campbell, 91.
9 Edward Gordon Craig, "The Actor and the Über-Marionette," in *Theatre and Performance Design: A Reader in Scenography*, ed. Jane Collins and Andrew Nisbit (London: Routledge, 2010), 259.
10 Stanisław Ignacy Witkiewicz, "From On a New Type of Play," in *Twentieth Century Theatre: A Sourcebook*, ed. Richard Drain, trans. Daniel Gerould and C.S. Durer (London: Routledge, 1995), 36.
11 Benjamin Boretz, *If I Am a Musical Thinker* (Barrytown, NY: Station Hill Press, 1985), 9.
12 Leo Tolstoy, "What Is Art?," in *Dramatic Theory and Criticism: Greeks to Grotowski*, ed. Bernard F. Dukore, trans. Aylmer Maude and Louise Maude (New York: Holt, Rinehart, and Winston, 1974), 182.
13 Richard Wagner, "The Art–Work of the Future," in *Dramatic Theory and Criticism: Greeks to Grotowski*, ed. Bernard F. Dukore, trans. William Ashton Ellis (New York: Holt, Rinehart, and Winston, 1974), 778.
14 Wagner, "Art–Work," 779.
15 Witkiewicz, "New Type of Play," 36.
16 *Where Elephants Weep*, composed by Him Sophy, libretto by Catherine Filloux, dir. Robert McQueen, set design by the author and costume design by Camille Assaf, prod. John Burt and Amrita Performing Arts, Chenla Theatre, Phnom Penh, KH, 2008.
17 *Party People,* by Universes (Steven Sapp, Mildred Ruiz-Sapp, and William Ruiz a.k.a. Ninja), dir. Liesl Tommy, set design by the author, costume design by Meg Neville, projection design by Sven Ortel, and composition, music direction, and sound design by Broken Chord Collective, The Public Theatre, New York, US, 2016 (previous iterations at Oregon Shakespeare Festival, Ashland, US, dir. Liesl Tommy, set design by Clint Ramos, costume design by E Sousa, video design by Pablo N. Molina, and composition, music direction, and sound design by Broken Chord Collective, 2012, and Berkeley Repertory Theatre, Berkeley, US, dir. Liesl Tommy, set design by the author, costume design by Meg Neville, projection design by Alexander V. Nichols, and composition, music direction, and sound design by Broken Chord Collective, 2014).
18 *Pass Over,* by Antoinette Chinonye Nwandu, dir. Danya Taymor, set design by Wilson Chin, costume design by Sarafina Bush, and sound design by Justin Ellington, Broadway, The August Wilson Theatre, New York, US, 2021 (with previous iterations at Steppenwolf Theatre, Chicago, US, with set design by Wilson Chin, costume design by Dede M. Ayite, and sound design and original music by Ray Nardelli, 2017, and Lincoln Center Theatre LCT3, New York, US, with set design by Wilson Chin, costume design by Sarafina Bush, and sound design by Justin Ellington, 2018).
19 Tolstoy, "What Is Art?," 181.
20 James O. Young, *Cultural Appropriation and the Arts* (Chichester, UK: Wiley–Blackwell, 2010), 40.
21 Lois Tyson, *Critical Theory Today: A User-Friendly Guide*, 3rd ed. (London: Routledge, 2015), 205.
22 Tyson, *Critical Theory Today*, 206.
23 *Les Mamelles de Tirésias,* composed by Francis Poulenc, libretto after *Les Mamelles de Tirésias* by Guillaume Apollinaire, dir. Ted Huffman, chor. Zack Winokur, set and costume design by Samal Blak. A coproduction between Snape Maltings, Festival d'Aix-en-Provence, and Queen Elisabeth Music Chapel with the support of enoa and the Culture Programme of the European Union, Aldeburgh Music, Aldeburgh, UK, 2012, Festival d'Aix-en-Provence, Aix-en-Provence, FR, 2013, La Monnaie/De Munt, Brussels, BE, 2014, Dutch National Opera, Amsterdam, NL, 2015, and Palau de les Arts Reina Sofia, València, SP, 2019.
24 R.G. Collingwood, *The Principles of Art* (Oxford: Clarendon Press, 1938), 15.
25 Collingwood, *The Principles of Art*, 15–17.
26 Collingwood, 22.

27. Jason Farago, "Good Artists Copy, Great Artists Steal," *BBC Culture*, November 12, 2014, www.bbc.com/culture/story/20141112-great-artists-steal.
28. Jan Meyer and Ray Land, "Threshold Concepts and Troublesome Knowledge: Linkages to Ways of Thinking and Practicing within the Disciplines," *Enhancing Teaching-Learning Environments in Undergraduate Courses Project, Occasional Report 4* (Teaching and Learning Research Programme, Economic and Social Research Council, University of Edinburgh, Edinburgh, May 2003), 1.
29. Meyer and Land, "Threshold Concepts," 1.
30. Meyer and Land, 10.
31. Meyer and Land, 4–5.
32. Oscar Hammerstein II, "You've Got To Be Carefully Taught," *South Pacific* (New York: Williamson Music, n.d.), 77.
33. Glynis Cousin, "An Introduction to Threshold Concepts," *Planet* 17, no. 1 (December 2007): 4. DOI: 10.11120/plan.2006.00170004.
34. Meyer and Land, "Threshold Concepts," 5.
35. *Othello*, by William Shakespeare, dir. Arin Arbus, set design by Peter Ksander, costume design by Miranda Hoffman, and sound design by Matt O'Hare, Theatre for a New Audience, New York, US, 2009.
36. William Shakespeare, *Othello, the Moor of Venice*, in *The Complete Works of Shakespeare*, ed. David Bevington, 4th ed. (New York: HarperCollins Publishers, 1992), 2.1.2–4.
37. Shakespeare, *Othello*, 2.1.70–75.
38. The first two ideas postdate Shakespeare, of course, but a rose by any other name …
39. Meyer and Land, "Threshold Concepts," 6–11. Here Meyer and Land are citing David Perkins, "The Many Faces of Constructivism," *Educational Leadership* 57, no. 3 (November 1999): 6–11.
40. Pina Bausch, "What Moves Me," *Pina Bausch Foundation*, accessed December 17, 2020, www.pinabausch.org/en/pina/what-moves-me.
41. Wassily Kandinsky, "On the Question of Form," in *The Blaue Reiter Almanac*, ed. Wassily Kandinsky and Franz Marc, documentary edition ed. and with an introduction by Klaus Lankheit, trans. by Henning Falkenstein (1912; repr., Boston, MA: MFA Publications, 2005), 149.
42. Kandinsky, "Question of Form," 149.
43. August Wilson, "The Ground on Which I Stand," *American Theatre*, June 20, 2016, www.americantheatre.org/2016/06/20/the-ground-on-which-i-stand/.
44. Wilson, "Ground."
45. Konstantin Rudnitsky, *Russian and Soviet Theatre 1905–1932*, ed. Lesley Milne, trans. Roxane Permar (New York: Harry N. Abrams, 1988), 52.
46. Yevgeny Vakhtangov, "Two Final Discussions with Students," in *The Vakhtangov Sourcebook*, ed. and trans. Andrei Malaev-Babel (London: Routledge, 2011), 153.
47. Vsevolod Meyerhold, "From the Reconstruction of the Theatre," in *Twentieth Century Theatre: A Sourcebook*, ed. Richard Drain, trans. Edward Braun (London: Routledge, 1995), 100.
48. Clement Greenberg, "Modern and Postmodern," William Dobell Memorial Lecture, Sydney, Australia, October 31, 1979, reproduced in *Arts* 54, no. 6 (February 1980): 65.
49. Kenya Hara, *White*, trans. Jooyeon Rhee (Zurich: Lars Müller Publishers, 2012), 61.
50. This is where the *Field of Dreams* argument comes in. If we make innovative theatre, will the audiences appear and pay for it, or do we need to make theatre that we believe our audiences will want to get them to come? For more on this charged topic, speak to Artistic and Managing Directors everywhere.
51. Young, *Cultural Appropriation*, 157.
52. Lewitt, "Sentences," 637.
53. Kendall L. Walton, "Categories of Art," *The Philosophical Review* 79, no. 3 (1970): 352.
54. Samuel Y. Edgerton, "The Mirror, the Window, and the Telescope: How Renaissance Linear Perspective Changed Our Vision of the Universe," *Nexus Network Journal* 12, no. 1 (2010): 149–152, doi.org/10.1007/s00004-010-0020-x.

55 August Strindberg, "Preface to Miss Julie," in *Dramatic Theory and Criticism: Greeks to Grotowski*, ed. Bernard F. Dukore (New York: Holt, Rinehart, and Winston, 1974), 564.
56 August Strindberg, "Preface to Miss Julie," 566.
57 For a deeper dive into this particular school of criticism, see chapter 7 of Tyson, *Critical Theory Today*.
58 Tyson, *Critical Theory Today*, 199.
59 *King Lear*, by William Shakespeare, dir. Arin Arbus, set design by Riccardo Hernández, costume design by Susan Hilferty, composition by Michaël Attias, and sound design by Michaël Attias and Nicholas Pope. Theatre for a New Audience, Brooklyn, US, 2014.
60 *La Traviata*, composed by Giuseppe Verdi, libretto by Francesco Maria Piave dir. Arin Arbus, set design by Riccardo Hernández, and costume design by Cait O'Connor. A coproduction between Lyric Opera of Chicago, Chicago, US, Canadian Opera Company, Toronto, CA, and Houston Grand Opera, Houston, US, from 2013 through this writing.
61 *Linda Vista*, by Tracy Letts, dir. Dexter Bullard, set design by Todd Rosenthal, costume design by Laura Bauer, sound design by Richard Woodbury. *Linda Vista* premiered at Steppenwolf Theatre, Chicago, US, in 2017, then Center Theatre Group, Los Angeles, US, in 2018, and on Broadway at Second Stage's Helen Hayes Theatre, New York, US, in 2019.
62 Young, *Cultural Appropriation*, 66.
63 Georgii Kovalenk "Alexsandra Exter," in *Amazons of the Avant-Guarde*, ed. John E. Bowlt and Matthew Drutt, published in conjunction with an exhibition of the same title at the Guggenheim Museum in New York, September 8, 2000–January 7, 2001 (New York: Guggenheim Museum, 2000), 131–141.
64 Young, *Cultural Appropriation*, 61.
65 Young, 32, 83–84.

3 The Spectator

Rooms by the Sea, 1951
By Edward Hopper
Oil on canvas
29 1/4 × 40 in. (74.3 × 101.6 cm)
Yale University Art Gallery
Bequest of Stephen Carlton Clark, B.A. 1903

DOI: 10.4324/9781003206460-4

Spectare

Theories of spectatorship are as important to a designer as the definition of an artwork or the artist because the first person to see our own work is ourselves. "Look," after all, is the next step in the process after "make." Positioning ourselves in the place of a spectator allows us to critically examine how one might engage with our work, what its impact might be, and, consequently, whether or not the work is actually doing what we want it to.

When I reflect on myself as a spectator, I identify a process or activity that, in the best cases, goes something like this: I look at Edward Hopper's painting *Rooms by the Sea*, which is to say that I engage (an active verb) with the painting. I do not do this automatically, rather, I have to be in the mood to engage, and I have to want to engage. I get distracted easily, and for me, being a good spectator takes a lot of effort. (I do not understand people who have the mental energy to take in an entire grand museum in one go!) But when I do engage, I do it across multiple spectrums: I think about the art and I experience emotion. Standing before Hopper's painting, I think about the absence of shore, the openness/emptiness of the room in the foreground and the quotidian nature of the sliver of the room I see on the left. What I think and what I feel are interdependent, connected by what I am bringing to the conversation with the work at that moment in time and the work itself. I cannot quite make sense of the shape of the light on the wall and the floor. I find that I feel unsettled. I think: "everything is not as it appears to be, is it?" I ruminate; I make meaning from my experience with the artwork.

I am drawn, like many others, to the word spectator specifically because it is the agent-noun of the verb spectate. I want spectate to include the many ways of seeing, hearing, watching, and/or experiencing—in short, engaging with and critically analyzing—artworks. I also want, in the context of theatre, to draw attention to the notion of spectacle. Specifically, that spectator and spectacle both stem from the same Latin word: spectare, which means to look at, see, or watch. Here, I will make a distinction between a spectator and an audience—after all, this is a book about theatre. A spectator is an individual, and an audience is a mass of spectators in a room watching a thing.

Two aspects

It seems to me that spectating involves two aspects that have both subjective and objective components: The personal and the transactional.

The personal aspect has to do with what the spectator brings to the moment of engagement with an artwork; their competencies and their background. Their competencies are the skills they bring to bear in that engagement. Their background is the sum of their identities, cultures, and life experiences that might influence the way they engage with an artwork. It is one thing to watch the second scene of *La Traviata* if one has not had one's heart broken, and quite another if one has. Our experiences affect our ability to empathize and understand. Therefore, different people bringing different experiences to the way they view the artwork will generate different perceptions. Neither is better than the other, they are merely different. This multiplicity is a good thing.

The transactional aspect has to do with the actuality of engaging with an artwork in person and making meaning from that experience. One engages with the artwork through the senses, intellect, and emotion. One sees, one hears, and one might touch, taste, or smell—processes which help us take the work in. One engages with it intellectually, through critical analysis, and emotionally, through how it makes one feel. Through this engagement, the spectator begins to understand the artwork, to describe and classify its components for eventual understanding. These processes happen in parallel at both conscious and unconscious levels as the spectator begins to make meaning, for themselves, from the artwork. There is a feedback loop where meaning-making might engender more nuanced engagement, which in turn creates new meaning, etc. However, meaning-making does not just happen at the moment of engagement—it continues after the fact. Sometimes, rumination takes time.

Interest

You will notice many echos of the methodologies proposed in "Beauty" in this chapter. That is because beauty, in its many forms (formal, contextual, affective), demands that the spectator pay attention. Philosopher and classicist Paul Woodruff, in his book *The Necessity of Theatre,* calls audience members watchers and states that "A good watcher pays attention."[1] We can, for this moment, equate watcher with spectator, say that the first step in caring is that the spectator has to want to pay attention—without attention, an artwork is, as I have oft repeated from Hickey, doomed to inconsequence. But, in terms of the transaction of spectating, paying attention is just the start of engagement. Interest, I think, is the natural next step toward caring. As Woodruff says, "Beauty is the reason for watching, but not for caring."[2] If, after the spectator's attention is caught, and they are interested in the artwork, it follows that they will want to care about it. Sometimes, it is possible to force a spectator's hand and make them engage. A sharp spotlight cutting through a dark stage on a singer in a sequined gown is going to be hard to not pay attention to, but a spectator's attention, and whether that turns to interest, is fickle. Interest has to be genuine for it to be lasting. Genuine interest is related to who the spectator is and what their competencies

Quinn Kelsey and Ekaterina Siurina in *La Traviata*

Canadian Opera Company, 2015
Photograph by the author

are, and has to do with things they already care about or things they are curious about.

I think that interest can be categorized as intrinsic or extrinsic. Intrinsic interest has to do with things one already knows or subjects about which one already cares. For example, a particular interest of mine is British and French naval architecture at the end of the 18th and beginning of the 19th centuries around the Napoleonic wars. Because of this, I might be curious about Thomas Birch's *Caught in a Gale*. It requires more than just a casual glance to see the barge of sailors at the stern, the wreckage in the foreground, and the fact all the topmasts are gone. It is at this point that I fully grasp the peril of the scene, and with that, I have an emotional response. I see the ship being destroyed and I care about the men in the painting. I also might know a thing or two about color and this intrinsic interest is the reason I am drawn to the work of Mark Rothko. The paintings are not necessarily only about color fields, but that is my hook. Once I am hooked, I contemplate the emotional content of the work and care about how it makes me feel.

Extrinsic interest is tied to curiosity about things one does not know or subjects in which one might not already be interested. I contend that curiosity is an innate trait and that some people are more curious than others, so this is very much a subjective thing, but the outcome is the same as intrinsic interest. If I did not already care about naval architecture but was curious about it, or if I did not know that much about color theory but was interested in it, the results are likely to be the same in terms of my interest in the paintings. Even if something is beautiful, and even if a spectator is possessed of both intrinsic and extrinsic interest, it still may not be possible to pay attention, and thus no transaction will be possible.

Transaction

What I mean by transaction is that there is a flow between the artist, via the artwork, and the spectator. I do not think that it is as simple as "the artist means x," and so the act of spectating will allow the spectator to learn "x." This smacks of the kind of inegalitarian relationship between artist and spectator that French philosopher Jacques Rancière seems to be railing against when he says, "It is not the transmission of the artist's knowledge or inspiration to the spectator. It is the third thing that is owned by no none, whose meaning is owned by no one, but which subsists between them, excluding any uniform transmission, any identity of cause and effect."[3] The artist, for Rancière, is not a teacher and the spectator an ignorant student rather they are peers in the process of making meaning.

I do, however, think that meaning-making has to take into account the artist's intent, which is where I depart from what I understand to be

Rancière's conception of the artwork/spectator relationship. I do not think that the "third thing" and its meaning are owned by no one or that it excludes transmission or cause and effect. I think meaning is owned, if a concept so feathery can be owned, by the spectator. That it is the effect of the artwork—no reaction happens without a catalyst—and that something flows from the artist via the vessel of the artwork to the spectator in the transaction of engagement. I agree that it is a "third thing." The artist means "x," the spectator brings "y," and the transaction results in "z."

The spectator, however, is not a passive receptor of the artist's intent, rather, they are an active participant in the artwork's efficacy. Rancière refers to this spectator as 'emancipated.' While I do not agree with his theory in totality, I do agree that the spectator is of equal intellectual value as the artist, and the boundary between those who act and those who look is blurred.[4] Rancière writes of this relationship,

> Like researchers, artists construct the stages where the manifestation and effect of their skills are exhibited, rendered uncertain in the terms of the new idiom that conveys a new intellectual adventure. The effect of the idiom cannot be anticipated. It requires spectators who play the role of active interpreters, who develop their own translation in order to appropriate the 'story' and make it their own story.[5]

A logical consequence of this perspective is that an artwork does not have a fixed meaning outside of the experience of the spectator; that it does not reach its apotheosis without engagement (what Wagner might refer to as "The moment of its liveliest embodiment"—!).[6] I think this is true, and as a convenient parallel for explanation, I turn to another form of literary critique: reader-response theory. Reader-response covers a broad spectrum of criticism and has to do with analyzing the act of reading as well as the actual words being read. As Tyson explains, "Reader-response theory ... maintains that what a text is cannot be separated from what it does," furthermore, "reader response theorists share two beliefs: (1) that the role of the reader cannot be omitted from our understanding of literature, and (2) that readers do not passively consume the meaning presented to them by an objective literary text; rather they actively make the meaning they find in literature."[7] I think that these ideas are easy to extrapolate from reader and text and apply to spectator and artwork.

For example, a sub-set of reader-response is affective stylistics. Affective stylistics analyzes text as an event in time that is a product of being read rather than a fixed thing and investigates how the text affects the reader. Tyson explains that "many practitioners of affective stylistics do not consider the text an objective, autonomous entity—it does not have a fixed meaning independent of readers—because the text consists of the results it produces, and those results occur within the reader."[8] If one substitutes reader and text with artwork and spectator, one gets this: the artwork is not an objective, autonomous entity. It does not have a fixed meaning independent of spectators because the artwork consists of the results it produces, and the results occur within the spectator.

In fact, there is another arm of the octopus of reader-response that concerns itself almost exclusively with the subjective response, but I think that takes it too far because it minimizes the importance of—you guessed it!—the formal elements of an artwork.

That is why I am drawn to some of the ideas contained in literary theorist Louise Rosenblatt's transactional reader-response theory, a theory that is a major influence on my own thinking. It is the reason why I have co-opted the word "transaction." Rosenblatt asserts that what she calls a poem (which I take as a stand-in for any literary work of art) "comes into being in the live circuit set up between the reader and 'the text.'"[9] She continues, "The finding of meaning involves both the author's text and what the reader brings to it."[10] Again, I contend that all these ideas can be extrapolated from a study of literature to spectating of all art forms. I read this as an assertion that the words (artwork) are as important as the reader (spectator) in terms of meaning-making, where the 'poem' is the meaning.

Furthermore, Rosenblatt puts forth that there are two ends to the "reading transaction" continuum.[11] On one side, there is the efferent; the facts, the information contained in the text, and on the other side, the aesthetic; how what we are reading makes us feel. Tyson further maps those two things to two kinds of meaning every text offers: determinate (efferent), meaning facts clearly indicated on the page, and indeterminate (aesthetic), meaning gaps in the text up for interpretation.[12] Rancière, too, considers the notion of the poem within his contemplation of theatre when he says that the spectator "observes, selects, compares, interprets," the "poem" that is the theatrical event, as "she links what she sees to a host of other things that she has seen on other stages, in other kinds of place. She composes her own poem with the elements of the poem before her."[13] It is the *spectator* who brings the determinate/efferent together with the indeterminate/aesthetic to create meaning.

Why is this all so important to me? Because it sets forth a kind of equality between an efferent/determinate mode of engagement with an artwork, which I think is objective, and an aesthetic/indeterminate mode of engagement with an artwork, which I think is subjective. Rosenblatt says that one ought to adopt a stance appropriate to how one wants to engage.[14] I do not know if this is a disagreement or a subtlety of interpretation, but I think part of spectating involves using *both* modes at the same time. It is the process of both recognizing how a tune is deployed *and* having an emotional reaction to it. Engaging both ways at the *same* time is critical to a lighting designer: they must be a good spectator to their own work and that of their collaborators, so they can always and at once make, look, evaluate, and adapt.

This might also imply that any way of spectating is as good as the next. Not really. As critic E.D. Hirsch writes in "Validity in Interpretation," that "Validity of interpretation is not the same as inventiveness of interpretation."[15] The salient takeaway is that while most forms of spectating can result in some manner of interpretation, there is some sort of qualitative continuum of interpretations. I argue that the more complex in scope the interpretation is, the better. Thus the notion of good spectatorship.

Competency

A good spectator has to know how to engage with an artwork. This often requires particular competencies. Like the features defining an artwork, competency can be defined as an activity that exists along a spectrum. At one end is bad spectating and at the other end is the perhaps unattainable state of perfect spectating. Somewhere in the middle is good spectating, and good spectating is delineated from bad spectating by the markers that describe basic competency. Basic competencies are fundamental and minimal—but sufficient—capacities with which to effectively engage with an artwork, and they are dependent on what the artwork is.

For example, a required competency for spectators prepared to watch the Claude Régy production Sarah Kane's play *4:48 Psychosis* presented at the Brooklyn Academy of Music 2005 was fluency in French. As the competencies advance, the quality of spectating advances. High school French may have allowed a basic entrée into this production, but mastery of conversational French would have allowed for a much more nuanced experience. The production was stunning in its simplicity and I suspect I would have loved it had I been able to understand what was going on. Alas, the supertitles were less than minimal and I am not fluent in French. Therefore, it was impossible for me to be a good spectator of the work and I did not care a fig for the show.

Education

That many basic competencies are a product of education is beyond dispute. Reading, for example, is a basic competency for being able to engage with literature. A good spectator fits the notion of an informed reader; someone who has attained a certain level of literary competency that allows them to engage a text in a particular way.[16] A society that advances the study of liberal arts is a society that makes good spectators. Setting aside the very big issue of access to and quality of education for the moment, I will focus on how we gain the competencies that allow us to become successful spectators in more advanced, art centric, topics of study: visual art, literature, music, fine, and performing arts.

Harkening back to the formalists and new critics, one can make the argument that mere exposure to enough examples of artworks will lead to competency.[17] Indeed, this is an argument that Hickey advances in the first page of his essay "Formalism."[18] As I wrote in the "Beauty," I do think that there is much to be gained objectively speaking from a formalist critique, but I also think that it requires training for the spectator. Mere exposure can make one more inclined to like one thing over another, but it is less helpful in understanding why. Form theorist Paul Hekkert and psychologist Pier Van Wieringen show in their paper "Beauty in the Eye of Expert and Nonexpert Beholders: A Study in the Appraisal of Art" that non-experts and experts judge art differently. Non-experts tend to judge art semantically, on content, whereas experts tend to "interpret, classify, and judge works of art, irrespective of content, in terms of formal, stylistic, and relational properties."[19] Education leads to the ability to engage with an artwork on multiple levels beyond just subject matter and is necessary for the judging of aesthetic quality. Art theorist Rudolf Arnheim explains in his essay "What is Aesthetic Fact?" "To evaluate a particular work, one relies on the standard one has derived from what one has found in the styles and principles of the arts elsewhere; but to obtain those standards and principles in the first place, one must have gathered them from what one has known."[20] This is not to advocate that a novice should not be let into a museum. Quite the opposite! How else can a novice build their vocabulary of what is "known?"

But, I do think a spectator that has certain competencies with aesthetic properties of, say, fin de siècle painting will be able to identify what Walton would call standard and variable features of that particular style. This aesthetic perception, in turn, will allow the spectator to identify the contra-standard. Which, in turn, will allow the spectator to categorize the artwork within the context of other similar artworks. Which, I then contend, will then allow them to engage with the artwork in a more meaningful way. Walton acknowledges the importance of education when he says, "Perceiving works in a certain category or set of categories is a skill that must be acquired by training, and exposure to a great many other works of the category or categories in question is ordinarily, I believe, a critical part of this training."[21] An expert is likely to get more out of any given artwork than a novice.

Basic competencies are not exclusively the result of formalized education, they can also be learned cultural norms. Watching intently and without disturbing one's neighbors is a normative way to experience contemporary Eurocentric theatre just as quiet contemplation is a normative way of looking at a painting in a museum for Eurocentric cultures. A good spectator is aware of these norms and adheres to them, especially in the company of others, in venues where this behavior is expected. These behaviors are a result of experience and exposure. It may be bougie to suggest that a good spectator is quiet at a concert of Verdi's *Requiem* because that is the best way to hear as much of the music as possible, but I do think the ability to remain quiet and listen intently are basic competencies required to get the most out of it. (This behavior does have a benefit, too, in that it is also considerate to one's fellow patrons.) Whether or not one likes it, it is a fact of life that these norms exist and that they exist for rational reasons. However, the existence of these norms also acknowledges the artist's right to choose whether to embrace these norms. This is what allows Banksy to exhibit mostly on stolen walls or for Riccardo Muti to hold the downbeat until the auditorium is silent. Both are equally correct.

Privilege

Still, any discussion that advantages education about and exposure to the arts is bound to encounter the issue of privilege. The argument is that those who have access to that education and exposure constitute a privileged few in society. And an extension of that argument is that because of that, one part of being a good spectator has to do with being privileged. This line of reasoning cannot be refuted because it is, sadly, true. Let me be clear, though: when I say that it is true that access to arts and arts education is confined to a privileged few does not mean that I think that that is *right*. It is elitist because the public education system treats it as elitist. I think that it is a crime against humanity that in the United States a basic education that includes arts literacy is seen as a luxury commodity. For a well-functioning society, art should *not* be something hung on the wall for decoration by the privileged few. It should be the material from which *everyone's walls are built*. As of this writing, at least, the society in which I live is not well-functioning in this regard in the least bit. (Somewhere, Nero is tuning his fiddle.)

No less than John Adams acknowledged the importance of the arts when he wrote,

> I must study Politicks and War that my sons may have liberty to study Mathematicks and Philosophy. My sons ought to study Mathematicks and Philosophy, Geography, natural History, Naval Architecture, navigation, Commerce and Agriculture, in order to give their Children a right to study Painting, Poetry, Musick, Architecture, Statuary, Tapestry and Porcelaine.[22]

He fought a revolution so that his grandchildren could study art. If there is a call to arms to be found anywhere in this book, let it be this: Education is the magic bullet. Good education is a universal right and an *essential* component of a good education is arts literacy.

Meaning-making

I do not think that there is only one right way to engage with an artwork, but I do think that there are better or worse ways. When I look at my influences above and synthesize them into my own perspective, I certainly think that it is not a question of learning what is the *correct* way to engage with an artwork but that once one has learned basic competencies, one can learn ways that are more efficacious than others. Basic competencies allow one to be a good spectator of *The Raft of the Medusa,* but a study of French romanticism makes one better. This is not a moral or binary judgment. It is more like baseball: one can be really good at it, or terrible at it (like me), or somewhere in between. Being a good spectator takes work. It is not a passive process of looking at something pretty, rather, it is a process of critically engaging and making meaning. This is hard work!

As I wrote in "Artist/Artwork," part of what makes an artwork is that it is both a vessel to express the artist's point of view—as a communicative act—and that it has troublesome knowledge embedded in it. This implies that there is some flow in the engagement. A good spectator is able to engage critically with an artwork both objectively and subjectively and intellectually and emotionally in order to make meaning from the experience. Sometimes that meaning is new knowledge or understanding, and sometimes, most times, I think it is seeing a path. Understanding is a process here, not an endpoint.

In the transactional process between artwork and spectator, it is important that the spectator engages in both the objective and the subjective modes, synthesizing the two in their meaning-making. This is an active process; the spectator has to think. Finding meaning, Hirsh says, "is an affair of consciousness."[23] The first mode allows the spectator to understand that when the ever increasing tempo of ba-duh, ba-duh, ba-duh starts happening in the score of *Jaws*, they are hearing a leitmotif, and the second mode engenders fear. And, the meaning-making happens when the big, bad fish with the sharp teeth shows up: the spectator understands that in the world of this movie, sharks are bad. I am pretty sure John Williams meant that. That is a simplistic example to illustrate a point. The more abstract the artwork, I contend, the more difficult it is to make meaning.

The thing is, of course, that the objective framework from which the spectator engages with Williams's score is that of Western classical music.

What if a spectator engaged via a non-Western framework, you ask? Well, the meaning would be different. Is that better or worse? As I have said, I contend that it is better to objectively engage in the framework that the artist is likely to have intended (which, here, is pretty clear to me). In Woodruff's words, "Successful theatre is a collaboration between performers and audience, and the two groups must share—or at least be willing to learn—a culture that allows them to practice the same art from different sides of the line."[24] Shared context engenders deeper understanding.

But what is meaning if not bringing order to the chaos of input? "As Rorschach tests demonstrate, the human animal is obsessed with making meaning," writes dramaturg Tori Haring-Smith, "Show us a blob of ink, and we see a goose. Show us a random collection of objects, and we can impose a narrative that explains their relationships. We impose form to create meaning."[25] Everything encountered in both modes of transactions are signs of some sort and the same conventions and symbols an artist must learn and deploy are the ones the spectator uses to determine meaning. Because the transaction is co-dependent on the spectator's context, spectating is necessarily synthetic and like any synthetic conclusion, your milage may vary.

Untitled, 2016

Photograph
Abdalrhman Ismail/Reuters Pictures

Take, for example, this photograph by Syrian photographer Abdalrhman Ismail that appeared on the cover of the *New York Times* on April 29, 2016, which was brought to my attention by Horowitz. Do I find it beautiful? I do, very much so, in a sublime way. I am attracted to its monochromatic nature, with a splash of red like a Clyfford Still painting, and that it is lit both directly, from over the subject's left shoulder, and indirectly, from bounced light. I am curious about the circumstances of the photograph and have a hard time understanding that it was not staged, although the forearm visible on the right side of the frame makes me believe it was not. These are my objective understandings of the photograph. It also unsettles me. I ask myself if I should feel shame that I find it so beautiful even though it is a moment of trauma for the subject. I feel sympathy for this woman who has had to endure years and years of violence (I cannot empathize with her, never having been bombed) and wonder what the emotional toll must be. I also wonder, has she lost someone? And who does that arm belong to? These are my subjective responses. When I put them together, I make meaning for myself from the photograph. The immediacy and difficulty of human conflict is laid bare before me. Human suffering is writ large via a single individual. And as a theatre maker, someone who's work traffics in emotion and routinely deals with the most difficult aspects of humanity, I immediately think, "Ah! So, this is Brecht's Mother Courage."

Evaluating

As a member of the creative team, being able to position oneself as a spectator to one's own work and to the production as a whole is a critical skill. It makes us better artists. Looking from the perspective of the audience—both from the objective/efferent/determinant and the subjective/aesthetic/indeterminate perspectives—allows one to anticipate how the production will engage (or does engage if the show is in previews) with an audience *and* what the consequent meaning-making might be (or seems to be). A facility with many modes of spectatorship will allow one to quickly examine the work from multiple perspectives in the process of making. A simplistic version, returning to our spotlit, sequined star, has to do with the articulation of the spotlight: a hard-edged spotlight might engender one meaning while a soft-edged spotlight might engender another. Looking from a spectator's perspective and evaluating possible meanings—performative vs. non-performative, audience aware vs. fourth wall, etc.—will allow one to make choices that best support the objectives of the production. In other words, understanding the possible meanings from the spectator's perspective is a profound part of the "evaluate" step in the make, look, evaluate, and adapt process.

Notes

1 Paul Woodruff, *The Necessity of Theatre* (Oxford: Oxford University Press, 2008), 142.
2 Woodruff, *Necessity*, 153.
3 Jacques Rancière, *The Emancipated Spectator*, trans. Gregory Elliott (London: Verso, 2009), 15.
4 Rancière, *Emancipated Spectator*, 10, 19.
5 Rancière, 22.
6 Richard Wagner, "The Art–Work of the Future," in *Dramatic Theory and Criticism: Greeks to Grotowski*, ed. Bernard F. Dukore, trans. William Ashton Ellis (New York: Holt, Rinehart, and Winston, 1974), 777.
7 Lois Tyson, *Critical Theory Today: A User-Friendly Guide*, 3rd ed. (London: Routledge, 2015), 162.
8 Tyson, *Critical Theory Today*, 167.
9 Louise M. Rosenblatt, "From *Literature as Exploration* and *The Reader, the Text, the Poem*," *Voices from the Middle: Remembering Louise Rosenblatt* 12, no. 3 (March 2005): 30.
10 Rosenblatt, *Literature as Exploration*, 30.
11 Louise M. Rosenblatt, "From *Viewpoints: Transaction versus Interaction*," *Voices from the Middle: Remembering Louise Rosenblatt* 12, no. 3 (March 2005): 56.
12 Tyson, *Critical Theory Today*, 165–166.
13 Rancière, *Emancipated Spectator*, 13.
14 Rosenblatt, *Transaction versus Interaction*, 57.
15 E. D. Hirsch, Jr., "Validity in Interpretation," in *Art and Its Significance: An Anthology of Aesthetic Theory*, ed. Stephen David Ross, 2nd ed. (Albany, NY: State University of New York Press, 1987), 348.
16 Tyson, *Critical Theory Today*, 178–180. See the discussion concerning the "informed reader" and "literary competency" in the "Defining Readers" section.
17 Paul Hekkert, Clementine Thurgood, and T. W. Allan Whitfield, "The Mere Exposure Effect for Consumer Products as a Consequence of Existing Familiarity and Controlled Exposure," *Acta Psychologica* 144, no. 2 (2013): 411–417, https://doi.org/10.1016/j.actpsy.2013.07.015.
18 Dave Hickey, "Formalism," in *Pirates and Farmers* (London: Ridinghouse, 2013), 83.
19 Paul Hekkert and Piet C.W. Van Wieringen, "Beauty in the Eye of Expert and Nonexpert Beholders: A Study in the Appraisal of Art," *American Journal of Psychology* 109, no. 3 (1996): 391, https://doi.org/10.2307/1423013.
20 Rudolf Arnheim, "What Is an Aesthetic Fact?," in *The Split and the Structure* (Berkeley, CA: University of California Press, 1996), 68.
21 Kendall L. Walton, "Categories of Art," *The Philosophical Review* 79, no. 3 (1970): 366.
22 In a letter to his wife, Abigail. "John Adams to Abigail Adams, 12 May 1780," *Founders Online*, National Archives, https://founders.archives.gov/documents/Adams/04-03-02-0258. Original source: *The Adams Papers*, Adams Family Correspondence, *April 1778–September 1780*, ed. L.H. Butterfield and Marc Friedlaender (Cambridge, MA: Harvard University Press, 1973), 3: 341–343.
23 Hirsch, "Validity in Interpretation," 344.
24 Woodruff, *Necessity*, 146.
25 Tori Haring–Smith, "Dramaturging Non-Realism: Creating a New Vocabulary," *Theatre Topics* 13, no. 1 (March 2003): 46, doi:10.1353/tt.2003.009.

4　Theatre

Ithiograph of the set design for act two of *Orfeo ed Euridice* for the 1913 Festspielhaus Hellerau production, 1926

By Adolphe Appia
Swiss Theatre Museum Bern, Inventory No. Appia 18B.
Courtesy of Richard Beacham

Definition

Here I want to reiterate my earlier comments about the transactional aspect of spectating. In the singular case of a static artwork—a book, a painting, a sculpture—meaning-making is largely unidirectional: it flows from the artist through the artwork to the spectator. In the collective case of theatre broadly writ—live artwork where there are humans performing in front of other humans—meaning-making is omnidirectional: it forms a feedback loop between the artwork that is the performance and the spectators en masse as an audience *and* between the spectators that comprise the audience. This meaning-making feedback loop is central to the efficacy of theatre.

My definition of theatre is quite simple: stories performed in a specific style by one group of people in front of another group of people in a specific time and place. This definition is tight—and this chapter is short—because there are direct corollaries in the theatre to the ideas I have advanced about artists, artworks, and spectators in previous chapters. As you may have guessed, they are:

1 Artist to creative team
2 Artwork to production
3 Spectator to audience

The nuances to the mappings, of course, bear explanation because the definitions in previous chapters are modeled on singularities, whereas theatre is, at its very beating heart, a collective endeavor.

Story

I acknowledge the complication of the word "story" because it seems to preclude forms like happenings, improv, postdramatic theatre, and performance art. Theatre and story, for me, are inextricably intertwined. While I think that many of the designerly ideas contained in this book are transferrable to other events on stages, my point of view on how to make good lighting for the stage has so much to do with understanding story that my definition of theatre must necessarily include the word story. The OED defines story as "a narrative of imaginary or (less commonly) real events composed for the entertainment of the listener or reader; a (short) work of fiction; a tale."[1] Implied in this definition is the notion of plot, an arrangement of a story with a beginning, a middle, and an end (even if not presented strictly in chronological order, e.g., Harold Pinter's *Betrayal*, Jason Robert Brown's *The Last Five Years*), and a narrative.

We need stories to help us understand our own reality and human nature in general. This includes our inward facing reality, versions of our own experiences (which is a sort of micro perspective), and our outward facing reality, those experiences of the world around us (which is a sort of macro perspective). Stories help us categorize, interpret, understand, judge, and grow by introducing threshold concepts. There are those, including Christopher Booker in his tome *The Seven Basic Plots*, who argue that storytelling is coded into humans evolutionarily, connecting our unconscious to our conscious:

> The real significance of our capacity to imagine stories, as we have seen, lies in the extent to which stories emerge from some part of the mind which is beyond the storyteller's conscious awareness. ... The very fact that they follow such identifiable patterns and are shaped by such consistent rules indicates that the unconscious is thus using them for a purpose: to convey to the conscious live of our mind a particular picture of human nature and how it works.[2]

This is not unlike Campbell's artist and mystic, both of whom bring their "inmost truth" to consciousness.[3] In this regard, the storyteller is as much an artist as a painter or composer.

No matter what the mode, and no matter how based in truth the plot of the story is, I contend that all theatre is fictional by virtue of being put on a stage. At the base level, the audience knows that the people on stage are not the characters they are playing and that they are acting out a story, so everything that stems from that is make-believe. It is make-believe, but we also believe it is truthful, as Walton asserts in *Mimesis as Make-Believe*. He calls this "fictional truth."[4] Fictional truth allows a path for the audience to become engaged and carried away with the story, which we know is a laudable goal for theatre makers. Fictional truth also calls for a buy-in, a suspension of disbelief, such as a willingness to accept that in opera, people singing to each other is a perfectly normal way of communicating.

I am not the first to say this by a long shot, but it seems that all stories involve some sort of conflict and a move toward some sort of resolution or a return to a state of equilibrium. In good theatre, this conflict is most successfully embodied in relationships between people. Even if the performers are playing archetypical characters, they are still humans. Whether the conflict is grand, as Lear vs. Regan and Goneril, or somewhat specific, as in Wheeler's conflict with his own set of evolving (or devolving as the case may be) values in *Linda Vista,* the central conflict is human in scale. This is important because human-to-human is the primary method of empathetic connection. Empathetic connection creates a shared space where, to riff

Chantal Thuy and Ian Barford in *Linda Vista*

The Steppenwolf Theatre Company production presented on Broadway by Second Stage Theatre at the Helen Hayes Theatre, 2019

Photograph courtesy of Joan Marcus

on Hickey again, the problematic content of a story can be valorized.[5] In other words, made worthy of consideration.

To preempt your question, this has everything to do with being a designer. The more intimately one can understand the structural basis of a story—the conflicts present, how the story moves toward resolution or equilibrium, how this story is similar to other stories, etc.—the more one is prepared to be an effective collaborator. One has to know the story before one can tell the story. This does not always happen; it is not like there is a binary between not understanding and understanding, rather, it is all on a spectrum of nuance. Some storytellers do a better job than others. This has to do with the way an artist sees the world. One has to know what is important in that particular story in order to develop a point of view as an artist.

Time and place

By time, I mean that the story happens at a particular time and lasts as long as it needs to. Simply put, the curtain rises at 8:00 pm and falls when the story is over. Now, it doesn't have to be at 8:00 pm, but both the audience and the performers have to agree, mostly implicitly, that the performance will commence at such and such time. Usually, this is dictated by local performance culture or the show's producer and everyone goes along for the ride.

Every story has a beginning, middle, and end, and measured against the clock on the wall, it takes a finite amount of time to be told. More abstractly speaking, as Thornton Wilder lays out as one of his four fundamental conditions of the drama, "On the stage it is always now."[6] Meaning that the story always happens in present tense. The action unfolds before the audience and it is always the first time this particular action has unfolded. Even when the play specifically tells us that there is repetition (Wilder's own *The Skin of Our Teeth*, for example), something about *this* instance is always meant to be different.

By place, I mean a specific location that is suited to the story at hand. This encompasses architecture devoted to a specific relationship between the performance and the audience. This can have to do with a variety of venues including those with a specific proscenium layout, such as most Broadway houses; uniquely shaped stages, like the Wurtele Thrust Stage at the Guthrie Theatre in Minneapolis; theatres in the round, like The Steppenwolf Theatre Company's new theatre in Chicago; and those that allow for a production specific arrangement, such as TFANA's Polonsky Shakespeare Center in Brooklyn. However, it is not restricted to stages in theatre buildings, it can also be any place occupied by performers: "In the twentieth century we began to see theatre space defined by action," writes

Woodruff, "Wherever the actors go, they carry the stage with them."[7] Both the backstage at the Harris Theatre in Chicago and an unspecified spot of green in a park can be redefined as presentational places by the presence of performers.

By place, I also mean design—sets, props, costumes, lighting, sound, and projection—and the myriad requisite details therein that coalesce with the performers to do all the things that good design does to reimagine a given venue or location, to make it unique to the particular production.

Implicit in this model is that the event is live. This is uncomplicated and requires little explanation other than to say that the live nature of theatre is necessary for the meaning-making feedback loop to exist and that because the audience changes with each performance, even though the production remains the same, each performance is a unique event. It is always a new night. But having an audience is not unique to theatre, and is, therefore (strictly speaking) not an identifier of theatre alone. Cinema also has an audience, but, like static forms of art (painting, sculpture, etc.), there is no possibility of a feedback loop between those artworks and their spectators. It is a one-way street.

People

I here break from my word-by-word explanation of this definition of theatre because the idea of one group of people in front of another group of people, referring, of course, to performers in front of an audience, is so intertwined that it would be cumbersome to try to separate them. The paradox, to riff on a word from Rancière, is that performers and audience members do not exist without one another.[8] A performer is not a performer unless there is someone watching and an audience is not an audience unless they are watching something. (Even an actor practicing lines in a mirror at home has themselves for an audience.)

Their humanity is why I think performers are so central to the definition of theatre—they are the embodiment of the performance in terms of human-to-human interaction. Even in the instance of a puppet or a mask, where there is still a human involved. This might seem odd coming from someone who has devoted their life to the theatre but not as a performer, yet I am not the first to do so and I will not be the last. No less than revolutionary Broadway designer Robert Edmund Jones asserted in *The Dramatic Imagination* that the aim of good design is to enhance the work of the actor:

> The designer creates an environment in which all noble emotions are possible. Then he retires. The actor enters. If the designer's work has

been good, it disappears from our consciousness at that moment. We do not notice it any more. It has apparently ceased to exist. The actor has taken the stage; and the designer's only reward lies in the praise bestowed upon the actor.[9]

Yet, I am still a designer and I firmly believe that those myriad requisite details are as critical for the actor's work as the actor themself (without light, after all, the audience sees nothing!). The designer is there to contextualize, they aid, they push back—they create a living space. Swiss scenographer and lighting advocate Adolphe Appia—who's thinking has greatly influenced my work and aesthetic—presents a useful hierarchy in his 1919 essay "Actor, Space, Light, Painting:" "the *actor* presenting the drama, *space* in three dimensions, in the service of the actor's plastic form; [and] *light* giving life to each" (italics in original).[10] The creative team is as crucial as the performers in shaping the production.

So, to take my definition of the artist and map it to the creative team, each individual artist brings their point of view to the table, and, as a team, the creative team forges a common point of view through collaboration to guide how they make the production. This is difficult, often messy, and happens over time—from preproduction to opening night. There are so many variables—a shift in a moment of staging in a transition might mean a change in speed of a scenic element, which then might dictate alterations in sound and lighting and affect how much time a quick change has. Even though each member that forms the creative team is working toward a specific goal, they each have an accomplished craft they bring to bear on the process the variables mesh. The singer sings, the lighting designer lights, and in the best of cases, the process of making is a dialog between the accomplished crafts that makes the whole more than the sum of the production's parts.

Theatre is the most efficacious art form in terms of fulfilling my concepts surrounding the artist, artwork, and spectator because, in large part, of collaboration. The foundation of my thinking on collaboration is informed by Wagner, who wrote, "Each separate member," read as collaborator, "may lift himself to the exercise of this dictatorship," which Wagner, in typical Wagnerian hyperbole is referring to the particular work of each member of a production team, "when he bears a definite message which so far answers to his individuality that in its proclamation he has power to raise it to a common purpose," in other words, each person has their part to play in the whole. Wagner continues, "For in that artistic fellowship," the creative team, "which combines for no other aim than the satisfaction of a joint artistic impulse," with the outcome being a show, "it is impossible that any other thing should come to definite prescription and resolve than that which compasses the mutual satisfaction of this impulse: namely,

Art herself ..."[11] This is pretty flowery, but at its base, it is a call for every member of the production to check their ego at the door and work toward the mutual goal.

Before I continue, I must address the fact that Wagner is both a huge influence on my aesthetic and someone who has a deeply problematic history. There is no doubt that some of his views were repulsive. He was an anarchist, an anti-Semite, and a proto-fascist that is incessantly and inexorably tied to Adolph Hitler and Nazism. His work is full of German nationalism and, when viewed through a contemporary lens, is sometimes cringe-worthy—I think specifically of the way my skin crawls when I hear the "Heil! Heil!" chorus in *Tannhäuser*.[12] His music is also awe-inspiring and magnificent and even as I write this thinking about the pilgrim's chorus in the same opera, I get goose bumps. His contributions to the advancement of the form are manifold. He coined the term *Gesamtkunstwerk* (often translated as "total work of art"), and not only did his work demonstrate the integration of forms—musical, textual, visual, and performative—in his day, but it still continues to inform successive generations about the integration of forms in opera and elsewhere.[13] According to music critic Alex Ross in his treatise *Wagnerism*, Wagner was a critical player in the "rapid evolution of the modernist arts," he "revolutionized theatrical architecture and practice" and showed "a way beyond naturalism."[14] To contend with Wagner is to contend with both facets of his legacy. As Ross writes, "To blame Wagner for the horrors committed in his wake is an inadequate response to historical complexity: it lets the rest of civilization off the hook. At the same time, to exonerate him is to ignore his insidious ramifications."[15] It is complicated because, objectively speaking, his impact on opera, and other art forms, is massive. So, even if one wants to cancel the man, it is impossible to cancel the lessons learned from him. There are too many. They reverberate too deeply. Just one example is how much influence he had on Appia, who's work is a cornerstone of modern stagecraft and who, as I have said, is a major influence on my aesthetic. The influence is not just through Appia's writing though. Appia influenced Jones, who in turn influenced his assistant Jo Mielziner who went on to become a Broadway legend in his own right. Mielziner then influenced his assistants, including Ming Cho Lee, who went on to become arguably the most influential set designer in the United States. Lee, of course, then had an outsized influence on one of his students: me. So, you see that it is not easy to get away from Wagner's impact on the world of design. I take the good and disregard the bad.[16]

The kind of collaboration Wagner calls for is really hard. It involves subordinating oneself and one's aesthetic to a common aim, which is seemingly counter-intuitive as an artist. A lighting design is not an artwork in and of itself, it is the "exercise of dictatorship" toward a common purpose.

Rather, the common purpose of the production is the artwork. In that regard, the lighting design is an exercise of craft. Not only that, but the subordination of self to the group is a powerful lesson that I did not quite understand until I encountered Wagner: a good idea is a good idea no matter where it comes from and it avoids a lot of Sturm und Drang to think not in terms of 'I' statements, but 'we' statements in all aspects of collaboration. In discussing his work with Handspring Puppet Company, South African artist William Kentridge said of collaboration: "One of the things collaboration does, even outside of the specifics of a particular work, is that it allows one to understand the making of a kind of applied arts, art in the service of some other, larger work, but which nonetheless also has an autonomy on its own."[17] One's work in one's specific discipline of design is one's own, but ownership of a design idea is irrelevant because the idea ought to be in service to the larger artwork that is the production; the audience sees the whole mise en scène and rarely, if ever, walks out humming the lighting design.

This brings up a common point of debate: whether theatrical designers are artists. After all, are not artists exclusively in control of their work? And, because theatre is a collective endeavor, doesn't that mean no one has exclusive control? (And how many times has someone come up to the lighting table and asked, "Can you turn that light over there up a bit?" Where's the exclusive control in that!?) I have a definitive point of view on this question: Yes, designers and, by extension, other members of the creative team are artists. Being an artist, as I have said, has as much to do with a way of thinking as it has to do with making a thing, and it has very little to do with exclusive control. A good designer thinks as an artist and brings that thinking to the room with the other collaborators in order to focus that thinking on the collective endeavor at hand.

You can see, too, that I am drawing a boundary between the creative team and the many other extraordinary and necessary people that are required to successfully mount a production. This is because I do not think that a technician, an electrician, for example, when doing the job that they do on a show is doing the job of an artist. The work of the electrician does not require the perspective of an artist. The perspective and skill of a craftsperson, to be sure, but not that of an artist.

To witness

On the other side of the proverbial footlights, a good audience member is a kind of spectator *plus*. A good audience member needs to possess all the characteristics of a good spectator: to come to the theatre ready to witness, experience emotion, and think about the performance. As my colleague Anna D. Shapiro has said, a play is an open circle until an audience closes it. To extend the metaphor, the closed circle corresponds to the all-important feedback loop between the performance and the audience.

The phrase 'witness, experience emotion, and think about a performance' is a tricky one grammatically. I do not know whether to include more 'ands' and less commas because I think these three things can, but do not necessarily need to, happen at the same time. Ergo, some explanation is required.

My concern here is how witnessing creates or removes distance between the audience and the performance and what that has to do with feeling and thinking. Theatre scholar Caroline Wake, in her article "The Accident and the Account: Towards a Taxonomy of Spectatorial Witness in Theatre and Performances Studies," proposes a taxonomy of witnessing that I find particularly useful as a starting point. In brief, she identifies three layers of witnessing, which I paraphrase here:

1   A primary witness is a witness to an event.
2   A secondary witness is a witness to the account of an event.
3   A tertiary witness who witnesses the act of the witnessing of others.[18]

One might be tempted to say that in a play, one actor could equal a primary witness, another could equal a secondary witness, and the audience the tertiary witness. This is an oversimplification. I think there are as many permutations to this are there are combinations of trumpet valves. It is easy to see how in an opera, for example, there might be a combination of all three (think of how often a chorus is a tertiary witness within the world of fiction). Similarly, I think it is completely reasonable to think of an audience as being able to occupy each role both in that they can move between levels *and* that they can occupy them at the same time.

Take, for example, an experience of being an audience member of a performance of the play *graveyard shift* (The Goodman Theatre, 2020),[19] as I was during previews. We, the audience, were primary witnesses to the confrontation between Janelle and Brian as it happened. It is a horrible thing with visceral impact. We were also secondary witnesses alongside Elise when she and Brian talk about the traffic stop later in the play. And at both moments, we were tertiary witnesses for two reasons. For the first, by virtue of being in a theatre alone, we were witnessing an account of the event. For the second, we were witnessing the account of the event as it is told between two characters. What is important about this taxonomy, as far as I am concerned, is that the primary witnessing end of the spectrum is conducive to emotional responses, while the tertiary end of the spectrum is conducive to thinking responses. Because it is possible to occupy multiple

Aneisa J. Hicks in *graveyard shift*

The Goodman Theatre, 2020
Photograph courtesy of Liz Lauren

states of witnessing at the same time as an audience member, it is also possible to feel emotion and think at the same time.

The point, of course, is that by occupying the space of a tertiary witness, a good audience member thinks about the performance both as they are watching it and after the fact too. Meaning that a good audience member will think about the tragedy of Sandra Bland's last days when they watch the traffic stop scene from *graveyard shift,* and they will reflect on it later. Thinking and feeling come together in the process of meaning-making, part of the work of the spectator.

Experiencing emotion

In thinking about emotion in the theatre, I think about Woodruff and empathy. What I have written earlier about pleasure and the sublime as affective components of beauty and the necessity of a spectator caring about an artwork neatly corresponds here in a bit of aesthetic string theory, meaning that they might look far apart in the linear layout of this book, but when the ideas exist on top of each other as they do in practice, as they do in reality outside the pages of this book, these concepts are right on top of each other. With regards to empathy, it is hard for me to remember having any understanding whatsoever of the critical nature of an audience feeling empathy in the theatre before I read Woodruff. So, it is curious that in thinking about emotion, I disagree with him on one critical point—the efficacy of lighting design. So it goes, I suppose.

First, the root of Woodruff's thinking on empathy is thus: "Good watchers pay attention because they are emotionally engaged with what they are watching, and the best kind of emotional engagement is a form of empathy that involves understanding."[20] He calls this cognitive empathy. According to Woodruff, two lesser forms of emotional engagement are congruence, where emotions are not directly connected to the action, and identification, which is akin to fantasy. I agree that cognitive empathy is important with regards to a good audience member experiencing emotion; it is a way to engage at an emotional level and still think critically about what one is watching. Where I disagree is that I do not think that cognitive empathy is the *most important* way: Woodruff asserts that one component of congruence—a lesser form of emotional engagement in his taxonomy—is what he calls tonal sympathy, which includes things like music, dance, and lighting. Things that call up emotion that do not directly spawn from character or plot.[21] According to everything I have set forth in my manifesto, this clearly will not do!

My read of this is that Woodruff is placing plot and character at the pinnacle of theatre. This is problematic to me because it asserts the primacy of the text over any other aspect of theatre, as discussed in "Beauty," and, after all, there are many more aspects than text that make up a theatrical production. If the point is to express a vision as a communicative act, and emotional engagement is key for meaning-making by an audience member, why is a lighting state not a valid method? Or a musical moment? Why else would Richard Strauss write, "Orestes stands by the gate of the courtyard, in black relief against the last rays of the sun" in the midst of such frenetic music if not to create the overall impression of impending danger upon Elektra's increasingly agitated condition in the eponymous opera?[22] It is important to not know who Orestes is until he reveals himself to his sister, and the drama of the moment requires tension for the revelation to be a release. In the production I designed for Seattle Opera (2008), Orestes, yet unidentified, entered through a door downstage right with an enormous shaft of white light, the whitest in the entire opera thus far, casting his shadow on the opposite wall.[23] At the moment of recognition, with the hammering of horns, a huge expansive change in the light shifted the space, revealing everything. It was the entire stage picture that created the impact of the moment, not only the plot and character. The same with Williams's score for *Jaws*—the point is to be scared by it. The movie does not have the same impact without the music, just as a production of *Elektra* does not have the same impact without good lighting.

In the end, a good audience member should feel emotion as they engage in the feedback loop of watching a performance, and any aspect of the production that engenders that—including lighting—is both good and valid. All roads lead to Rome.

Liminal space

While Rancière might shudder at this, I do think it is important for good audiences to learn things from the stories told in theatres, otherwise, what is the point? These things are the threshold concepts discussed previously in the section on troublesome knowledge in "Artist/Artwork." Ideas that once learned cannot be unlearned. Emotions felt that cannot be unfelt. In that section, I introduced Meyer and Land's idea of the liminal space, a space between levels of understanding. This is precisely the space I think a good audience occupies between the downbeat and the final blackout. They become a community united in between two states of knowing. That which they knew when the curtain went up, and that which they will know when it goes down. That liminal space can be terrifying and equally enjoyable. It is both French dramatist Antonin Artaud's agitated "… tremendous masses, convulsed and hurled against each other …"[24] and German dramatist Bertolt Brecht's "… pleasurable learning, cheerful and militant learning."[25] Quite the expansive experience.

Artwork redux

A production is the artwork of the theatre. I assert that a good production has the same four key characteristics of an artwork as discussed in "Artist/Artwork"—it is beautiful, it is more than a functional object, it confronts the audience with troublesome knowledge, and it is innovative.

Beauty inherent in a production can come from any number of sources, but it must fulfill the same obligation, that of engagement. As Woodruff says, "... since no one *needs* to watch anything in particular, theatre must be done well, so as to make people want to watch" (italics in original).[26] In this regard, if we agree with Meyerhold's notion of a Ford, "done well" can read as "beautiful." Formally speaking, the choreographic excellence of John Tiffany's production of *Black Watch* for the National Theatre of Scotland alone is enough to demand my attention. Likewise, the thunderous opening of *Tosca* makes my heart jump and my body lean forward; I find the music beautiful and want to engage. And in terms of context, I am drawn to Shakespeare because, to me, his use of language is consistently mesmerizing. The list goes on.

That a good production is both a result of and situated within many cultures almost goes without saying by now; they are the constituent cultures of the creators and the audience. What is worth noting here that an audience's dominant culture can change from night to night, having a significant impact on the feedback loop between audience and performance. All other things being equal, a delightfully raucous veterans' night final dress rehearsal at Steppenwolf is one thing, and a staid, quiet Sunday matinee is quite another. Because the meaning-making feedback loop is reliant on the audience, their culture will impact how any troublesome knowledge embedded in the production is manifest.

Whereas a painter may direct their thinking to expressing their individual point of view via a painting, theatre artists direct their thinking to shaping and expressing a collective point of view via a production. And what is a production if not an artwork wrought from the collective point of view? Not only is a production created with an intent to express a point of view, but it is created out of play, the childlike fruits of imagination, the answer to a series of what-ifs, and in that regard, is more than an object of function, even if it is theatre for instruction. A good production embraces this.

Similarly, I think it is easy to see how a good production can move the form forward by some combination of applied and conceptual innovation. Like a threshold concept, once an idea embodied in production is advanced, it is hard to go back. A cursory look at the development of the American Musical over the last 100 years shows this relentless drive for innovation: From *Show Boat* advancing a rather dark story through musical and lyrical content, and thus marking the transition away from the prevalent musical comedy and revues of the late 1920s, to the increasingly complicated themes of the golden age of the 1940s and 1950s classics like *Oklahoma!*, *West Side Story*, and *Guys and Dolls*, the form progressed to acknowledge the problematic complexity of our world in musicals from the 1960s onwards like *Cabaret*, *Hair*, *A Chorus Line*, *La Cage aux Folles*, *Rent*, and *Hamilton* and even spawned lavishly complex productions like *Starlight Express*, *The Phantom of the Opera*, *Sunset Boulevard*, *The Lion King*, *Wicked*, and *Spiderman: Turn Off the Dark*. Even this limited list of innovative productions shows artists pushing the form, and the list goes on and on and on.

On market value

It would be hard to talk about theatre without talking about the marketplace. After all, the art that sells is the art that lasts, right? And in the world of the performing arts, precious few organizations are lucky enough not to be concerned with selling tickets. This, of course, is why it is not called show *art*, it is called show biz, darling! And that is why we need to wrestle with the dueling concepts of the aesthetic virtue of an artwork and its value in the marketplace.

John Berger, via his groundbreaking book *Ways of Seeing*, has shaped my thoughts on this topic immensely. For me, it boils down to this: the market is a great barometer for value, but not aesthetic virtue. This is based in popular taste and supply and demand dynamics. Berger's influence on my thinking stems from his writing around the high period of representational oil painting (circa 1500 to 1900) and the corresponding emergence of the market for private ownership of art.[27] Once paintings were made on wood panels and canvases, as opposed to frescoes and on other immovable objects, it was possible for individuals to commission, buy, and sell them. And like anything that can be bought, they became status symbols. The market made "more insistent demands than the art" and the result was a lot of what he calls hack work (a term onto which I gladly glom); the mass of oil paintings produced in this period was not very good and, by extension, became commodities.[28] Here we introduce supply and demand economics, and *bang!* Value equals the price someone is willing to pay for an artwork; a measurement based on external factors that are not directly tied to the virtues within the artwork itself. Hickey takes this one step further and says that the market, in this case, personified by art dealers, does not care "what it means" as long as it sells.[29] If we are to believe this position, which I do, it means that the whole of the contemporary Eurocentric artistic tradition is built on a market-driven foundation, with walls that are mostly made out of bad art.

In fact, Greenberg cites "threats to aesthetic value" from the market as the primary motivator for the modernist art movement.[30] He writes, "Modernism has to be understood as a holding operation, a continuing endeavor to *maintain aesthetic standards* in the face of threats ... As the response, in effect, to an ongoing emergency" (my italics).[31] The threats were middle-brow taste and an unrestrained market—a Petri dish for hack work. I will return to this idea of maintaining certain aesthetic standards in later chapters, but I bring it up now because it supports my proposition of good art and bad art. If there are aesthetic standards, then if an artwork meets or exceeds the standards it could be seen as good, and if it does not, it could be seen as bad. Not only that, but a proliferation of bad art lowers the standards. Greenberg's worry was that "When the highest levels of quality are no longer upheld in practice or taste or appreciation, then the lower levels sink lower."[32] Who sets the standards? Well, it depends on a host of issues: the artist, the art form, the system of critique, and the spectator to name just a few. Nothing is easy when subjectivity is involved.

In the context of the essay mentioned above, Hickey is talking about the fact that beautiful art sells. I do not think that is a bad thing. In fact, it is a ray of hope because it means that good art sells too, and if an artwork sells itself (both figuratively and literally), then it is one step closer to efficacy and, therefore, one step closer to good. But what if the artwork is selling something else? Here we come to the meat of Hickey's argument: the beautiful sells something—either an idea or a thing. The beautiful selling itself in order to communicate an idea is a good thing, I think, definitely on the good art side of the spectrum. The beautiful selling something else, well, that is advertising and that does not seem very virtuous to me—bad art. Berger, too had definitive opinions on advertising (his word for it is "publicity"), devoting a chapter to decrying the relationship between publicity and capitalism—money money money.[33] This brings us to what I will call the Norman Rockwell conundrum.

If advertising is bad art, then a Norman Rockwell painting used as a cover of *The Saturday Evening Post* is bad art because it is being used to sell a thing, in this case, a magazine. But if the same painting is seen in a different context, then is it good art? As a specific example, take "Thanksgiving: Girl Praying." To me, viewed exclusive of its context as a magazine cover, this is an extraordinary artwork of great aesthetic virtue. The painting is situated within the absolutely devastating upheaval of World War II. The style is realistic ... or is it? The brush strokes are self-aware and the work is rife with symbolism. Its formal composition forces my eye to the lone potato in the pan (I think? A sad dinner at best), behind which I see the crumbling of rational thought as symbolized by the fallen column. Next to the column, I see a broken shackle and think of Lady Liberty with her broken chains. I see that the coat the girl of indeterminate age is wearing

Thanksgiving: Girl Praying, 1943

By Norman Rockwell
Saturday Evening Post cover, November 27, 1943 Issue
Oil on canvas
Printed by permission of the Norman Rockwell Family Agency
Copyright ©1943 the Norman Rockwell Family Entities
Illustration provided by Curtis Licensing

is that of a First Sergeant, who would have been a man of fatherly age, and who was apparently willing to give up his coat in the cool days of late European Autumn to a needy child. It jolts me and I am not able to un-think about it. I find it is all quite beautiful in a sublime way. So, is this beauty selling an idea or a magazine? Is the point to have value or aesthetic virtue? I acknowledge the messiness of this: with some things, it comes down to context. As I said, I do not think that the market is a great barometer for aesthetic virtue. (Poor Van Gogh, one laments.) Aesthetic virtue based on efficacy is in the hands of the artist and the spectator and is not a money-based transaction.

Aesthetic virtue

You might ask, well, if there are systems of criteria, why not make it binary and use the criteria to determine art or not art without creating a value spectrum? Good question. The reasons are fourfold. First, in order to advance the notion of good lighting, there needs to be a comparative structure between what is bad and what is good. Second, anything that has even a hint of subjectivity by nature does not fit well within a binary system. Third, the Norman Rockwell conundrum is created by context, meaning that where something is classified is subject to change. Fourth, because there is a lot of hack work out there that goes under the guise of art, but that, in my opinion, is not, so we need to be able to account for a mix of vices and virtues. Especially in the theatre, a production might have many positive characteristics (e.g., wildly entertaining or commercially successful) but that do not quite have the aesthetic virtues for which one would hope. What Suzan-Lori Parks might call "Theatre of Shmaltz."[34]

Aesthetic virtue and market value in the theatre are not, however, mutually exclusive. As we know well, a show can be of great aesthetic virtue and a total cash cow. In the context of the work of the designer, this makes me think of virtues of spectacle. In this instance, I use spectacle to describe something meant to be impressive, to wow an audience; like epic, gasp-inducing Franco Zeffirelli productions for The Metropolitan Opera. Is the spectacle meant to advance the production's aesthetic virtues or increase market value? Does it sell an idea or itself? For the moment, these questions are rhetorical, but it does make me think about how the role of songs in theatre began as standalone entertainments (in revues and the like, much like Molière's interludes) and evolved into meaningful storytelling elements that push the plot forward in contemporary musical theatre, to pose an interesting parallel.

All of this is salient because part of the job of the lighting designer is to understand the difference between aesthetic virtue and market value. At some point, every one of us is going to come up against a choice between the two—and it is better to go in with eyes wide open about the concepts, so we can determine for ourselves, and for the production, whether that L128 back light is a schmaltzy choice or not. This complex relationship between virtue and value is an essential concept to carry forward as one interrogates one's own design choices.

The efficacy of theatre

By this point, it is evident that I am completely biased. I think theatre is the most efficacious art form in terms of fulfilling my concepts surrounding artist, artwork, and spectator. I have shown above that there are a great many things the theatre does well because of its group nature, both in creation and in the person-to-person connection created when an audience engages with a performance. The feedback loop between performance and audience engenders community and engages feelings and thoughts that provide fertile ground for feeling emotion and thinking.

There are some things that theatre does not do well by virtue of its temporal form. Theatre, ephemeral as it is, does not last. No two performances are the same and once Wilder's perpetual now is complete, it can never be the same again. No matter how universal a production might claim to be, it is still rooted in its own time and place and as time goes on, productions move from being novel to being archeological artifacts. *Les Misérables* was groundbreaking in its time, but now after 14,000 performances on the West End, it is a bit dated.

I think this ephemerality a good thing. This is why we can return again and again to Shakespeare, for example, and continue to find contemporary resonance. I have designed several productions of *Hamlet*, and I hope I will be able to do several more because with each new production, I discover new intricacies and connections. This is because the older I get, the more diverse experiences I have to bring to bear on the text *and* the society around me is different now than it was a year ago. This is also why, while I do think that there is good theatre and bad theatre, I do not think there is one right way to make good theatre. This is *the* topic that successive generations of theatre artists have wrestled since time immemorial and will wrestle with forever. Since culture is an ever-evolving entity, so theatre must be.

Production style

As I bring this chapter to a close, I want to reiterate why I think an understanding of this kind of aesthetic theory is required to being a good lighting designer. Our ability to think critically about the role of the artist and artwork, what that might mean for the spectator, and how those ideas manifest themselves in the context of the theatre makes us better at our jobs. In the end, I think figuring out where to put the lights and when to turn which of them on is actually *not* the most important part of being a lighting designer. The *most important* is bringing one's artist-self to the collaboration, taking one's place at the collaborative table and working with a team to tell a story. Only after that does it make sense to think about the specifics of the lighting design.

So, now that we have a story, we need to tell it. In the theatre, the telling is the artwork—the production. The mode of storytelling that we choose is a critical part of the process because stories need to be told in a manner understandable to the audience in order to have efficacy. This is why the first question after "Why are we telling this story?" in a production process ought to be "How are we telling this story?" In the theatre, how the story is manifested is the central question in the design process, and the answer to it is a metric against which all design and production choices can be measured. If pseudo-realistic, how authentic is it? If abstract, are the boundaries of the abstraction clear to everyone? Once the boundaries of abstraction are clear, then the question becomes "What specific vocabulary are we using to tell this story?" This dictates the stylistic vocabulary of the production. Depending on the source material, many of the answers to this question are determined by the writer and/or composer and/or director and/or choreographer, but eventually, each member of the creative team's personal style impacts the overall production style. This harkens back to the ideas of sign systems that I discussed concerning accomplished craft, the agency of beauty, and artistic intention. See how it is all coming together?

Notes

1 *Oxford English Dictionary Online*, s.v. "story, n," accessed April 13, 2021, www.oed.com/viewdictionaryentry/Entry/190981.
2 Christopher Booker, *The Seven Basic Plots: Why We Tell Stories* (New York: Bloomsbury, 2004), 553.
3 Joseph Campbell, *The Inner Reaches of Outer Space: Metaphor as Myth and as Religion* (Novato, CA: New World Library, 2002), 91.
4 Kendall L. Walton, *Mimesis as Make-Believe: On the Foundations of the Representational Arts* (Cambridge, MA: Harvard University Press, 1990), 39.
5 Dave Hickey, "Enter the Dragon: On the Vernacular of Beauty," in *The Invisible Dragon: Essays on Beauty, Revised and Expanded* (Chicago: University of Chicago Press, 2009), 9.
6 Thornton Wilder, "Some Thoughts on Playwriting," in *Dramatic Theory and Criticism: Greeks to Grotowski*, ed. Bernard F. Dukore (New York: Holt, Rinehart & Winston, 1974), 892.
7 Paul Woodruff, *The Necessity of Theatre* (Oxford: Oxford University Press, 2008), 112.
8 Jacques Rancière, *The Emancipated Spectator*, trans. Gregory Elliott (London: Verso, 2009), 2.
9 Robert Edmund Jones, *The Dramatic Imagination: Reflections and Speculations on the Art of the Theatre* (New York: Routledge, 2004), 24.

10 Adolphe Appia, "Actor, Space, Light, Painting," *Adolphe Appia: Texts on Theatre*, ed. Richard Beacham (London: Routledge, 1993), 114.
11 Richard Wagner, "The Art–Work of the Future," in *Dramatic Theory and Criticism: Greeks to Grotowski*, ed. Bernard F. Dukore, trans. William Ashton Ellis (New York: Holt, Rinehart &Winston, 1974), 794.
12 Richard Wagner, *Tannhäuser*, ed. Feliz Mottl (Leipzig: C.F. Peters, 1974).
13 Krisztina Lajosi, "Wagner and the (Re)mediation of Art: Gesamtkunstwerk and Nineteenth-Century Theories of Media," *Frame* 23, no. 2 (2012): 42–60.
14 Alex Ross, *Wagnerism: Art and Politics in the Shadow of Music* (New York: Farrar, Straus, and Giroux, 2020), 659.
15 Ross, *Wagnerism,* 659.
16 Acknowledgment is due to director Louisa Muller who, in conversation, helped me articulate my point of view on this issue.
17 William Kentridge and Jane Taylor, "In Dialog," *Handspring Puppet Company,* ed. Jane Taylor (Johannesburg, ZA: David Krut, 2009), 205.
18 Caroline Wake, "The Accident and the Account: Towards a Taxonomy of Spectatorial Witness in Theatre and Performance Studies," *Performance Paradigm* 5, no.1 (May 2009): 82–100.
19 *graveyard shift,* by korde arrington tuttle, dir. Danya Taymor, set design by Kristen Robinson, costume design by Montana Levi Blanco, and sound design and composition by Richard Woodbury, The Goodman Theatre, Chicago, US, 2020.
20 Woodruff, *Necessity,* 165.
21 Woodruff, 175.
22 Richard Strauss, *Elektra,* libretto by Hugo von Hofmannsthal (London: Boosey & Hawkes, n.d.), 151.
23 *Elektra,* composed by Richard Strauss with libretto by Hugo von Hofmannsthal, dir. Chris Alexander, set design by Wolfram Skalicki, and costume design by Melanie Taylor Burgess, Seattle Opera, Seattle, US, 2008.
24 Antonin Artaud, *The Theatre and Its Double,* trans. Mary Caroline Richards (New York: Grove Press, 1958), 85.
25 Bertolt Brecht, "Theatre for Pleasure or Theatre for Instruction," in *Brecht on Theatre: The Development of an Aesthetic,* ed. and trans. John Willet (New York: Hill and Wang, 1964), 73.
26 Woodruff, *Necessity,* 24.
27 John Berger, *Ways of Seeing* (London: British Broadcasting Corporation and Penguin Books, 1972), 84, 88.
28 Berger, *Ways of Seeing,* 88.
29 Hickey, "Enter the Dragon," 7.
30 Clement Greenberg, "Modern and Postmodern," William Dobell Memorial Lecture, Sydney, Australia, October 31, 1979, reproduced in *Arts* 54, no. 6 (February 1980), 66.
31 Greenberg, "Modern and Postmodern," 65–66.
32 Greenberg, 66.
33 Berger, *Ways of Seeing,* See chapter 7.
34 Suzan-Lori Parks, "From *Elements of Style,*" *The America Play and Other Works* (New York: Theatre Communications Group, 1995), 6.

5 Theatrical Abstraction

August Strindberg, 1893
By Christian Krohg
Oil Painting
49 1/2 × 50 in. (126 × 127 cm)
Photograph by Haakon Harriss
Courtesy of Norsk Folkemuseum

DOI: 10.4324/9781003206460-6

Spectrum

In my manifesto, I state that lighting for the stage is an abstract form. Here, I expand the thesis to advance the idea that the theatre itself is an inherently abstract form. Thus, choices made in the theatre exist on a spectrum of theatrical abstraction, which, like that of good lighting, is bounded by pseudo-realism on one side and pure expressionism on the other. In this, the spectra are the same. To understand one is to understand the other. I contend that this spectrum applies to all other aspects of theatrical choices in both macro and micro ways. In order to make the concept useful in practice, these terms must have commonly understood definitions. In my experience, they do not. Concepts like realism, naturalism, abstraction, and theatricality are employed often in collaboration but without precise, commonly understood definitions. Realism and naturalism, for example, are often used interchangeably, which I think is problematic.

Precision matters in language. In the theatre, in the context of collaboration, precision is critical. Even when research or sketches are employed, language is the primary mode of communication about lighting up until the point where the lighting designer can *actually* show the work in context. The more precise we can be about our choices up to that point, the better the work will be. In order to bring clarity to the spectrum, one must first understand its components. That is the work of this chapter.

Interrogating -isms

To begin, art movement -isms—e.g., realism, naturalism, expressionism, and so forth—are inherently problematic. This is because any one -ism can mean many different things to many different people. And, as a knock-on consequence of that, any one -ism can also mean many different things depending on the medium of the artwork. Expressionism in painting is different than expressionism in the theatre and so forth. It is hard to pin these things down. Yet, these words exist because we need them to qualify the myriad modes of artistic expression that are available to us as artists. Sometimes these -isms are coined by artists, so there is convenient documentation on which to base our usage, like Dada. Other times, the -isms are after-the-fact impositions by academics or critics, so the one-step-removed interpretive lenses can distort things, like cubism. That is why I think that in the theatre, especially in the context of design for theatre, a common understanding of what we mean when we say something like "realism" is a critical component of production concept development and design. If the words we are using to describe ideas do not line up, then the conceptual foundations start out off-kilter. This can be especially problematic during technical rehearsals when time is short and a common vocabulary is critical to a smooth process.

There are a lot of -isms to contend with in lighting design. The biggest, I think, is realism. First, because it is generally agreed that so-called realism is the foundational style of contemporary Eurocentric theatrical design, and second because it is the theatrical -ism that irks me the most. At this point, I think it is important to situate—*in extremely broad terms*—some of the -isms to which I have previously alluded. Modernism arose in the late 19th century, parallel to the industrial revolution, and, according to Greenberg, in answer to the crisis of "a certain confusion of standards brought on by romanticism," as discussed in "Beauty."[1] Modernists advanced the idea (perhaps not so explicitly) that modernism was attempting to codify rules; the one right way to make things, expressed in their most elegant form. Hara writes that the foundation of modernism is to take the basic elements of color, form, and texture and entrust the shaping of them "to the rational, lucid consciousness, whose aim it is to organize those elements."[2] Within 20th-century modernism, there are all sorts of movements which aesthetic theorist Ihab Hassan, in his seminal 1987 essay "Toward a Concept of Postmodernism," proposes can be divided into three modes: avant-garde, modern, and postmodern. These are not necessarily temporal distinctions; they are better understood as clusters of modes that overlap. The avant-garde, for Hassan, describes "those movements that agitated the earlier part of [the twentieth] century."[3] Examples include cubism, futurism, constructivism, and Dadaism. As subsets of modernism, these movements, which some would call radical, were characterized by extreme energy and they eventually exhausted themselves. So, while the avant-garde ran out of steam as it were, the broader tenets of modernism proved more hardy and resulted in what I will hereinafter refer to as high modernism: a period characterized by minimalism, abstraction, technology, and design that peaked around the 1960s, but whose aesthetic impact continues to inform contemporary art—both as an influence and as something to react against.

Perhaps the most over-arching unifier of 20th-century art is that it is messy and difficult to categorize, especially if one is inclined to try to date things precisely. The art critic and curator Tony Godfrey characterizes it thusly,

> Crudely speaking, modernism had been seen as a relay race: Gustave Courbert, the first off the blocks, had handed the baton to Manet, who had handed it to Cézanne, who had handed it to Picasso, who had handed it to Jackson Pollack, who had handed it to another abstract painter ... but then confusion! The baton had been dropped. There was no longer a race going in one direction, no evident line of progression.[4]

So, there is much argument about the precise moment when the mode of postmodernism arose, but let us call it (somewhat arbitrarily) at, say, 1975. As its name implies, its definition is in dialectical opposition to that of modernism and thus equally as messy to pin down. While Greenberg's high modernism was concerned with maintaining aesthetic standards, postmodernism can be seen as the democratization/commercialization of the same, Hassan's postmodernism is "playful, paratactical, and deconstructionist ... less cliquish, and far less aversive to the pop, electronic society of which it is a part, and so hospitable to kitch."[5] Seen through these lenses, the after-effects of high modernism and postmodernism are operating in parallel, under the umbrella of contemporary art. Okay, so when did contemporary art start? Dating it is also an imprecise endeavor. There are, however, some clear catalysts: certain expositions in the 1960s as well as the globalization of the art market that started in the 1970s and, by the early 1980s, it was damning the torpedoes and running full steam ahead.

-isms and design

These modes/periods are important to lighting designers for two reasons. First, they are navigational markers. It is useful to understand art history to contextualize how a particular piece of fits within the larger development of the form. Take, for example, Ibsen and Strindberg's growth beyond naturalism and what that means in practice for a lighting designer. The two were dramatic rivals and, surprisingly, the portrait of Strindberg by Christian Krohg at the beginning of this chapter hung in Ibsen's study. Ibsen was reported to have said of the painting, "He shall hang there and keep watch ... because he is my mortal enemy."[6] Similarly, Strindberg supposedly said that Ibsen "cost me my wife, children, fortune, and career."[7] Knowing about this rivalry and that Strindberg's *The Father* was, in a sense, a rebuttal to Ibsen's *A Doll's House* provided useful context for me when I was lighting a 2016 double bill of the plays at TFANA—it allowed me to understand how the ideas debated in the two plays connected, which unlocked a way of seeing them as more symbolic than naturalistic.[8] The visceral presence of the portrait as a symbol of this rivalry had a direct impact on my lighting choices for the two plays, opening up a level of abstraction: Nora's final monologue in *A Doll's House* was accompanied by an expressionistic bleached-white sunrise, and the final act of *The Father* was lit in equally expressionistic fractured light from no apparent source. The portrait unlocked my understanding of how these two plays were situated in their respective -isms and, because of that, the trajectory of my designs.

Understanding these movements is also important because they each brought forth a confetti of ideas, especially having to do with precedents regarding abstraction. To enumerate them all would be tedious, but there are a few ideas so important that it would be impossible to continue a discussion of good lighting for the stage without proper acknowledgment. These are precedents established by Appia and Craig, who contemporaneously advocated for nonrealistic staging practices, and later by Jones, who many consider to be the father of modern stage design in the United States.

One precedent is that any lighting idea in a lighting design should have expressive intent to contribute to the artwork that is the production. Light for 'visibility' does not qualify as expressive. Appia was evangelical in his call for the use of light as an expressive design element rather than just illumination. He wrote, in "Music and the Art of the Theatre" (in 1899, mind you, ahead of his time) that "... light is not merely 'visibility' ... light is distinguished from 'visibility' by its expressiveness. And if there is no expression, there is no light."[9] He continues, "The realism of lighting, therefore, is not the realism of forms arranged in space, since these are set up in imitation of a particular phenomenon, while light is based on the existence of an *idea*" (italics in the original).[10] Light used thus, expressive and in service of an idea, is abstracted. From that, as a practicing designer, I would also extrapolate: to see faces is not sufficient justification for hanging a system of front light. That front light needs to be part of an *idea*.

Another precedent is that on stage, an abstraction, a 'sense' of something is often more efficacious than trying to accurately reproduce something detail by detail. Craig argued for abstraction when he wrote in "The Artists of the Theatre of the Future" in 1907, "By means of suggestion you may bring on the stage a sense of all things—the rain, the sun, the wind, the snow, the hail, the intense heat—but you will never bring them there by attempting to wrestle and close with Nature... Actuality, accuracy of detail, is useless upon the stage."[11] In this regard, it would be better to evoke the storm in *King Lear* through expressionistic means than to try to make it rain and blow wind.

Yet another precedent is that stage design can be magical in the figurative sense, that it can have both an enchanting, mystical sense and be surprising. This is not just theatrical sleight of hand. Magic here also means that authentic objects can and should be expressive elements within a stage design. As I wrote earlier, by virtue of being on stage, any element has meaning, and it is up to the designer to determine the expressive potential of those objects. Jones, in 1941, wrote, "Do not think for a moment that I am advising the designer to do away with actual objects on the stage. There is no such thing as a symbolic chair. A chair is a chair. It is in the arrangement of chairs that the magic lies."[12] It is up to the designer to understand not just the authentic arrangement of the chairs for a particular situation, but what about an abstracted arrangement of the chairs can or does make them magical. Similarly, it is up to the lighting designer to understand that it is not in *what* the light is revealing but in *how* it is revealing it that the magic lies.

Naturalism

Now then, if one is to contend with the idea of realism in the theatre as a production style, one must contend with naturalism as a movement. This is because, at least in my experience, these words are often used interchangeably in conversation with an imperceptible distinction between the two.

There is a difference between them, albeit subtle, which I think is important. This difference gives specific meaning to the word "realistic," a word we encounter over and over in the theatre. Before I dig into this topic, I do want to acknowledge that there are about as many opinions about realism and naturalism, their pros and cons, and their precise origins as there are stars in the sky. So, my opinions on this topic are not orthodox. Rather, they arise from repeated collision with the concepts in production and in the classroom, my own rooting around in the dirt for understanding, and conclusions I have made regarding realism and my own aesthetic.

Back to the point at hand: naturalism is a broad term for an early-modern art movement that emerged in the latter half of the 19th century that was, like all art movements, reactionary to its predecessors and fed by the zeitgeist. By the mid-19th century, historical dramas and melodramas, such as the well-made plays of Eugène Scribe, dominated the stages of the self-styled Western world. At the same time, huge advances in the physical and social sciences were pushing the boundaries of humanity's understanding of itself and of the natural world. Christopher Innes, in his introduction to *A Sourcebook on Naturalist Theatre*, cites Darwin's 1859 *On the Origin of Species*, Claude Bernard's 1865 *Introduction à l'étude de la médicine experimental*, Karl Marx's 1867 *Das Kapital*, and the work of Sigmund Freud, including his 1900 *The Interpretation of Dreams*, as well as, "... the emergence of materialistic capitalism and the rise of middle-class democracy" as primary influences on naturalism.[13] Science was in the air, and discontent between advances in human understanding of the natural world and our place in it and what was currently being produced on stage was growing.

Conveniently, there is a primary resource to examine regarding naturalism in the theatre: Emile Zola's preface to his play *Thérèse Raquin* (1873), in which he rails that, "We must look to the future and the future is the human problem studied within the bounds of reality; it is the abandonment of all legendary tales; it is the living drama of characters and the environments, purged of all nursery tales, historical rag bags, magniloquence, trivialities, and conventional heroes."[14] He wanted plays about real people in real situations, relying not on plot but on the inner conflict of the characters and the external forces acting on them. Carl E. W.L. Dahlström explains, "The proper situational complex in Zola's naturalism is one in which the forces are exclusively biological and social, observed and studied objectively in the actions of specific men and women in specific milieux."[15] This seems like a very scientific examination. He continues, "In other words, the fundamental conflict or situation should arise through collisions of interest among actual people in actual environments."[16] This is very different than, say, a kidnapping in a melodrama or a singing contest in the Wartburg as the main point of conflict because the stakes hit closer to home.

Zola, of course, was not the only artist of the time whose work concerned itself with societal pressures and collisions of interests. Major players here include playwrights Strindberg (his early work), Anton Chekov (also his early work), George Bernard Shaw, and Ibsen, who said, "My task has been the *description of humanity*" (italics in original).[17] This movement also included directors like André Antoine of the Theatre Libre and Konstantin Stanislavski of the Moscow Art Theatre. This list is by no means exhaustive. And while the pervasive influence of naturalism continues even today, Innes considers the period between 1881 and 1904 to be the movement's high point.

In the theatre, the manifestation of the naturalist movement called for a realistic stage environment rather than the codified painted drop and footlight settings of the day. Zola, in "Naturalism in the Theatre," argues that because the characters in naturalistic drama are influenced by their environment, the settings need to be an "exact reproduction of the environment."[18] In other words, the realistic set and props are an integral part of the storytelling, rather than mere background. Again, this was reactionary and, as Kim Solga reminds us through the use of the phrase "avant-guard realism and naturalism" in her book *Theory for Theatre Studies: Space*, also revolutionary for its time.[19] As to the distinction between naturalism and realism, I again rely on Innes, who proposes that realism be used to refer to the intended effect—what actually ends up on the stage, the design—of naturalism rather than the movement itself.[20] This distinction makes sense to me because while naturalism was supplanted by the many -isms that have followed in the intervening nearly-century-and-a-quarter, one lasting effect with regards to stage design is that realistic staging practices have proven themselves very durable, for better or worse.

It seems to me that realism with regards to production practice, especially that which is informed by Zola's naturalism in its strictest sense, has run its course. One can argue, as Innes does, that the exemplary naturalistic plays are now historic pieces precisely because they were written so responsively to then-current conditions.[21] Yet there are exemplary naturalistic plays—*The Father* and *A Doll's House* to name but two—whose content continues to resonate with contemporary audiences. Perhaps this is because of what might be the most lasting impact of naturalism, one that survived the onslaught of the avant-garde through to our current postmodern moment: introspective societal criticism. As Innes writes,

> What give naturalistic plays historical status is, in fact, their position in the history of ideas; and paradoxically, it is on this level that they are most contemporary. The challenge to social orthodoxies, which naturalistic playwrights introduced into the theatre, is a characteristic feature of much twentieth-century art and thought.[22]

To be clear, I think the challenge of social orthodoxies continues to be one of the most important facets of theatre as an art form, so let us not throw the baby out with the bathwater here. My argument is not to stop doing the good naturalistic plays whose content is still meaningful, but that they certainly should not be done in the kind of late 19th-century-influenced realistic style that is, by now, anachronistic on our stages because it is undesirable, aesthetically inefficacious, and downright boring in the here and now.

Realism (Blergh)

I have problems with the concept of realism in this strict sense as related to design, which leads me to want to abandon the word altogether.

The first relates dramatic intent and stage-worthiness, which are intertwined in my mind. There seems to me to be very little room in Zola's exact reproduction of an environment for the design to have any curated dramatic intent. A stage design must participate in telling the story, therefore, the choices that make up the design need to have dramatic intent. Furthermore, a faithful rendering of a "real" kitchen on stage would probably have very bad sightlines, the practical light fixtures would not be bright enough for the audience to see, and maybe a color that is not very useful, rendering the entirety of the setting not very stage-worthy at all. If, that is, one manages to see through a suddenly literal fourth wall. A more expressionistic kitchen, on the other hand, can still fulfill the essential requirements of kitchen and *also* have dramatic intent while also having good sightlines, etc. What the exact details of this theoretical kitchen would be are, of course, totally dependent on the dramatic needs of whatever piece is calling for it.

The second, and perhaps more important, problem has to do with the virtue of the proscenium and the hand of the artist: the mere fact of putting something on stage implies a choice—whether or not to include a thing that is part of a 'real' environment—and this choice, made by the creative team, is an act of *curation*. The moment an object is put on the stage it is given, by virtue of its position behind the frame (figurative or literal), aesthetic significance. Playwright and critic Bert O. States agrees in his *Great Reckonings in Little Rooms:* "theatre—unlike fiction, painting, sculpture, and film—is really a language whose words consist to an unusual degree of things that *are* what they seem to be" (italics in the original).[23] He continues, "as a consequence, the medium becomes the message: the form winks at the content."[24] A kitchen sink, for example, purchased directly from a kitchen sink store has the identity of a 'real' kitchen sink when it is still in its box. But that changes when it is part of a design. Brecht, on the realistic, wrote: "Just to copy reality isn't enough; reality needs not only to be recognized but also to be understood. The scenery accordingly must have *artistic merit* and give evidence of an individual handwriting" (my italics).[25] By the intercession of the artist, once it is put onstage, the kitchen sink is more than itself—it is also a component of a larger idea, an idea *expressive of dramatic intent*. The kitchen sink has now become theatrical!

So, I think we should stop using the word 'realistic' altogether. If this seems like a semantic argument it is because it *is* a semantic argument. Again, precision matters in language. If one says "blue" and if another says "blue" without qualifiers, are they talking about the *same* blue? If they say "daylight blue" (or, better yet, Lee 501), they get closer to what they are after. So if realism in actuality is not possible onstage, why bother with the word and its associated vocabulary at all? Removing the word from our vocabulary removes the temptation, as Haring-Smith says, to "impose realist expectations."[26] While we are at it, we should probably abandon the word naturalistic and its associated vocabulary as well.

Yet, for better or worse, some of these plays, etc., continue to be written in the naturalistic mode, and they must, as Jones would say, be wrought appropriately. Since I have already outlined why I think realism on the stage is both undesirable and impossible, I am proposing in this book a shift in vocabulary around the way design for projects like these are conceptualized: Instead of "real," as in "a real object," I favor the words "authentic" and "evocative." Likewise, instead of "realistic," as in a mode or aesthetic, I favor the notion of the "pseudo-realistic." As always, precise definitions are in order and this time, the dictionary definitions—when taken together—will do. Authentic can be variously defined as "possessing the characteristics of the original" and "truthful, accurate...having the quality of verisimilitude, true to life."[27] In the case of our kitchen sink, an "authentic" kitchen sink is a sink that is made to possess the characteristics of a kitchen sink or, more easily, a potentially functional kitchen sink bought from a store. To evoke is "to call (a feeling, faculty, manifestation, etc.) into being or activity."[28] In the case of our kitchen, the single architectural gesture of warm cross light from the example above works because it evokes the desired sense of light symbolically. Finally, "pseudo-," as a combination form word, means "apparently but not really, falsely or erroneously called or represented, falsely, spuriously."[29] The term "pseudo-realistic" acknowledges the word "realistic"—something I think is probably necessary simply because "realistic" is, sadly, so commonly used in design discussions (is there no getting away from it?)—while maintaining that it is apparently, *but not really*, real. Like the relationship of realism to naturalism, the authentic and evocative are the means, and the pseudo-realism is the end.

To cite examples of this vocabulary in practice, I will dissect my lighting designs for the Broadway transfer of *Linda Vista* and for a production of *True West* (Seattle Repertory Theatre, 2020),[30] because these plays make firm demands that their lighting be "very realistic," which is to say (for my purposes), that the lighting should be *pseudo*-realistic. Reminder:

these demands coincide with one boundary of the spectrum of theatrical abstraction. For each production, the authentic tools needed to index—in the symbolic sense—the realistic settings the play demands formed the starting point of my designs as practicals, real fixtures that are the equivalent of the kitchen sink from the store. Those choices are rooted in authenticity, but practicals alone have no dramatic intent, they have not been elevated into the artistic realm beyond objectness. To paraphrase Jones, it is in the arrangement of the practicals that the magic lies. It was how I used those authentic elements, in combination with the other ideas in the light plot, that moved the lighting designs beyond a mere articulation of place and time of day to designs with expressive intent.

Linda Vista is written in the realistic mode and requires the actors to interact with very specific items. The set design was a study in authenticity: Todd Rosenthal's set consisted of a revolve divided into three wedges. One, the biggest, was central character Wheeler's apartment living room and kitchen (with the requisite kitchen sink), and the other two wedges were variously a camera shop, a karaoke bar, and a few different restaurants. The revolve was situated within a vast chalky-blue space, above which hung a massive billboard featuring an image of San Diego. A few scenes—a park, a home office, a locker room, and a bar—were played downstage of the revolve. Each location was meticulously rendered with authentic objects and design elements, from the menus on the fridge in the apartment to the equipment in the cases of the camera shop and the soda dispenser at the Panda Express. Equal detail was given to the specificity of the clothing.

It was important that the lighting supported this general point of view, and as such, I tried to make the starting point of the lighting as authentic as possible. This meant including many practical sources in each locale. The apartment had sconces, under counter lighting, and can lights; the karaoke bar had illuminated beer signs; the camera shop had an illuminated Nikon sign, work lights, and cabinet lighting; etc., etc. Authentic elements like these not only give light themselves, but their presence also "sells" the stage lighting. If one sees a sconce on the wall, it is easier to believe that the light illuminating the actor is coming from the sconce. It grounds the light—it makes it local—by providing a believable source. In terms of the sign systems I have been writing about, this sconce is a lighting index: in the same way that smoke implies fire, the presence of the sconce implies that the light in the space comes from it (when it is on, of course). This is not only true of whether there is light but also of the characteristics of the light. In the karaoke club, the illuminated beer signs featured neon blues and reds. Because those colors were extant in the setting, it allowed me to light the scene with saturated purples and warm whites. The signs indexed the rest of the light, and it all seemed right.

Theatrical Abstraction 103

Zachary Ray Sherman and Kevin Anderson in *True West*
Seattle Repertory Theatre, 2020
Photography courtesy of Alan Alabastro

Similarly, my lighting for *True West* is an example of a design rooted in authentic elements. For better or worse, Sam Shepard is very specific about what the set should look like. He goes so far as to include the following note in the acting edition of the script:

> The set should be constructed realistically with no attempt to distort its dimensions, shapes, objects or colors. No objects should be introduced which might draw special attention to themselves other than the props demanded by the script. If a stylistic "concept" is grafted onto the set design it will only serve to confuse the evolution of the characters' situation, which is the most important focus of the play.[31]

The point is not whether I agree with the aesthetic merits of such a prescriptive note about "realistic" elements (as you may suspect, I do not) rather, the point is that Shepard is demanding authenticity from the environment like the naturalists who came before him. He is as specific about the lighting as he is about the set. The text is full of references to time of day, to lighting elements like candles and moonlight, and to specific states like "very early morning, between night and day" and, perhaps my favorite, "now starkly visible in intense yellow light, the effect should be like a desert junkyard at high noon, the coolness of the preceding scenes is totally obliterated."[32] These stage directions add up to a road map for a lighting design that needs to be very pseudo-realistic indeed! Like *Linda Vista*, this design relied on a number of practical fixtures to index the lighting: sconces, can lights in the ceilings, refrigerator, and stove lights, as well as candles on the dining table (amplified by a cleverly hidden source). A translucent backdrop visible through windows served as an icon for time of day. These elements allowed me to use the not-so-natural angles in the light plot (it was a tricky set with a very shallow playing space and a ceiling) to evoke the times of day that Shepard calls for.

My perspective on naturalism and realism argues for three things: First, in moving on from naturalism, perhaps there is room for a further revisiting of its philosophical roots as a form of new or neo-naturalism informed by a postmodern perspective (an endeavor beyond the scope of this book, but which might have the worthy outcome of a few less plays having being written that would have been better off as scripts for TV or film, mediums wherein the realistic seems to be the only production style, save a few particular examples). Second, we should develop a more precise vocabulary with which to situate our designs on the spectrum of theatrical abstraction. And third, our design vocabulary should also overtly embrace the idea of deliberately stylistic theatricality.

Abstraction

In actuality, my lighting designs tend to be both pseudo-realistic *and* expressionistic. This spectrum of theatrical abstraction is most useful in terms of understanding the outer limits the design will occupy rather than a fixed point. For example, the lighting vocabulary for a particular production of *A Doll's House* might be built out of authenticity and not very expressionistic, which would put its boundaries deeply into pseudo-realistic on one side and not so expressionistic on the other. On the other hand, the lighting for a particular production of *Measure for Measure* might be extremely expressionistic and not concerned with authenticity in the least bit, which would place its boundaries deeply into expressionistic on one side and maybe only on the verge of the pseudo-realistic side on the other. In both of those productions, a good lighting design will slide along the spectrum, and, in the best cases, it is difficult to tell where the line between pseudo-realistic and expressionistic is, often because, recalling States, often the pseudo-realistic *is* the expressionistic. They each wink at the other.

The importance of abstraction—what Italian futurist scenographer Enrico Prampolini called interpretive equivalents of realities—in the theatre is nothing new.[33] In fact, deliberate abstraction of some sort or another seems to have been the common characteristic of the nonrepresentational -isms that made up the avant-garde movements that reacted to/grew out of naturalism. Even Strindberg himself moved toward abstraction with his later work; hence his "Author's Preliminary Note to *A Dream Play*" from 1903. So, it is inevitable that abstraction became part of theatrical vocabulary, especially since many artists in the Eurocentric theatre cross pollinated with other forms of artistic expression, despite the lingering tendency toward naturalistic stories. The spectrum I have introduced takes as a given that lighting (and by extension, all stage design to one extent or another) is abstract and that the utility of the spectrum is in situating not *if* something is abstract but *how* abstract that something is. A pseudo-realistic lighting state for an inside room might have a sense of source from a practical lamp, whereas a purely expressionistic one might be a single backlight on at full, but in neither instance are they 'real.'

A proper definition of abstraction is in order. For that, it is useful to consider Ernst Gombrich's 1951 essay *Meditations on a Hobby Horse or the Roots of Artistic Form*.[34] The hobby horse to which he refers is the toy; a stick with a representation of a horse's head at one end that a child straddles and pretends to ride. In the essay, he dissects what about the toy gives it its horse-ness. Two conditions are required: that it can be 'ridden' and that riding it matters to the person 'riding' it. The function of the hobby horse is more important than the form of the hobby horse. He continues by saying that understanding the hobby horse as a representation of an actual horse requires some work on behalf of a person interacting with it; that they are disposed to see it in the required way. And for that to happen, there is a 'minimum image,' a version with sufficient defining features to allow it to be seen in the required way.[35]

Extrapolating this idea into stage design, this means that an abstracted design element must have a sufficient minimum number of features to fulfill the function prescribed by the script, its own minimum version. If a horse is to be abstracted on stage and the only need is for it to be ridden, then the hobby horse (as described above) will be a sufficient minimum version. However, if the horse has to also eat and emote, it will require a mouth and a certain amount of expressive features. So, the greater the function required from a design element, the more details are required, which creates an inversely proportional relationship between the extent of abstraction possible and the amount of functions required. In other words, the greater the function required, the more likely it is that the design element will need to be pseudo-realistic, whereas the less function is required, the more expressionistic it can be. Take, for example, this kitchen I keep going on about. Once version of the lighting for this kitchen might need to be replete from a dramaturgical standpoint, and therefore the minimum version might require multiple practical fixtures, a sense of diffuse incandescent warmth from many stage lights, and maybe something coming through the window. Whereas another version of the lighting for the same fictional kitchen might not need such a complex minimum version, calling instead only for the right color. Perhaps revealing the performers and the kitchen in a single architectural gesture of warm side light is enough.

The parameters of the minimum version are dictated by the needs of the moment, which, in turn, are dictated by both the source material and the choices of the production. Thus far, the kitchen example implies that architectural, spatial, or structural needs are the most important. However, the needs for the minimum version also include, and indeed should be driven by, the more expressive requirements of a moment. Plainly put, how the production wants the spectator *engage* with a moment—physically through the senses and mentally through cognition and emotion—should be the driving factor behind the method of abstraction each design element uses to reach an efficient, essential minimal version. As a practical example, in 2011, I helped develop a play with Sabab Theatre called *The Speaker's Progress*.[36] It was, in part, a response to the then-recent uprisings of the Arab Spring. Through the course of the story, a revolution ensued and by the end, the carefully curated world of the play was in tatters. The last scene, where two women who have survived the revolution make the decision to forge a new life together, was lit with two lone footlights. The light

Theatrical Abstraction 107

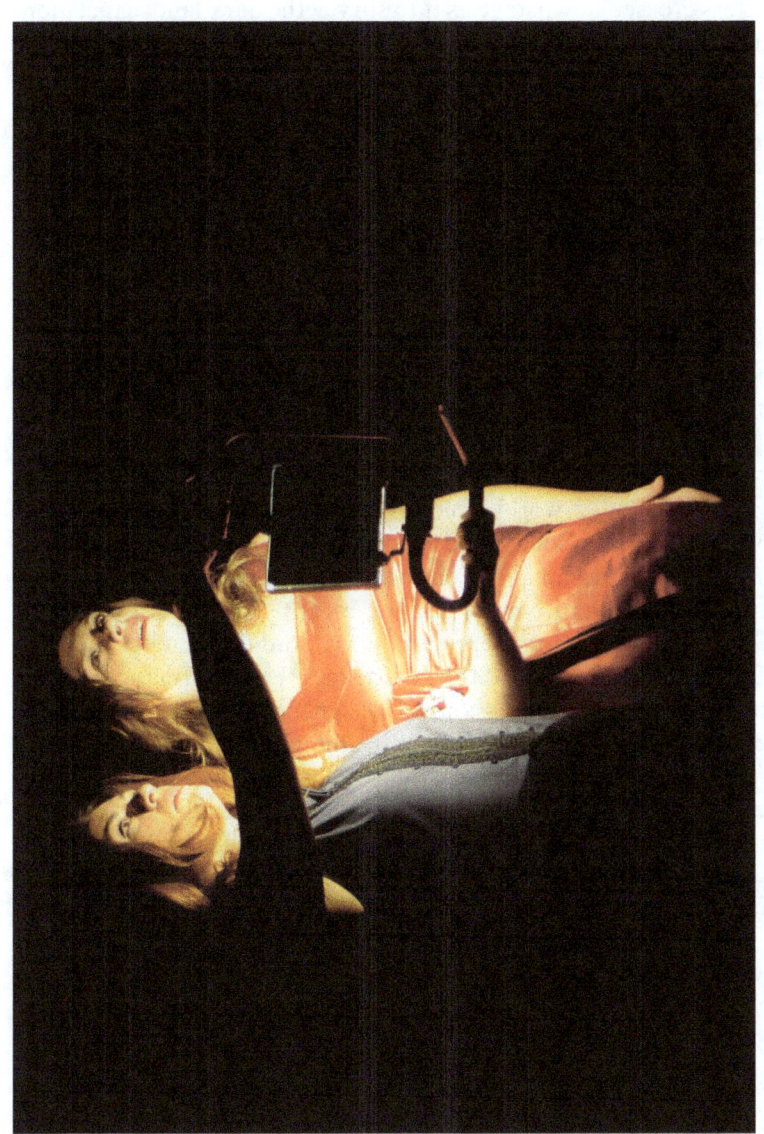

Amal Omran and Carole Abboud in *The Speaker's Progress*
Arts Emmerson, 2011
Photograph © Mike Ritter

was aggressive, indiscriminate, and from an unnatural angle, all appropriately ugly for the scene. There was no pretense to make the fixtures appear as anything other than what they were, two simple incandescent work lights, the sort used to illuminate construction sites. At the last moment, the characters crossed downstage as if to survey the dark landscape, alone but together. As they passed the work lights, they picked one up and held it like a lantern, which lit their faces. It worked because, for this moment in the play, a sufficient minimum version of a lantern had two requirements: that it emitted light and that it could be held in the manner of a lantern, a gesture recognizable across many cultures. This simple gesture of the work light as a "lantern" transformed the landscape of devastation into a strikingly beautiful final image.

Expressionistic

Whereas authenticity is rooted in objects and features, expressionism is rooted in mood, emotion, and what Wagner might call tone. Historically, according to the *Oxford Dictionary of Literary Terms*, expressionism was an avant-garde movement that, "in extreme reaction against realism or naturalism, present[ed] a world violently distorted under the pressure of intense personal moods, ideas, and emotions: image and language thus express[ing] feelings and imagination rather than represent external reality."[37] Expressionistic, as I employ it here, means that the impetus for a design idea is not rooted in the representational, rather, it excites the emotions and influences how a spectator experiences the performance.

For example, my mostly expressionistic design for *Tosca* (Virginia Opera, 2001)[38] keyed off the low brass chords of the intense opening music with a bed of deep red backlight and a shaft of light from high above illuminating the statue of the Madonna as Angelotti furtively searched for the key of the chapel in which he was to hide. Then, as the high strings climbed with the entrance of the Sacristan, the red give way to golden white. I have never seen a chapel that is blanketed in red light, but that does not mean it was not right from an expressionistic standpoint for the orchestral fortitude of the opening moments of this opera. Thus defined, exclusively expressionistic lighting is freed from practical concerns such as time of day or other such verisimilitudes and able to concern itself with emotion, mood, and tone.

As previously discussed, this is why I respectfully disagree with Woodruff. He does not think very highly of tone—music, lighting, dance—because of its ability to call up emotional reactions that are independent of reactions caused by the plot and characters.[39] As a lighting designer, I am biased. I think the tonal nature of lighting design and its expressionistic ability to call up emotional responses, independent of plot and character but in service of the overall dramatic intent of the production, is its strongest feature as a design tool. Theatre that relies on plot and character alone by eschewing all of the other elements that constitute the theatrical is, at minimum, not the kind of theatre I would want to make.

Just like one has to define where the boundary of a lighting design is on the pseudo-realistic side of the spectrum, one also has to determine where the boundary of a lighting design is on the expressionistic side. The easy part of this has to do with how expressionistic the source material is in the first place. *A Doll's House* is one thing, and *Elektra* is another. The perhaps less easy part is that the lighting designer must access their artist self. I refer to my definition of the artist as a kind of mystic who has a way of seeing both the world as it is and a world beyond rational, objective understanding, with a singular point of view, who is possessed of a need to express that vision as a communicative act and does so by making artwork utilizing an accomplished craft. In this analogy about lighting design, the pseudo-realistic can be correlated to the world of rational, objective understanding: a practical is a practical. The lighting designer as an artist must reach beyond the practical as a practical and use the practical as an expressive tool as a part of a collective communicative act. Only if the lighting designer understands their point of view—singular *and* informed by the collective work of the creative team—can they then determine how expressionistic the design needs to be and, by extension, what tools are needed to manifest it in production.

By now, it should be evident, given how I have railed against realism and championed abstraction, that the lighting designs for *Linda Vista* and *True West* were not exclusively concerned with being pseudo-realistic. Pseudo-realism was the starting point, for sure, but each design, in its own way, was also expressionistic. *Linda Vista* is the story of a middle-aged man who has made some bad choices and is seemingly getting his life together, but who ultimately makes more bad choices that relentlessly move him to emotional devastation by the end of the play. The play is also very funny. It was important to playwright Tracy Letts that the world be fresh, alive, and bright and that it had an analog sensibility. Conceits for the lighting included large volumes in bright tints of blue and yellow for day and warm interiors within a surround of velvet blues and lush purples for night. This was all in addition to the authentic elements mentioned above.

Part of the reason for large volumes of light, rather than surgical precision, was that the set—the revolve in a field of blue—functioned as a sort of Petri dish for Wheeler. So, even though it was several rooms and locales, it was also a sculptural element in space. Treating it as such relived the need for abject verisimilitude in lighting—fortunately, as expected, the practicals did a surprising amount of that heavy lifting on that front—freeing the design to breathe and contract in concert with various tension points in Wheeler's journey: for example, the bar where he struggles to connect with another character is a constrictive box of light in a sea of deep color (with the billboard above lit in a dark, tense magenta), a state of light in that was in dialog with Wheeler's loneliness. The overall color journey of the production, too, was expressive of Wheeler's emotional state. It started lush and through the progression of the second act, as things became more and more dire, the light bleached and became more intense through the climax, leaving the denouement drenched in raw, oppressive fluorescent white. Treating the revolve as a sculptural element also allowed for very expressive lighting in transitions, often picking Wheeler out with a single gesture distilled from the previous scene that captured the set architecturally. The billboard, too, was a veritable pathetic fallacy; functioning as sky and commenting emotionally on Wheeler's anti-hero journey.

Likewise, the design for *True West* was subtly expressive. The play becomes a cage match to the death between Lee, a man for whom the true "West" is the desert, highway, and lawlessness, and his younger brother Austin, a man for whom the true "West" is city, culture, and safety. The action of the play is feral, full of animal tension, and constantly off balance. The lighting design echoed this tension and imbalance via two major points of departure: The first was the work of Gregory Crewdson, a photographer with a particularly keen sense of subtle color imbalance whose work is a huge influence on my aesthetic, and the second was Shepard's own note about how the sound of coyotes in the play modulated toward the climax. I wanted the lighting to feel as if it were a tourniquet getting tighter and tighter on a limb throughout the play until, at the climactic moment, the limb exploded. So, at the beginning of the play, the lighting for the night scenes was primarily evocative of candlelight, with footlights softly extending the gesture from the candle on the table in the dining area stage right to make it seem as if the entire space, all the way into the kitchen stage left, were lit from it. Likewise, the day scenes were bright, with angle and intensity keyed off the windows stage right and the bright translucent backdrop. I also embedded a series of color changing systems in the plot: low ideas from the front-of-house sides that swept through the set, unifying it, and several hidden rows of LED tape on the downstage soffit of the ceiling and under all the counters. Influenced by the tension in Crewdson's photographs, I used these systems to subtly twist the color as the play progressed in lockstep with the progressing tension of the coyotes. At the beginning of the play, the shadows were filled with neutral color from these systems, and as the tourniquet tightened, I twisted the color in the shadows moving it from cool white to acid green and finally to the relentless yellow Shepard calls for in his stage directions. All the while, the intensity was just barely below noticeable. I wanted the effect to be unconsciously surreal. It wouldn't work if it were overt, the expressionistic bent of the design had to be hidden within the construct of verisimilitude.

Theatrical

Theatrical, as a term, is multivalent depending on context. From a designer's standpoint, I use the word theatrical to describe a self-referential aesthetic of theatre-making. This aesthetic acknowledges itself to be both *in* the theatre and *of* the theatre. It is embodied by an abstract sign system that is form-based rather than rooted in a specific production of a specific piece. And as Thomas Postlewait and Tracy C. Davis contend in *Theatricality*, it is both a practice and a theoretical concept.[40] Theatrical design embraces all of this.

In some form or another, the idea of theatricality seems to have been foundational for much of the avant-garde, and it is ubiquitous today. Brecht's embrace of theatricality in his Epic Theatre is maybe the most visible—and cited—example of this aesthetic in practice, but it is not his exclusively. My goal is not to assert the use of this aesthetic as a novelty—it has already been in use for over a century—rather, it is to add some precision to its usage (and maybe celebrate it a little). I should admit that for a long time, I was irritated by the word. I felt it so all-encompassing as to lose any sense of specificity as a descriptor or rationale for a production choice. This was around the same time that I was really getting bothered with the notion of realism on the stage. It was while I was trying to get a handle on these words that I came across Vakhtangov's "Two Final Discussions with Students," in which he critiques the divergent approaches of Stanislavsky and Meyerhold and champions the idea of "true and necessary theatricality" over what he called "vulgar theatricality."[41] For Vakhtangov, vulgar theatricality is a result of mediocrity. Whereas true theatricality embraces theatrical means; it does not try to make people forget they are in a theatre rather it celebrates the painted curtain, the uniformed ushers, spectacular sets, and virtuosic actors. With true theatricality, Vakhtangov said, "an audience should not, even for a second, forget that they are at the theatre."[42] Theatricality, for me, suddenly became very specific. The curtain, the ushers, the sets, and the actors *are* the theatrical sign system; both in and of the theatre. And like any aesthetic sign system, the icons, indexes, and symbols of which it is comprised can be applied well (true) or poorly (vulgar).

Viewed through the lens of a theatrical aesthetic, an act curtain is an act curtain, but it is also an abstract icon of presentational performance. It serves its function—to hide and reveal—but it also valorizes itself in the way it is used. That an act curtain is used, and how it is used, is as important as what is upstage of it. The grand reveal is a theatrical gesture, a scenic equivalent of a presentational flourish. Likewise, a follow spot with a hard edge can be viewed as a symbol; the signifier is the sharp circle of light, and the signified meaning is that this is an overtly performative moment. (Whereas a follow spot with a soft edge is light where one wants it and not where one does not, a precision tool which works best when unnoticed.) Because the mechanics of the theatre are so specific, the sign system of theatre is very specific to itself, and because theatre, of course, not only relies on design elements but people as well, the sign system of theatre is partially dependent on the type of source material being played by those people: The sign system of a verismo opera has commonalities with, but is also very different from the sign system of Noh theatre.

The lighting design for the 2017 production of *The Skin of Our Teeth* at TFANA[43] is a model example of how deliberately mixed styles of authentic, pseudo-realistic elements and evocative, expressionistic elements come together under the umbrella of theatricality to form a cohesive design. The play itself is an exemplar of the theatrical aesthetic: there are near-constant acknowledgments of the audience, scenery breaks and falls, the stage manager walks out, actors break character and fight, and the list goes on—including a bizarre turn of events where dinosaurs are kept as pets. There is no pretense in the writing that the audience is anywhere but in a theatre. And there really is no way for an even a halfway decent production to avoid a theatrical aesthetic in practice. A key feature of a theatrical aesthetic is that it is not exclusive. It lends itself neatly to coexisting with other aesthetic points of view. Dramaturgically, *The Skin of Our Teeth* flows between Brechtian and Arthur Miller-esque in its awareness of being in the theatre, thus, the lighting also needed to flow between theatrical and representational. In our production, we wanted the light to move between performative, self-aware, and expressionistic at certain moments and unobtrusive, (somewhat) diegetic, and pseudo-realistic at others.

The lighting for act one was overtly theatrical: it began with a hard-edged spotlight on the announcer reading the news events of the world. As the curtain opened revealing the Antrobus's home, an abstract, iconographically shaped box with a peaked roof and no upstage wall, the light was driven by warm footlights. This angle has become an icon of performance—think of the term "across the footlights"—because it quotes pre-naturalistic theatre. This angle also has the virtue of doing precisely what Appia and Craig hated: throwing shadows on the backing. Just think—a cloudy sky with shadows on it, what a travesty! The footlights also contributed to the design because they are now, to my eye, an expressionistic tool—there is very little that is realistic about that angle. Even though I was treating the backing as sky, I was contradicting myself with the shadows, yet *it all worked together* because nothing was meant to be 'real,' and yet it *seemed* real. The dominant interior color was warm white, while the exterior of the

Arthur French, Robert Langdon Lloyd, then clockwise from left to right, Sam Morales, Mary Lou Rosato, Jessie Shelton, Max Gordon, Fred Epstein, Eric Farber, Storm Thomas, Andrew R. Butler, and Austin Reed Alleman in *The Skin of Our Teeth*

Theatre for a New Audience, 2017
Photograph courtesy of Gerry Goodstein

house was lit in arc white cold. With the arrival of the refugees, the lighting became starker, cooler, and more aggressive. Aside from the footlights, the space was lit almost exclusively by low angle side light—head highs and the like—and a big starkly directional architectural gesture from upstage right. Much of that choice was dictated by architecture of the set since low angle side light was the most efficient way to light the interior. It worked thematically as well, the compression and tension in the composition echoed the claustrophobic despair of this moment in the story. In this instance, the expressionism of the light is what gave significance to a seemingly pseudo-realistic choice.

As an addition to the text, the transition from act one to act two was a musical number, sung by Mrs. Antrobus and the cast, while the company changed the set in full view of the audience. The ceiling flew out, the walls fell over to create a long runway from the extreme right to the extreme left, and a gold and green mylar half curtain flew in upstage. The light for this transition blossomed to reveal everything that was happening, including the addition of the houselights. There was to be no illusion: the cast was performing a song and a set change in the same room at the same time as the audience.

Act two was a more baroque affair—deeply expressionistic and still overtly theatrical. It began similarly to act one in that the Announcer was in a hard-edged spotlight, which continued for the opening speeches. The entrance of the Conveeners was a rowdy musical bit, which revealed the boardwalk proper, lit with bright jewel tones driven by a dominant golden amber gesture from stage left—a pseudo-realistic idea drawn from hot sunlight on a summer's day at the beach. Yet, it deliberately clashed with the green and yellow of the mylar, a choice driven from the imbalance of the story during this act. As the storm approached, the lighting began a shift to echo the cool ending of act one. The dominant gesture became arc white from stage right, and the lighting became atmospheric, with deep variations in visibility, and was dissonant in rhythm, meaning that the timing of lighting changes and the timing of corresponding events on stage were not the same. When the flood came, the backdrop fell and the ceiling of the act one house flew into the floor, the peaked shape evoking an overturned boat. As the cast clambered atop it, the lighting completely fractured and became elemental—the only nod to the pseudo-realistic was the occasional lighting flash and aside from that, the rest of the light was designed to evoke chaos through disjointed angles and seemingly random movement.

The backdrop that fell—an enormous stormy sky painted in black and white—is an excellent example of how a design element can be understood from a sign-based perspective. In this instance, it was both a symbol and an icon. It was a symbol in that it represented vastness, even though one could see the tattered edges and the bar from which it hung. It was also an icon in that it looked like a stylized version of the thing it was meant to represent, which was the sky. And even though it fell halfway through the first act and again at the end of the second, it still evoked the sky when it was in trim. When it was seen as both a symbol and an icon throughout the production was important because it allowed me to make aesthetically appropriate choices depending on the moment. For example, at the end of act one, when the drop functioned as an icon of night sky, I lit it in deep blue to enhance its vastness (itself a symbolic gesture, a theatrical nudge-nudge shared between the audience and production: the real night sky is black; in the theatre, it is represented symbolically in blue), but when it fell during the storm and thus contextually became both literal and iconic broken scenery, I lit it using a broad single source gesture to enhance it as a sculptural object instead.

The lighting for act three was minimalist in the extreme. It was lit using four soft lights from multiple angles to give the sense of diffuse, cool, source-less light. The opening moment was broken by the entrance of the stage manager, and the rehearsal moment and resumed with the entrance of Mrs. Antrobus and Gladys. Through the course of the act, in long slow evolution, the diffuse light was broken by a sharp gesture of light from stage right. The later character breaks in the act were not met with lighting changes, rather they were subsumed into the whole movement of light from diffuse to sharp. Those beats were tying the story of the actors in the play to the story of the characters in the play, and it seemed to make the most sense to let it be under one long change in lighting. By Bailey's entrance to recite Spinoza, the space was sharply revealed in the dawn of a brighter future. After the house was reset, as is called for in the script, the light was exactly that from the top of show, nodding to the idea that we are right back where we started.

Choices

As the lighting for *The Skin of Our Teeth* shows, making theatre is all about making choices. It is my hope that the language and clarifications I have advanced here will bring clarity to collaborative discussions about those choices. I have introduced this language in my own practice and just like pointing to a blue swatch and saying "that blue," pointing to a theoretical point on the spectrum of theatrical abstraction and saying "that abstract" has helped me communicate ideas to my collaborators in more concrete and understandable terms. In making a production, it is never a question of *whether* to do the work as a creative team to find a unified aesthetic (I hope), but *how close* a team can get to it in the given amount of development and rehearsal time with a given amount of effort. Time will be lost if the team is casting about for common vocabulary. However, precise language, such as I have put forward in this chapter, can launch a creative team off the blocks a lot faster as they develop their work. The end result of which is more tightly integrated aesthetics, more efficient time in the theatre, better work overall, and Godfrey's baton much further down the track by opening night.

Notes

1. Clement Greenberg, "Modern and Postmodern," William Dobell Memorial Lecture, Sydney, Australia, October 31, 1979, reproduced in *Arts* 54, no. 6 (February 1980), 65.
2. Kenya Hara, *Designing Design*, 4th ed. (Zurich: Lars Müller Publishers, 2014), 24.
3. Ihab Hassan, "Toward a Concept of Postmodernism," *The Postmodern Turn: Essays in Postmodern Theory and Culture* (Columbus: Ohio State University Press, 1987), 90.
4. Tony Godfrey, *The Story of Contemporary Art* (Cambridge, MA: MIT Press, 2020), 47.
5. Hassan, "Concept of Postmodernism," 91.
6. Janike Sverdrup Ugelstad, "The Mortal Enemy on the Wall," in *A Thing or Two about Ibsen: His Possessions, Dramatic Poetry and Life*, ed. Anne-Sofie Hjemdahl (Oslo: Andrimne, 2006), 187.
7. Michael Billington, "The Troll in the Drawing Room," *Guardian*, February 15, 2003, https://www.theguardian.com/stage/2003/feb/15/theatre.artsfeatures.
8. *A Doll's House*, by Henrik Ibsen and *The Father*, by August Strindberg, both dir. Arin Arbus, set design by Riccardo Hernandez, costume design by Susan Hilferty, composition by Daniel Kluger, and sound design by Daniel Kluger and Lee Kinney, in repertory, Theatre for a New Audience, Brooklyn, US, 2016.
9. Adolphe Appia, "Music and the Art of the Theatre," *Adolph Appia: Texts on Theatre*, ed. Richard Beacham (London: Routledge, 1993), 53.
10. Appia, "Music," 55.
11. Edward Gordon Craig, "From the Artists of the Theatre of the Future," in *Twentieth Century Theatre: A Sourcebook*, ed. Richard Drain (London: Routledge, 1995), 241.
12. Robert Edmund Jones, *The Dramatic Imagination: Reflections and Speculations on the Art of the Theatre* (New York: Routledge, 2004), 23.
13. Christopher Innes, "Introduction," in *A Sourcebook on Naturalist Theatre*, ed. Christopher Innes (London: Routledge, 2000), 6.
14. Emile Zola, "Preface to *Thérèse Raquin*," *Theatre/Theory/Theatre: The Major Critical Texts from Aristotle and Zeami to Soyinka and Havel*, ed. Daniel Gerould, trans. Kathleen Boutall (New York: Applause Theatre and Cinema Books, 2000), 355.
15. Carl E.W.L. Dahlström, "Strindberg's 'Naturalistiska Sorgespel' and Zola's Naturalism: VI. 'Fröken Julie': Conclusion," *Scandinavian Studies* 18, no. 5 (February 1945): 189.
16. Dahlström, "Naturalistiska Sorgespel," 189–90.
17. Henrik Ibsen, "Speech at the Festival of the Norwegian Women's Rights League, Christiana," in *Dramatic Theory and Criticism: Greeks to Grotowski*, ed. Bernard F. Dukore, trans. Arne Kildal (New York: Holt, Rinehart, and Winston, 1974), 563.
18. Emile Zola, "Naturalism in the Theatre," *Theatre/Theory/Theatre: The Major Critical Texts from Aristotle and Zeami to Soyinka and Havel*, ed. Daniel Gerould, trans. Jane House (New York: Applause Theatre and Cinema Books, 2000), 361.
19. Kim Solga, *Theory for Theatre Studies: Space* (London: Methuen Drama, 2019), 61.
20. Innes, "Introduction," 6.
21. Innes, 16–17.
22. Innes, 18.
23. Bert O. States, *Great Reckonings in Little Rooms: On the Phenomenology of Theater* (Berkeley, CA: University of California Press, 1985), 20.

24 States, *Great Reckonings*, 32.
25 Bertolt Brecht, *Brecht on Theatre: The Development of an Aesthetic*, ed. and trans. John Willet (New York: Hill and Wang, 1964), 233.
26 Tori Haring–Smith, "Dramaturging Non-Realism: Creating a New Vocabulary," *Theatre Topics* 13, no. 1 (March 2003): 45, doi: 10.1353/tt.2003.0009.
27 *Oxford English Dictionary Online*, s.v. "authentic, *adj.* and *n.*," accessed May 22, 2021, www.oed.com/viewdictionaryentry/Entry/13314.
28 *Oxford English Dictionary Online*, s.v. "evoke, *v.*," accessed May 22, 2021, www.oed.com/viewdictionaryentry/Entry/65437.
29 *Oxford English Dictionary Online*, s.v. "pseudo-, *comb. form*," accessed May 22, 2021, www.oed.com/viewdictionaryentry/Entry/153742.
30 *True West*, by Sam Shepard, dir. Braden Abraham, set design by Timothy Mackabee, costume design by Deborah Trout, sound design by Mikaal Sulaiman, Seattle Repertory Theatre, Seattle, US, 2020.
31 Sam Shepard, "Note on Set and Costume," in *True West* (New York: Samuel French, 1981), 5.
32 Sam Shepard, *True West* (New York: Samuel French, 1981), 51, 60.
33 Enrico Prampolini, "From Futurist Scenography," in *Twentieth Century Theatre: A Sourcebook*, ed. Richard Drain (London: Routledge, 1995), 23.
34 Ernst H. Gombrich, "Meditations on a Hobby Horse or the Roots of Artistic Form," in *Meditations on a Hobby Horse and Other Essays on the Theory of Art* (New York: Phaidon, 1963), 1–11.
35 Gombrich, "Meditations," 7–8.
36 The Speaker's Progress, written and dir. Sulayman Al-Bassam, production design by Sam Collins, costume design by Abdullah al Awadi, sound design and composition by Lewis Gibson, SABAB Theatre, al-Maidan Cultural Centre, Salmiya, KW, 2011, Theatre Tournesol, Beirut, LB, 2011, Brooklyn Academy of Music Next Wave Festival, Brooklyn, US, 2011, Arts Emerson, Boston, US, 2011, Journées Théâtrales de Carthage, Tunis and Souse, TN, 2012, D-CAF Festival, Cairo, EG, 2012, National Arts Council, Salmiya, KW, 2012, Holland Festival, Amsterdam, NL, 2012.
37 Chris Baldick, "Expressionism," in *Oxford Dictionary of Literary Terms*, 4th ed. (Oxford: Oxford University Press, 2015), 129.
38 *Tosca*, composed by Giacomo Puccini, libretto by Luigi Illica and Giuseppe Giacosa, dir. Dorothy Danner, set design by Michael Yeargan, Virginia Opera, Norfolk, US, 2021.
39 Paul Woodruff, *The Necessity of Theatre* (Oxford: Oxford University Press, 2008), 175–176.
40 Thomas Postlewait and Tracy C. Davis, "Theatricality: An Introduction," in *Theatricality*, ed. Tracy C. Davis and Thomas Postlewait (Cambridge: Cambridge University Press, 2003), 1.
41 Yevgeny Vakhtangov, "Two Final Discussions with Students," in *The Vakhtangov Sourcebook*, ed. and trans. Andrei Malaev-Babel (London: Routledge, 2011), 150.
42 Vakhtangov, *Sourcebook*, 152.
43 *The Skin of Our Teeth*, by Thornton Wilder, dir. Arin Arbus, set design by Riccardo Hernadez, costume design by Cait O'Connor, sound design by Stowe Nelson, projection design by Peter Nigrini, Theatre for a New Audience, Brooklyn, US, 2017.

6 On Design

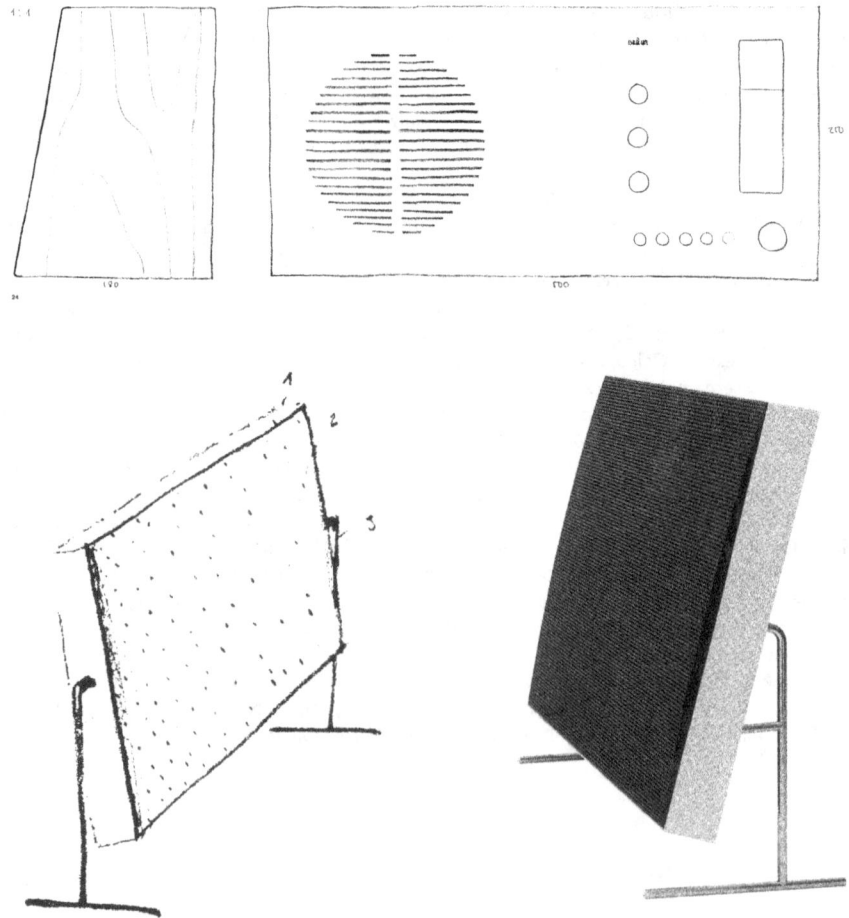

Design sketches by Dieter Rams

Courtesy of Dieter und Ingeborg Rams Stiftung (Dieter and Ingeborg Rams Foundation)

DOI: 10.4324/9781003206460-7

Applied art

Design, in general, is neither craft nor artwork. In many regards, the object of design (verb), being a design (noun), can be seen as a craft object as described in "Artist/Artwork." As I wrote, a craft object is a means to a predictable end, and because its form is dictated by its function, any aesthetic considerations—beauty, for example—are secondary. For example, light that is necessary to illuminate a parking structure is a craft object, the predictable end being that the parking structure has adequate visibility. This does not mean, however, that a design *must be* devoid of aesthetic concerns. Rather, a design's function is its *chief* concern, but, strictly speaking, the act of designing has to do with planning for the making of something functional that *can* choose to be concerned with aesthetic criteria.[1] In other words, in design, aesthetic virtues *can* matter. Thus it is possible for the lighting of a parking structure to also be pleasing. It is this consideration of aesthetic criteria that separates the notion of design from the notion of craft (in both the verb and noun sense). However, a design is strictly speaking not an artwork either, since its aesthetic virtues are not its primary concern. Thus, design exists within a space between the two categories.

For a moment, I would like to concern myself with design as a verb. Design, according to Rams, is in all instances a thinking process: "Working for me," says Rams, "does not mean so much designing in the usual sense of the term, but more contemplation, reading and talking."[2] This thinking process is a process of identifying, understanding, and proposing a solution to a problem. In our world, the play, opera, dance, or what-have-you can be seen as the problem. Therefore, the act of designing lighting for the stage begins with identifying and understanding the "problem." This is the biggest undertaking in the theatrical design process. Without understanding, no sense can be made. Then, it might be tempting to say that logically speaking, the lighting design would be the solution, but this is not the case. The production is the solution. The lighting design is a component of the solution. To reiterate what I have said before in slightly blunter contextual language, a lighting design for live performance is not an artwork in and of itself. The production is the artwork.

Yet, to slightly complicate the matter, a lighting design for the stage *must be* concerned with aesthetic virtues in order for it to fulfill its role, which makes it more than just a design (noun). It is, to borrow the term from Kentridge, a kind of applied art in service of the artwork that is the production. A lighting design for the stage has a function and it is obliged to interact with the production as whole, which means it needs to have at least some predictable ends in order to fulfill that function. But, since its aesthetic virtues are a component of *how* it interacts, the aesthetic virtues of a lighting design not only can matter but *do* matter. It can not fulfill its function without its aesthetic virtues. For example, a lighting design for the stage must be beautiful in itself in order to contribute to the beauty of the production. (Conversely, if it is beautiful, but where the performers and the space are not appropriately lit—as defined by the production's aesthetic—it is a failure.[3]) So, even though it includes the word 'design,' a lighting design should be seen as an applied *art* because of its aesthetic value. It is an articulation of the lighting-designer-as-artist's vision: formally, using tried and true principles of design and composition, and expressionistically, through their point of view, as a component of the total artwork of the production.

Part of the joy (pain?) of writing this book has been an examination into my own understanding of how lighting design concerns itself with aesthetic value as an applied art and what that means for its interaction with myriad other points of view coming from the other artists involved in a given collaboration. In order to be articulate about what aesthetic virtues are important to me, I have had to examine the hitherto unremarked upon dueling influences of modern and postmodern aesthetics—both through education and exposure—on my own development as a contemporary artist. The result is that I have come to understand my aesthetic as a kind of contemporary abstract essentialism.

Essentialism

The common denominator among the major influences on my aesthetic is that they all, to some extent or another, argue for the efficacy of the "sufficient minimum version," as discussed in "Theatrical Abstraction." In other words, the essential. By now, you will have remarked that the word "essential" appears in key places: In my manifesto, when asserting that good lighting for the stage is precise, minimal, and unobtrusive, and in my thoughts on abstraction, where the end result of abstraction should be an efficient, essential minimal version. Taken together, they describe an essentialist perspective which dictates that every component of a design is carefully considered and only that which is deemed indispensable for the production to do what the creative team intends makes it to opening night. As Brecht says, when discussing the work of his collaborator, the designer Caspar Neher, "whatever does not further the narrative, harms it."[4] Only the essential components in a design are included, and if one is removed, the design fails. My draw toward an essentialist aesthetic came from many sources and was catalyzed by my work with Arbus, many produced by Horowitz at TFANA, beginning with the production of *Othello* described in "Artist/Artwork" and continuing to this day. The central questions we grapple with on every production are: Why are we telling this story? What does that mean for the production vocabulary? And how can we defend each choice as essential?

James Newcomb in *Measure for Measure*
The Goodman Theatre, 2013
Photograph courtesy of Liz Lauren

Essentialism is not easy. In fact, it is counter-intuitive. Recent research points to human propensity to lean toward additive problem-solving rather than subtractive problem-solving.[5] When given a choice, people overwhelmingly choose to add things—concepts, objects, rules, procedures—in order to accomplish specific tasks. We are only more likely to choose subtractive solutions when directly prompted with comments like "make this shorter" or "less is more," and subtractive solutions seem to be harder to find. When thinking of the design for a play, an opera, or a dance as a problem, the corollary is clear: it is harder and more counter-intuitive to reduce than to build up. This tendency toward addition is very dangerous for a lighting designer; essentialism makes the hard part of lighting a show not figuring out what lights to turn on but figuring out what lights to turn off and, more importantly, what lights to not hang at all.

I think aesthetic essentialism is a matter of attitude more than anything. Greg McKeown, in his book *Essentialism: The Disciplined Pursuit of Less*, sums it as, "A non-essentialist thinks almost everything is essential. An essentialist think almost everything is nonessential."[6] Does it help tell the story? No? Cut it. Is it superfluous or decorative? Yes? Cut it. Do you worry about focusing the plot in an eight-hour call? Maybe? Cut some systems. This attitude has led me to believe that no production is so complicated that it resists an essentialist aesthetic in its design. However, this needs qualification on two fronts: First, essential is a relative term. Essential for my lighting for *Othello* mentioned above is one thing, essential for my lighting for an epic *Measure for Measure* at The Goodman (2013)[7] is quite another. The sheer scale of the set for this production, along with the expansive staging of the large cast, demanded a light plot equal to the task (including 72 practical channels and over 430 discreet lighting elements). Sometimes essential is quite baroque! Second, while many modernists who have influenced my work could be called essentialists, I do not see essentialist thinking as directly analogous to modernist thinking. Rather, on the flow chart of process, it follows as a barometer for measuring the absolute necessity of choices within a lighting design regardless of their geneses and is directly related to creating sophisticated meaning within the narrow gradations appropriate for the production.

Legacies

When I think about the designers whose work and teaching have impacted me the most, I see work in search of elegant design solutions that "make sense" within a given rule system. Unsurprisingly, this work tends to be characterized by crisp and extremely thoughtful minimalism that not only takes structural/functional concerns into consideration but also aesthetic concerns—broadly characteristic of a high-modernist sensibility.

A hybridized approach where form does not follow function, nor does function follow form. As Parks aptly describes this kind of relationship: "Form is not something that 'gets in the way' of the story but is an integral part of the story ... the container dictates what sort of substance will fill it and, at the same time, the substance is dictating the size and shape of the container."[8] So, form and function, interdependent, approach a zenith of unity.

By now, you will see that the impact of Rams's work on my thinking cannot be undervalued. His methodical approach to lasting industrial and product design, and, indeed, his ten principles of good design, here condensed, are a huge influence in my conception of the role of the designer.

For Rams, good design is:

1 Innovative
2 Makes a product useful
3 Aesthetic
4 Makes a product understandable
5 Is honest
6 Is unobtrusive
7 Is long-lasting
8 Is thorough down to the last detail
9 Is environmentally friendly
10 Is as little design as possible[9]

Echos of these principles can be seen in my manifesto and thus throughout this book, especially those having to do with good design being innovative, thorough, and minimal. Rams's design sensibility is rational and feasible, both with regard to the product's ability to meet the demands of the user and with regard to the product's ability to be brought to market in an efficient way. While his focus was on products, the point was that the products were going to be used by people: "Rams is always at pains to stress," says his biographer Sophie Lovell, "that the duty of industrial design is first and foremost to users and the users are, generally, human beings with all their complexities, habits, ideas and idiosyncrasies."[10] For me, the parallels to designing lighting for the stage are clear: a good lighting design is rational in that it can meet the needs (dramaturgical, physical, metatextual, visual, and rhythmic) of the production and it is also feasible in that it can be manifested within whatever limitations (time, budget, resources, etc.) are put on it. And, to stretch the comparison a bit more, if the user is the audience and users are riddled with complexities, a good lighting design will account for the evolving complexities inherent in the making of theatrical works of art. In other words, a lighting state that works for a moment at one level of understanding might not work when the complexities surrounding a moment in a play are better understood. Again, design is first a thinking process.

Another of Rams's propositions that have impacted my aesthetic addresses visual pollution: chaos that comes from misplaced priorities. For him, it has to do with the presence too many things. Lovell describes it thus: "Our world is filled with too many products with superficial attractions and little or no use."[11] Substitute "world" with "production" and "products" with "lighting," and one can see how the idea of visual pollution manifests itself in a lighting design. Rams's minimalism is well thought out; if an element does not serve the overall need of the product, it probably shouldn't be there. Likewise, if a fixture is included on a plot for no reason or if a light cue seems superficial, it probably is. In fact, if I had a dime for every superficial cue or fixture of little or no use I have cut from a show, I would be a rich man.

I have already cited Hara's minimalist influence, as his meditations on the nature of white have made me understand the utility of white light anew. White, in pigment, is the absence of all color. In light, it is the presence of all colors. As such, it is special. Of course, there are many kinds of white light: clear, incandescent white, which to my eye feels like a color more than white; cool, slightly oppressive arc white; and thicker, more revealing corrected white light, like L501. And then there are the whites that appear white only when contrasted with something else—a hint green can appear white when next to saturate yellow, etc. Hara's influence does not only extend only to color; he has also reinforced the utility of rumination as an active part of the design process: the repetitive process of considering and assessing images. This takes time, but a lighting designer needs to be able to do that quickly in the context of technical rehearsal. This is an argument for limiting the palette for a production: "Design involves controlling differences," writes Hara, "Yet repeating the same jobs over and over taught me how important it is to limit those differences, retaining only those that are most *essential*. I came to believe that if I wanted to weave a tapestry that was meaningful, it was narrow gradations, not great disparities, that mattered" (my italics).[12] By extension, when creating a lighting design, one can work faster within a tight palette than within an infinite one simply because there are less possibilities from which to choose.

Apples and hats

Another late hitting influence on my thinking about design is the graphic designer Chip Kidd, whose iconic book covers belie a very sophisticated sense of how design serves narrative content. He has said, "A graphic designer gives form to content, but also manages a very careful balance between the two."[13] This is a powerful reminder that such balance is difficult and requires constant designerly attention. Kidd cited a lesson from his first day of design class in his TED Talk, "Designing Books Is No Laughing Matter. Ok, It Is," "Either you put a picture of an apple or write the word apple but if you put a picture of an apple and you write the word apple you are treating your audience like a moron and they deserve better."[14] This is very similar to what Arbus often says: as a creative team, there is no need to put a hat on a hat. Meaning, it is best when only the most efficacious element of the production carries the weight of a choice. Shakespeare is a classic example: if he wants the audience to know that it is night, a character will say it. In a contemporary setting, this frees the lighting designer from having to create a strictly pseudo-realistic state of light to convey time of day if the design is best served by a more abstract state. The text has already said, "apple." It is already wearing a hat.

As an aside, I would also say that the totality of this minimalist, essentialist thought reinforces my desire for a theatre that is not dominated by the text. Of course, this is not a new idea. According to Artaud: "A theatre which subordinates the mise en scène and production, i.e., everything in itself that is specifically theatrical, to the text, is a theatre of idiots, madmen, inverts, grammarians, grocers, antipoets and positivists."[15] Indeed, current articulation methods of stage design are such that it can, and by rights should be, a coequal expressive storytelling tool given equal agency alongside the actor and text. Visual dramaturgy, as those from Craig to contemporary puppet theatre-maker Eric Bass argue, is as important and expressive as movement and dialog. Bass writes,

> As writers of dialog, we put ourselves in the shoes of our characters to find their voices. As physical dramaturgs, we let our impulses lead us to discover the truth of a moment onstage. As visual dramaturgs, the space, our materials, the imbalance of our images, the actual transformation of our elements, all have the potential to contain dramatic tension ... Any and all of these can be the tools of our 'writing'.[16]

Words, music, people, movement, image—they are all apples, they are all hats, and they are all equally capable of storytelling.

Of course, the foundational influence on the modernist aspect of my aesthetic was that of my teachers at the Yale School of Drama in the late 1990s. It would be impossible for me to articulate how much I learned under their tutelage, but suffice it to say that in those days at the Annex, a high modern aesthetic was hot. If the room needed a door, there was a door. And if the room needed to have an 18th-century feel, it did. But if it did not need a door, there was not one, and if evoking a period was not essential then there was no molding—less is more visually allowed for less but *better* in execution. Finally, it might also be painted completely dove grey and lit with one kind of white light. The key was to have one Big Idea and a certain maintenance of 'accepted' aesthetic standards. Stage design historian Arnold Aronson describes the modernist aesthetic thinking that I experienced at Yale succinctly in his essay "Postmodern Design:" "Modern [stage] design functions by visually and metaphorically placing the specific world of the play within some sort of broader context of the world of the audience; it is a kind of meta narrative that attempts to encompass the world within a unified image."[17] Among my peer students, the best light plot was not the largest but the smallest possible to articulate the Big Idea. Every fixture had to have a reason to exist on the plot, and if it did not, it had to be cut. At the core, this incredibly complex pursuit of simplicity sent me off into the world of professional theatre working very, very hard at keeping my plots small and precise. To this day if the magic sheet covers too many pages, I take it as a sign that I should cut some ideas.

MTV

Moving a little further back in time, we travel to the inception of my postmodernist bent. In May of 1988, at the age of 13, when I was hit by a car and ended up with, among other injuries, a broken left leg. I was in a cast for nearly the entire summer, and, as such, I could not navigate stairs. So, I was summarily parked on the couch for my convalescence. As a concession to my inability to go outside and play, my parents finally acquiesced to letting me spend time watching music videos on MTV: Journey, Guns N' Roses, U2, Rick Astley, INXS, Huey Lewis and the News, Hall & Oates, Michael Jackson, Sting, Bobby Brown, Tracy Chapman, Bruce Hornsby and the Range, Van Halen, Steve Winwood, Joan Jett and the Blackhearts, George Michael, Gloria Estefan and the Miami Sound Machine, Information Society, Pet Shop Boys, Elton John, Run DMC, Chicago, Def Leppard (my absolute favorite at the time) ... and the list goes on and on. That accident was, and may very well be, the best thing that ever happened to my development as an artist. Every four minutes and eight seconds, I was bombarded with a new aural and visual experience. A mishmash of aesthetics beamed into my provincial mind from around the world, each valorizing its own point of view and value system. It was impossible to collate these into a single, cohesive aesthetic beyond its own indeterminacy (its inability to identify itself—clearly a critical imposition viewed through the lens of today). It scrambled my adolescent brains, and I loved it all! Little did I know how influential this TV channel would be on my aesthetic development.

Hassan, who presents a useful schema for modernism vs. postmodernism in *Toward a Concept of Postmodernism*, describes postmodernism with words like antiform, play, chance, and anarchy. These are apt descriptors of my experience of the videos on MTV.[18] From this vantage point, there is no

Rick Savage, Joe Elliott and Rick Allen of Def Leppard during the *Hysteria* World Tour, Hammersmith Odeon, London, 1987

Duncan Raban/Popperfoto via Getty Images

such thing as the one-right-way of Greenberg's modernism because, in the global audience of MTV, there was no one universal viewer. I have stolen the word "indeterminacy" above from Hassan, who elsewhere wrote: "By indeterminacy, or better still, indeterminacies, I mean a combination of trends that include openness, fragmentation, ambiguity, all conducive to indeterminacy or under-determination."[19] MTV, here, is both an actual aesthetic influence and a metaphor for my introduction to multiple cultures at large from the late 1980s onwards. Cultures too numerous and vast to name. There were so many things to look at, so many aesthetics bombarding me; it was as if Godfrey's baton—the one passed on from the Courbert that represents the serene continuation of strictly defined modernist aesthetics—not only got dropped but seemed to multiply itself exponentially with every bounce.

In an environment like that, one must pick and choose influences and intentionally define one's own aesthetic. "Perhaps, after all, postmodernism can be 'defined' as a continuous inquiry into self-definition," Hassan wrote in the months before the 9/11 attacks,

> The more interactive the globe, the more populations move, jostle, and grapple—this is the age of diasporas—the more questions of cultural,

religious, and personal identity become acute—and sometimes specious. In still another transposition of postmodernism into postmodernity, you can hear the cry around the world: "Who are we? Who am I?"[20]

This statement's relationship to 9/11 is important for a few reasons. First, if Godfrey's baton had been bouncing and multiplying during my adolescence and my formative years in the academy, it shattered when the World Trade Center fell. And second, that was when my urge for self-definition as a bi-cultural and bi-racial artist became palpable and urgent. Only in hindsight is it possible to see this marker in time as a pivotal moment. What a time to be starting one's career! What to do when all bets are off, the baton of artistic precedence is in shards around you, and you have one foot firmly planted in postmodernism and the other in modernism?

Coexistence

The reconciliation, for me, is to understand that my work—and therefore my conception of good lighting for the stage in general—occupies a space of coexistence between the two aesthetic movements, which, maybe, is postmodern in and of itself. In the words of cultural theorist and landscape architect Charles Jencks, "Postmodernism has the essential double meaning: the continuation of Modernism and its transcendence."[21] Because lighting is not composed of things, like a set, understanding these aesthetic pulls becomes about understanding process, tendencies, and articulation. To get at these two legacies in the context of a contemporary lighting design, I will examine my design process for *graveyard shift* and situate which choices I see to be essentially modern and which I see to be essentially postmodern. Again, I emphasize the difference between the two from Hassan's schema: form, purpose, design, and hierarchy on one side with modernism, and antiform, play, chance, and anarchy on the other with postmodernism.

The lighting for the first movement of *graveyard shift* was fairly pseudo-realistic in form and purpose—even though the set itself was quite abstract—evoking a series of day and night-time interiors. This was designed to set up a counterpoint for the progression of the design. This desire for rational structure is informed by my need for form and purpose. However, the practical act of writing cues for this show belied a reliance on postmodern play, chance, anarchy, and perhaps a little antiform as well. Even though I go into the room with a very specific idea of what each scene will look like, it almost always goes to hell (anarchy!) the moment I write the first cue. For me, the content of cue one informs cue two informs cue three, etc. If what I have planned for cue one changes, it dominoes down the design.

I find this anarchy a great space of experimentation. Where I am freed to create instinctively, from a place of emotion, and where logic is not the most important driver. I can propose what Aronson calls "a multiplicity of competing, often incongruous and conflicting elements and images" through light.[22] This is how I can access ideas that would not be possible to understand alone in the studio. In *graveyard shift* this is what allowed me to understand that Janelle's jail cell needed to be a square of light that echoed the squares of light I proposed for the traffic stop. This process of play, chance, and discovery is also how I came to the hitherto completely unexpected palette of the final movement of the play: Yellow side light contrasting with white fluorescents on a deep blue sky that, through a nine-minute-long multi-cue sequence, took the yellow away and replaced it with stomach-acid green shin-busters from one end of the runway stage and moved the sky through green to red, ending in a completely dissonant image for the penultimate scene. This scene was the moment of greatest fracture and discord in the play and it was important that the lighting echoed the discord of the story. To be clear, while some ideas are a result of anarchy, in practice, they are often then wrangled into considered choices through the process of iterative rehearsals, which moves it from antiform to a design. One does not just chance upon a nine-minute-long multi-cue sequence after all.

While there are many aspects that a production will reveal as determinate, I have come to believe that lighting itself is indeterminate because it is insubstantial and, therefore, cannot be identified in isolation from that which it is lighting. So, lighting is not so much concerned about *what* we are seeing as *how* we are seeing. And, of course, because I have advanced the act of spectating as the meaning-making transaction between spectator and artwork, no two ways of seeing will ever be the same. Aronson addresses this: "Postmodernism shifts the basis of the work of art from the object to the transaction between the spectator and the object and further deconstructs this by negating the presence of a representative objective viewer."[23] From the modernist perspective, the objective viewer might be seen as a sort of distillation of the 'idealized' spectator as a stand-in for a culture. Of course, the idea of only one way of viewing is a fiction, especially as we begin to recognize that the so-called idealized perspective has often been white, Eurocentric, and male. This inevitable multiplicity asserts the impossibility of a single, *exclusively objective*, definition of 'good' in lighting for the stage. Conveniently, it is a damn good defense of why it is okay for the stage to look different from house right and house left. While this may seem like a mere digression, it is in fact key: since there is not only exclusively objective right way to see, I am freed to play with the unanticipated inspiration that comes as a result of the domino effect and see what happens.

So, for me, to answer the question of what to do is to embrace both influences—the modern and the postmodern. I find that my thinking process tends to concern itself with things like form, purpose, design, and hierarchy and my articulation leans toward antiform, play, chance, and a little anarchy. Now, let me be clear that the latter does not mean that anything goes; on the contrary, everything still needs to both make sense within the context of the design and make sense for the production as a whole—wrangled like the palette for the end of *graveyard shift*—considering only those things that are required and that are not merely superfluous decoration.

Vocabulary

The realms of visual and musical composition rely on specific elements being brought together in specific ways, following established principles, to create meaning. This is analogous to words and grammar for language. Lighting design is no different. Even though design is a thinking process, it is also an articulation process and ideas are of very little practical value unless they can be put into action. Design implies function and good lighting for the stage follows established principles—the vocabulary and grammar of stage design if you will—to achieve this function. The manifestation of good lighting for the stage revolves around many things—dramaturgical acumen, collaborative understanding, technical know-how—but they must be coupled with an acute knowledge of these fundamentals, leading to insightful and innovative applications. These fundamentals are the essential tools of the theatre artist's mastery of craft. As Mr. Miyagi might have said to Daniel San, grammar is no good without vocabulary, so first we must wax the car and paint the fence to understand some fundamental vocabulary.

What follows is a list of elements and principles that I most often evoke in my process—both in terms of what lighting states look like and how the light moves across time. They come from multiple sources, including literary criticism, music, and the widely recognized principles of design and composition. I have divided them here into three major groupings—visual, music, and temporal—for clarity, although, as you will sense, many jump boundaries and hold multiple meanings. For the sake of these definitions, a composition can either be a single lighting state, multiple lighting states, or movement between lighting states and can refer to the lighting specifically or to the entire mise en scène.

Visual composition

The vocabulary of visual composition is best suited to describing the individual elements that make up a composition and how they fit together in the overall picture.

> Angle—where a lighting idea comes from in space, expressed in relationship to plan, section, or elevation orientation. E.g., front light, backlight, cross light, side light, etc.

Balance—the distribution of visual elements within a composition to create stability or tension. In visual compositions, balance may be symmetrical, asymmetrical, radial, etc. Balance also refers to the visual complexity of a composition.

Chroma—the intensity or purity of a color.

Color—the sum of values and intensities of all the hues within the visual spectrum.

Color Temperature—the measurement, in degrees Kelvin (where 0° is absolute zero), used as a descriptor for colors that exist on the line from red to yellow to white to blue. In stage lighting, commonly used to distinguish kinds of white.

Contrast—the juxtaposition of elements or degree of differentiation in a composition. In lighting, this could be contrast within a single lighting state or contrast between states. In color, high contrast colors are opposite to each other on the color wheel (complementary), whereas low contrast colors are closer to each other (analogous).

Depth—actual or implied distance from the viewer or relative distances of objects within a composition. Often discussed in terms of foreground, middle ground, and background. Depth can also be a useful term for discussing the degree to which something is done, for example, one might go deep into a color (meaning going very saturate).

Dominant/recessive—in light, dominant colors are those that hold their integrity in the presence of other colors. Recessive colors are those that tend to blend out easily in the presence of other colors.

Hierarchy—a ranking of order or importance. In a composition, elements can have hierarchical positions based on compositional rules; think of the figure of Christ in da Vinci's *The Last Supper*, where all elements of composition point to his head. Hierarchy is not limited to visual elements, however. For example, a moment of particular impact in a story (like a climax) could have a hierarchical relationship over other scenes.

Hue—of color, the name of the dominant wavelength used to identify a color, such as red, purple, green, etc.

Intensity—a measurement or relative relationship of brightness or darkness, including the brightness of a fixture on a scale from zero to full. Also a measure of emotional or cognitive impact in storytelling.

Line—the basic element used to express all visual compositions. Also, in math, the shape described by connecting two discrete points in space.

Movement—how the composition forces the viewer's eye through the visual space to focal areas and along paths of viewing (c.f., *The Last Supper*). In dynamic compositions, like effects sequences, this is literal.

Pattern—when a repeated symbol or element appears in regular rhythm within a composition. Works with repetition to breed visual familiarity.

Progression—the specific movement of elements from one composition to another.

Proportion—the way the visual elements within a composition relate to each other and help to create balance. On stage, the most important metric for proportion is the human figure.

Repetition—when a symbol or element appears in multiplicity in a composition.

Saturation—the depth of intensity of a particular hue.

Shape/form—an area defined by edges.

Space—the area between objects or elements in a composition. Usually expressed as positive or negative.

Tint—the degree of lightness of a particular hue.

Texture—the surface quality of a composition. In light, the implication of light passing through a partial obstruction.

Value—or chiaroscuro, the infinite gradations between light and dark, which imply a light source and show three-dimensional form. Used also to describe color as compared to a greyscale.

Variety/unity—the presence, or lack thereof, of multiple conflicting elements within a composition.

Musical composition

I have co-opted this vocabulary from the realm of music because, like light, music is ephemeral. I have found that because these definitions have been grounded through time, they tend to have widely understood meanings. This lends precision to discussions about lighting, a form that has very little widely understood vocabulary beyond the very technical. Musical vocabulary is also very useful when describing things that happen over time.

Articulation—the distinct expression of an idea. In music, how a note is played. For example, staccato means notes are detached with a slight empty space between them, whereas legato means the notes should be played connected and smoothly. These terms can be useful in describing how lighting states might transition—staccato might mean zero counts and legato might mean overlapping long fades. Articulation can also refer to the technical aspect of creating an idea, an example being a box of light articulated with a framing profile fixture.

Aria—an air, a piece of music often with a single or simple melodic line. In opera, usually a distinct solo piece. In lighting, I use this term to describe a distinct state or movement in light that is related to a long solo text, such as the lighting for the bartender's monologue in *Queens Boulevard (The Musical)* (Signature Theatre Co, 2007)[24], which was a soft pull in to him standing on a table and subsequent release over the length of the text.

Dynamics—how loud or soft a moment of music should be played; for example, pianissimo is very softly, forte is loudly, to crescendo is to gradually become louder, and to diminuendo is to gradually become softer. Its metaphoric use in lighting has to do with how visually or rhythmically "loud" a visual composition is. Dynamics can also have to do with the nature of movement in light.

Dissonant—the lack of harmony. In a visual composition, unusual or clashing combinations of angles, colors, patterns, etc. It also refers to how one proposition might purposefully not fit within, or even outright clash with, a series of propositions.

Emphasis—in music, when one note is stressed over others, either by attack or virtue of being higher than others. In a visual composition, when one element is given more prominence than the others. For example, within a three-dimensional space, this is often called foregrounding. Also, an emphasized step an effect loop creates in relation to an emphasized note or articulation (a cymbal crash, for example) in a repetitive musical gesture.

Harmony—the arrangement of parts together to create a pleasing whole. In some musical conceptions, this can mean a tuneful or pleasing sound. In a visual composition, this has to do with a non-dissonant relationship of elements. This is tricky because it calls into question the system of aesthetic values within which the proposition (or music) is being evaluated.

Leitmotif—popularized by Wagner, a musical theme that is associated with a particular character, situation, or idea. Like aria, this is a good word to borrow. It can be used when describing an idea of light that is associated with one of the elements above that repeats through a design. If all of Macbeth's asides are lit the same, that state or concept can be referred to as a leitmotif.

Rhythm—the combining of elements within a composition to create pattern, flow, and organization. Like music, visual rhythm can influence emotional comprehension. Variation in rhythm is a valuable tool and a good way of adding humor through lighting.

Tempo—the speed of a piece of music, also of lighting element (effects, etc.). Tempo has an influence on the emotional impact of a transition between lighting states or an effect; slow might be calming, whereas fast might impart a sense of urgency or energy.

Transition—the method of moving from one visual composition to another.

Unity—how harmonic or dissonant the elements within the composition are. Manipulating unity is a way of encouraging emotional responses. Within a temporal form, unity relies on memory as the perception of the whole can only be in retrospect.

Temporal composition

Finally, this vocabulary of temporal composition contemplates ideas that are *strictly* related to the fact that lighting happens over time. I acknowledge that there is a blurred distinction between temporal and musical, and in the instances where the idea is rooted in music, the element was listed under music to clarify its derivation.

Energy—the dynamics within a given visual composition. This is expressed profoundly over time.

Expectation—what the viewer expects given a certain string of visual compositions. If the first five scenes of a play have ended in a blackout, the expectation is that the sixth will. A production choice is whether to follow through with the expectation or to break it, for a good reason (of course).

Form—the description of the shape of a story or design. Usually used to show how something moves from the beginning through the middle to the end. In the sense of stage lighting, this has to do with the big-picture shape of the design; it could be described as moving from light to dark, colorful to stark, etc.

Flow—the way in which the elements or a visual composition or design move around each other. In a lighting, this has to do with how ideas or systems move through the form of a design.

Inertia—the weight in which one idea moves forward, contrasted with the weight required to change it. A lighting sequence, in a musical number perhaps, may have a lot of complicated elements built together, which would give it a great deal of momentum. A small change in the music would not have enough weight to change the momentum, whereas a big change (tempo, key, orchestration) would.

Intent—how the elements of the composition inform the programmatic intent of the composition.

Satya Bhabha, Emily Donahoe, Amir Arison, Bill Buell, Arian Moayed, and Jon Norman Schneider in *Queens Boulevard (The Musical)*
Signature Theatre Company, 2007
Photo by Richard Termine

Time—the fourth dimension of composition. How the elements of a composition evolve temporally, either an idea across the time of the design or cue movement between states of light.

Dramatic intent

As an applied art, a lighting design is obliged to interact with all aspects of a production in a well-structured way. Lest it seems, by my examination of *graveyard shift*, that my process is totally ruled by anarchy, I want to reiterate the point that while my choices may seem arbitrary, they are guided by a preexisting structure for the design—a framework within which to make decisions—and my aesthetic point of view. This structure is the result of a rigorous studio process that is intellectual, rational, and justified, which allows the design to be constructed with some manner of planned dramatic intent. All the choices that go into a good lighting design for the stage, from the coexisting pulls of modern and postmodern thinking to distilling essential choices to the formal use of the vocabulary and grammar of stage design, *have to* be made with dramatic intent in mind. In the end, theatre is storytelling and if the lighting design does not concern itself with the story, no amount of aesthetic virtue will make it successful.

Notes

1 *Oxford English Dictionary Online*, s.v. "design, v.," accessed June 10, 2021, https://www.oed.com/view/Entry/50841.
2 Dieter Rams, *Less but Better*, trans. Christopher Harrington, 5th ed. (Berlin: Gestalten, 2014), 145.
3 Lest my use of the phrase "appropriately lit" be misconstrued, I would like to be clear that it is *not* an argument for having the faces must be lit all of the time. Faces are important—as the old adage attributed to Craig Miller goes, "It's the face that sings!"—but sometimes not lighting faces, or bodies at all, *is* the appropriate way to light something.
4 Bertolt Brecht, "Stage Design for the Epic Theatre" in *Brecht on Theatre: The Development of an Aesthetic*, ed. and trans. John Willet (New York: Hill and Wang, 1964), 232.
5 Gabrielle S. Adams et al., "People systematically overlook subtractive changes," *Nature* 592 (April 8, 2021): 258–261, https://doi.org/10.1038/s41586-021-03380-y.
6 Greg McKeown, *Essentialism: The Disciplined Pursuit of Less* (New York: Crown Business, 2014), 46–47.
7 *Measure for Measure*, by William Shakespeare, dir. Robert Falls, set design by Walt Spangler, costume design by Ana Kuzmanić, and original music and sound design by Richard Woodbury, The Goodman Theatre, Chicago, US, 2013.
8 Suzan-Lori Parks, "From *Elements of Style*," *The America Play and Other Works* (New York: Theatre Communications Group, 1995), 7–8.
9 Dieter Rams, quoted in Sophie Lovell, *Dieter Rams: As Little Design as Possible*, 4th ed. (New York: Phaidon, 2014), 352–353.
10 Lovell, *As Little Design*, 343.
11 Lovell, 348.
12 Kenya Hara, *White*, trans. Jooyeon Rhee (Zurich: Lars Müller Publishers, 2012), 19.

13 Chip Kidd, "Designing Books Is No Laughing Matter. Ok, It Is," *TED*, March 2012, accessed June 10, 2021, www.ted.com/talks/chip_kidd_designing_books_is_no_laughing_matter_ok_it_is?language=en.
14 Kidd, "Designing Books."
15 Antonin Artaud, *The Theatre and Its Double*, trans. Mary Caroline Richards (New York: Grove Press, 1958), 41.
16 Eric Bass, "Visual Dramaturgy: Some Thoughts for Puppet Theatre-Makers," in *The Routledge Companion to Puppetry and Material Performance* (London: Routledge, 2014), 59.
17 Arnold Aronson, "Postmodern Design," *Theatre Journal* 43, no. 1 (March 1991): 2, https://doi.org/10.2307/3207947.
18 Ihab Hassan, "Toward a Concept of Postmodernism," *The Postmodern Turn: Essays in Postmodern Theory and Culture* (Columbus: Ohio State University Press, 1987), 91–92.
19 Ihab Hassan, "From Postmodernism to Postmodernity: The Local/Global Context," *Philosophy and Literature* 25, no. 1 (April 2001): 4, doi: 10.1353/phl.2001.0011.
20 Hassan, "From Postmodernism to Postmodernity," 6.
21 Jencks, Charles. "Postmodern and Late Modern: The Essential Definitions," *Chicago Review* 35, no. 4 (1987): 34, https://doi.org/10.2307/25305377.
22 Arnold Aronson, "Postmodern Design," *Theatre Journal* 43, no. 1 (March 1991): 2, https://doi.org/10.2307/3207947.
23 Aronson, "Postmodern Design," 2.
24 *Queens Boulevard (The Musical)* by Charles Mee, dir. Davis McCallum, set design by Mimi Lien, costume design by Christal Weatherly, and sound design by Ken Travis, Signature Theatre Company, New York, US, 2007.

7 The Box

Untitled, 2003–2008

Gregory Crewdson
Digital Pigment Print
57 × 88 in. (145 × 224 cm)
Edition of 6 + 2 AP
© Gregory Crewdson. Courtesy Gagosian

DOI: 10.4324/9781003206460-8

Gravity

Time is money, and once we are in the theatre itself, it is someone else's money, so we must work very quickly. Whereas in preproduction we have more flexibility with our time. I find that preproduction is the place to really investigate a piece and conceive of a design that is intellectual, rational, and justified. For me, the way I approach preproduction for each individual project I design is much like a Japanese tea ceremony—the steps are ritualized, specific, and minimal for a reason. Having practiced the steps—so I do not have to think about what step is next, how to do the step, or if I have forgotten a step—allows me to free as much mental energy and space as possible to think creatively, to "ruminate," as Hara would say.[1] My approach also helps provide rigor and discipline to my practice. *The New York Times* commentator David Brooks, writing of the creative processes of artists like Maya Angelou, W.H. Auden, and others, wrote that "creative people organize their lives according to repetitive, disciplined routines. They think like artists but work like accountants ... In situation after situation, this pattern recurs: order and discipline are the prerequisites for creativity and daring."[2] The truth of this has played out time and again in my own work, and that is why my design process is so rigorous and regimented.

In the introduction, I wrote that one does not often cry "eureka" in a moment of profound revelation, fully conscious of a permanent aesthetic shift in the making. This was, of course, qualified because sometimes it does happen; sometimes, one does have that sort of Campbellian "Aha!" moment. In fact, it once happened to me in a coffee shop in Williamsburg, around the corner from where I used to live. I was lighting a production of *Macbeth*, directed by Arbus (TFANA, 2011).[3] As she described it, "The play is highly theatrical in that the landscape is continually shifting – at times we are in actual locations, then it rapidly shifts to the interior of Macbeth's mind. Other times we enter a poetic territory of the supernatural, or the gates of hell and slide back into actual locations."[4] We met to hash out the vocabulary of the lighting design: the natural world of Scotland, the supernatural world of the witches, the inversion of time, and how the world becomes more twisted and macabre as the play moves along. It was a rainy day, it was hot inside, and as fate would have it the windows were steamy. The details of the conversation are sketchy at best, but I was trying to articulate my thinking about the arc of the lighting and remembered a two-dimensional image of gravity that I had seen in a *National Geographic* or something. It looked like the surface of a stretchy fabric with a ball sitting on it and pulling it down. I started squeaking circles in the condensation on the window. This is the witches, this is Banquo's ghost, this is 'steeped in blood,' etc. I proposed that each of those dramaturgical markers were balls of different size creating divots in the fabric, gravity wells, as it were. I started tracing a line in the condensation, like a marble rolling along the surface of the fabric. As the line passed an event (a ball weighing down the fabric), it got caught in that event's gravity and its trajectory changed; the bigger the ball, the stronger the gravity, the deeper the divot, and the larger the trajectory change. As I continued to draw, the line went off in a slightly different direction. That line represented the movement of light through the play, and by virtue of the dramatic events, its trajectory could not remain constant. The "eureka" moment was that every story event in *Macbeth*—or any piece for that matter—impacts the trajectory of the lighting design.

To wit, act two, scene one, with its famous "Is this a dagger which I see before me" soliloquy, happens at night:

BANQUO: How goes the night, boy?
FLEANCE: The moon is down. I have not heard the clock.
BANQUO: And she goes down at twelve.
FLEANCE: I take 't, 'tis later, sir.
BANQUO: ... There's husbandry in heaven;
Their candles are all out.[5]

This is a very specific, dark night—no moon, no stars, very late—during which Macbeth sees the dagger and goes to kill Duncan. This is a major moment of gravity in the action of the play. Act two, scene two follows immediately in time, where Lady Macbeth says, "Hark! Peace!/It was the owl that shrieked, the fatal bellman,/Which gives the stern'st good-night."[6] And later, "I heard the owl scream and the crickets cry."[7] Describing a night even more morbid, unearthly, and terrifying. How could this night remain the same before and after Duncan's murder? For that matter, how could the trajectory of the lighting design for the play remain constant with such a big event so clearly demarcated in Shakespeare's text? It could not.

Now imagine that marble is actually a cube, a space bounded in three dimensions, moving through the fourth dimension, time. The trajectory of the cube is like the trajectory of the marble above, influenced by the gravity of dramatic events. I call this conceptual cube "the box." It is the container of all the ideas that make up a lighting design. Its boundaries are defined by many influences: structure, needs, space, resources, and time. It is a conceptual construct, a map, conceived during two parallel processes: individual studio work and team collaboration (like the design meeting in the story above). These initial processes overlap and create feedback loops, and the results distill into ideas for the lighting design. Mystic vision, singular point of view, need, and innovative thought are all unable to combine to achieve their full potential without the ability for a lighting designer

John Douglas Thompson in *Macbeth*
Theatre for a New Audience, 2011
Photograph courtesy of Gerry Goodstein

to express them. That capability lies in the expertise of craft. To be made manifest, these ideas must be organized, brought together, and expressed in the box's physical manifestation—the light plot.

Roadmap

For me, pursuing the form of the box begins with distilling the findings of these varied forms of analysis into a single document somewhat uncreatively called a "structure," which collates information along the timeline of the source material. This is a tool that I learned from Tipton in graduate school and it has stayed with me since, like so many of her precedents. The structure, while a fundamental distillation of the dramaturgical aspect of the source material, is not analogous to what might be called a scene breakdown because it will continue to grow and hold ideas that span the entirety of the production as it develops across all dimensions—ideas that are individual *and* the result of collaboration. The structure functions as a roadmap to the design, occupying prime real estate on the lighting table during technical rehearsals. It is where I organize my analysis, research, and plans for the design. Without it, I would be lost.

Analysis

The first step in populating the structure, indeed in the design process altogether, is coming to an individual understanding of the piece at hand. An understanding that is intellectual, rational, and justified while *also* being aesthetic, emotional, and individual. Without this seemingly paradoxical understanding, nothing else matters. This includes understanding the nuts and bolts of the piece, envisioning the world, who the people are, what ideas are embedded in the story, what is between the lines, and why it is important to tell this story right here and right now—accounting for objective/efferent/determinate *and* subjective/aesthetic/indeterminate concerns. So the first step in preproduction toward making the proverbial box is analysis. To analyze well, a designer must first be a good spectator. This is because a designer's first engagement with a source material will be that of a spectator, albeit a spectator with a pretty deep file of competencies. One must make meaning for oneself and then with the production team before one can make meaning for an audience.

The lighting designer is responsible for every second of stage time, so having a firm grasp on the basics of the piece is critical for keeping mud off your face during the process. A rigorous individual process forefronts this. One way of doing this is to ask oneself a series of questions. For a framework, Aristotle is not a bad place to start: In *Poetics*, he writes that "Every tragedy," which we will here generously apply to all narrative material for the stage, "must have six parts, which parts determine its quality—namely, Plot, Character, Diction, Thought, Spectacle, and Song. Two of the parts constitute the medium of imitation, one the manner, and three the objects of imitation."[8] This method of initial story analysis is decidedly un-sophisticated because its simplicity allows me to get at the meat of the matter quickly.

Key questions to ask for each of Aristotle's Six Parts:

1. For Plot: What is the story? Where and when does it happen? Why does it happen? What is the sequence of events (gravity wells!) that allow the plot to unfold? What is the action? Is it funny, serious, happy, or sad?
2. For Character: Who are the people that inhabit the world of the piece? What are their virtues and foibles? What are the motivations for their actions? What do they want? Where do they come from? Who is the protagonist, antagonist, etc.?
3. For Thought: What are the big ideas? Is it entertaining or didactic? How did the ideas embedded in the source influence the characters? How are the characters agents of the ideas? How might have the work resonate in the period in which the work was created? What was that sociocultural context? What competencies would the original audience have had? How does the work resonate here and now (temporally, geographically, culturally)?
4. For Diction: How is the language—spoken, sung, musical, physical—used to make the piece? If text, is it prose or poetry? Is the movement modern, classical, or other? Where does the story fit on the spectrum of theatrical abstraction?
5. For Song: Are there songs in the commonly understood sense? What is the style of music? How is it orchestrated? How is it used? Does it propel the plot forward or is it embellishment? And regardless of whether or not there are songs, what is the rhythm of the piece?
6. For Spectacle: What about the piece is theatrical? What is the visual nature of the world? Is nature important? How can and could non-textual elements contribute to the storytelling? Are there diegetic concerns for the design?

Many of these questions really have a lot to do with figuring out the style of the source material.

Finally, I address two overarching questions that cross a lot of the boundaries above: What does the piece tell us about the human condition? How is this piece situated within the author/creator's entire body of work? All of these questions—and this list is by no means exhaustive—can be useful both for initial analysis and for collaborative discussion.

Dimensions

Concomitant with the play analysis method proposed above, understanding the multiple overlapping dimensions of the source material and production-to-be is an equally important component of preproduction analysis. These dimensions are dramaturgical, physical, metatextual, visual, and rhythmic. Each of these has a component to be studied in the studio process when conceiving of a design and another to be articulated in the process of making the lighting. Examination of dramaturgical and physical dimensions is heavily weighted toward the development phase of a production, where the visual and rhythmic dimensions, while considered in the studio, are only really understood in the space. The process of developing the metatextual dimension, because it is derived from the production itself, tends to span the entire process.

The dramaturgical dimension

The dramaturgical dimension deals directly with determinate ideas embedded in the source material for the work that will affect the lighting design. These can be diegetic ideas—details in the narrative that create the universe of the story—like time of day, specific location, a textual mention of lights turning on or off, etc. They can also have to do with how the story progresses; whether the play is one long scene or broken up into multiple scenes, and whether time progresses forward or if the scenes jump around the timeline. They can also have to do with authorial or compositional intent (to the extent that it is decodable). For example, take two productions of plays by Tracy Letts: the aforementioned *Linda Vista* and the *Mary Page Marlowe* (Steppenwolf, 2016).[9] In *Linda Vista*, time moves in a linear fashion, which lent itself to a design that not only addressed the concerns of each scene (times of day, comedic vs serious, etc.), but one that also expressed a long-form arc of light moving from bright, saturated states to stripped down, exposed, fluorescent bareness. In contrast, *Mary Page Marlowe* is a story told in a series of scenes out of chronological order and, as such, demanded a design that treated each scene as a vignette and relied on Letts's order of the scenes to organically provide an overall arc to the light.

Equally important in understanding the dramaturgical dimension are textual cues. Returning to *Macbeth*, Shakespeare peppers the text with very specific prompts for the sense of the world. In act two, scene three, Lennox describes the night:

LENNOX.   The night has been unruly. Where we lay,
          Our chimneys were blown down, and, as they say,
          Lamentings heard i' the air, strange screams of death,

	And prophesying with accents terrible
	Of dire combustion and confused events
	New hatch'd to the woeful time. The obscure bird
	Clamored the livelong night. Some say the earth
	Was feverous and did shake.
MACBETH.	'Twas a rough night.
LENNOX.	My young remembrance cannot parallel
	A fellow to it.[10]

From descriptions such as this (and those from *Macbeth* mentioned earlier), one can derive very specific needs for the lighting design. Lest it seem as though I am contradicting myself by proposing a hat on an apple, in this instance, the text is a springboard to determine what *kind* of night and how far away from a pseudo-realistic depiction the lighting can roam while still being "night." Where Letts's plays start right at pseudo-realistic, with *Macbeth*, one is already far along the spectrum of theatrical abstraction with plenty of rationale for expressionistic states. Therefore, night in *Macbeth* must, in one of the greatest understatements of all time, be rough. The lighting designer's work is to determine how to articulate "rough" and what that means for the overall design. This, in turn, informs the contents and shape of the proverbial box that is the lighting design.

The physical dimension

The physical dimension involves everything having to do with the physical environment of the production and the physical manifestation of the lighting design. This includes the architecture of the theatre, architecture of the set, costumes, content of any projections, and anything else having to do with where light can or does come from (for example, extant and added positions) and where light can or does go (for example, through a window or onto a drop). The physical structure, more than anything else, will determine the shape of the light plot itself. If the set has a ceiling and walls, that is one thing, if it is a wing and border situation, that is another. For example, a ceiling might be frustrating from a technical standpoint, but I find that sort of physical constraint exciting as it focuses on what is possible with the lighting. This was certainly the case with the production of *True West* which I described in "Theatrical Abstraction"—the low ceiling and position of the room in plan meant that, with the exception of lights through the windows and the practicals on set, all of the light was coming from downstage of the plaster line. This meant, by default, the lighting design was already pushed away from the pseudo-realistic end of the spectrum of theatrical abstraction.

The metatextual dimension

The metatextual dimension is inspired by a concept proposed by Edward Bond regarding actorly and directorial points of view, specifically ideas that they bring to the production that are not necessarily present in the text or subtext. He writes, "The text (and any subtext) is written but a metatext is not. It is inferred and created by studying and rehearsing the written texts. It may contain many ideas, actions and emotions—because it is open-ended—and some of these may be in the written text ... But some things will only be in the metatext."[11] For Bond, metatextual discoveries are of the moment of rehearsal and as such are production bound. For me, this has to do with what the production intends to communicate and where it can find its efficacy as an artwork. In lighting, I have extrapolated this idea to have to do with ideas, macro and micro, in design that come from production concepts, choices, and/or things that come up in rehearsal that are not necessarily related to text or subtext. The final image in the Broadway iteration of *Pass Over* was the result of metatextual choices. The stage directions simply read, "The sun begins to rise," and "MOSES takes in the promised land."[12] The creative team's exploration of the play and our desires for what the ending needed to feel like in *this* moment for *this* production led to the starkly lit reveal of a forested Eden that then transformed into a lush, joyous, self-styled Afrofuturistic palette—an expressionistic dawn breaking on the transcendent reality where the island of Manhattan had never been colonized and where Moses and Kitch were free to roam.

The visual dimension

The visual dimension, very simply, relates to how the lighting design uses the principles of design and composition to determine how things look. Turning such and such lights on because of their relationship to the dramaturgical or metatextual dimensions of a moment is appropriate, but a byproduct of that might be that the entire stage picture is an incomplete composition. For example, in the TFANA *Macbeth*, I used a slash of light for Macbeth's act two, scene one dagger soliloquy because it was appropriate for the metatext of the moment. However, the slash alone was an incomplete stage picture. As a purely visual concern, the background needed to be included. There were perhaps twenty ways to light the background in that light plot, but I chose a specific way because its compositional relationship to the slash of light lighting Macbeth was visually *and* metatextually *and* dramaturgicaly appropriate. It came from the opposite side of the stage as Macbeth's slash, so that as it completed the visual composition by illuminating the background, it *also* created a dissonant composition: Macbeth's slash and the light on the background came from two different directions, this was visually unsettling and subtly reinforced that it was a "rough" night indeed.

Namir Smallwood and Jon Michael Hill in *Pass Over*
Broadway, The August Wilson Theatre, 2021
Photograph courtesy of Joan Marcus

The rhythmic dimension

Good lighting is as much music as it is image, so how it moves from state to state is as critical as what the static stage pictures look like. It is a fundamental tenet of my aesthetic to consider stage lighting not as a series of static images that happen to cross-fade from time to time but rather as ideas of light that ebb and flow through time in much the same way that different sections of instruments will come and go in a symphony creating one long interconnected evolution. The rhythmic dimension addresses this by concerning itself with how the lighting design moves through time and how that design relates to any extant rhythmic concerns in the source material. For example, opera and musicals, to a large extent, dictate the rhythmic movement of light. Verse language does too, to a lesser extent. Returning to Cassio announcing Desdemona's arrival, the rhythm of Shakespeare's text can be the hook on which the series of cues taking us from storm to bright day can be hung. Sometimes rhythm is apparent, and sometimes it takes a little work to find it.

Overlap

While each of these dimensions can be theoretically viewed in a silo, in practice, they overlap, inform each other, and can be dominant or recessive as each aspect or moment of the production requires. My lighting for *Pass Over* illustrates how a design can address multiple structural concerns simultaneously. Dramaturgically speaking, the light was evocative, though not overly so, of the time of day where the majority of the play was situated—night—with multiple iterations depending on whether Moses and Kitch were alone or if the characters of Mister or Ossifer were on stage. Physically, the design was in dialog with the architecture of the set and space, with most of the light coming along the angle of the main platform of the set—parallel to the plaster line and along the rake—via systems of head-highs and shin-busters. The color was completely keyed into the dominant scenic gesture of the streetlamp. The lamp was rigged with color changing LED tape so that its color, and resultant tone of the space, could subtly shift between the crisp, sinister white of mercury halide for most of the show and the acid warm, yet slimy, tone of sodium vapor for Mister (both echoed with tints in the cross light), a metatextual choice. The visual structure of the lighting came from a minimalist approach; the design did not require anything other than carefully crafted cool and warm whites in symmetrical images for most of the play, with the intercession of arc white shin-busters for the scenes with Ossifer and the burst of color, texture, and lushness in the final moments as discussed above. The rhythmic structure found final form in the rehearsal process, where we understood that certain moments deserved zero-count, radical changes of space: flinches by Moses and Kitch, the cacophonic plagues sequence, and the reveal of the promised land, whereas other moments needed long, legato transitions, including a sunrise to sunset transition moment and the transformation to the final, vibrant image.

Research

A parallel process of preproduction, one that also bridges the gap between individual and collaborative work, is research. Research takes many forms and can be roughly divided into two broad camps: dramaturgical and visual. Dramaturgical research, as the name implies, has to do with answering a lot of questions that come up in the analysis process. For example, questions having to do with the period in which the piece was written or composed and the intended period of the story; *King Lear* was written circa 1606 CE and was set in ancient Britain, so it is helpful to come to an understanding of both of those periods. Since the play deals with a political power structure, it is useful to learn about 17th-century English politics to carry on a reasonable discussion about the play. Dramaturgical research can also reveal things about the world that might not be directly mentioned in the text but that are important to the design. This is an extreme—dare I say obvious—thing, but knowing that flame and nature were the only two sources of light in ancient Britain and in 17th-century England has a direct correlation to a design choice that might feature only warm incandescent point sources, redolent of candlelight, and broad swaths of 5,500° Kelvin (K) daylight white as the only two colors used, or at least that is what it means for me. That is not to say that every show set before the advent of electric lighting needs to restrict itself to that palette, but for the TFANA production of *King Lear*, where nature was such a powerful presence, using only flame, lightning, and sun seemed right.

Visual research has to do with how things look. This can be practical research dealing with diegetic matters such as daylight through a window, light in a phone booth in the middle of the night, etc. Visual research can also be intuitive/emotional research. This includes images that seem right based on either how they make one feel in relation to the piece and/or how one wants the audience to feel. The Crewdson photograph at the beginning of this chapter is an excellent example of a piece of research that bridges the gap between the two because it had both the look and the feeling I wanted to impart in the lighting design for *Visiting Edna* (Steppenwolf, 2016).[13] The image presents mundane domesticity with a ghostly twist; colors and sources are not quite what they should be. Why, for instance, is the vent above the closet glowing? To be honest, I cannot remember whether the image came from me or from set designer David Zinn. That is the great thing about good research, it becomes a shared resource and a touchstone of common vocabulary. The world of the photograph is spooky, remarkably lonely, and completely appropriate for a family drama that had characters who embodied Cancer and TV and an interlude featuring a violent angel. So, for this production, I distilled the many Crewdson images I had in my research to select a few and mapped those individual images to each scene in the play in my ever-evolving structure.

The great thing about really good research is that from there, it is easy to extract the conceptual boundaries of the box: Crewdson's twisted reality and color sensibility informed every aspect of my lighting for *Visiting Edna* and allowed me to push the light from what was a pseudo-realistic domestic space (albeit with an abstract sky box above) to a very expressionistic space. I wanted to be able to contort the comfort of the primary compositions without being too obvious about it, much in the same way the greenish white of the kitchen is uncomfortably offset by the strange blues and whites of the living room in the photograph. I also knew that the majority of the playing space would need to be treated in a pseudo-realistic manner. So, I created a plot with systems that could do that, keying off the multiple practical lighting fixtures in the space, the windows, and the sky box above to create warm white, expansive, daylight states and incandescent islands within a cooler framework for nighttime states. These needed to be fairly neutral whites to not oppress the palette of the set and costumes. To make the compositions uncomfortable, I relied on the background, which was an upstage wall up right, an entry alcove up center, and a bedroom box up left. I was able to "push" the composition to be more expressionistic by subtly shifting the tints of whites used to light those spaces: for example, for some scenes at night, the cool light in the background was just slightly greener than it ought to be. Imperceptible, but enough to make the composition formally uncomfortable for the audience (a technique I later repeated for the aforementioned production of *True West*). At other times, when the text was very abstract—like when Cancer or TV were dominating the stage—I painted those surfaces in saturated color. The box for this show was full of tricks like that. Sometimes lighting is overt, and sometimes it is a very sneaky form.

Outcomes

I think the individual analysis discussed above leads to four main outcomes for the creative team, especially the designers, in preproduction work. First, the team needs to find a common understanding of the piece at hand in order to create a shared point of view. This sounds simplistic, and for all intents and purposes, it is. But without it, the production will suffer. A common understanding can be found by revisiting the analysis questions and considerations of the multiple dimensions in group discussion. Ultimately, this will result in a shared point of view for the production, most commonly led by the director.

Second, to identify and/or create the metatext of the production—a process that will continue through all phases of creation and rehearsal. This is allied to the *why* of the production, the meaning the creative team intends to make out of the piece. Metatextual engagement is impossible without a shared point of view because metatext is related to the production's ability to meet the requirements of an artwork: demands engagement from the audience, is more than a craft object, confronts the audience with troublesome knowledge, and innovates. Without metatext, a production is doomed to inconsequence.

The Box 151

Debra Monk, Ian Barford, and Sally Murphy in *Visiting Edna*
Steppenwolf Theatre Company, 2016
Photograph courtesy of Michael Brosilow

Furthermore, these first two outcomes of the preproduction collaborative process are the foundations on which the production is built. If that foundation is shaky, every subsequent step in the process will be in jeopardy.

The third outcome is to determine a shared aesthetic that dictates the physical and ephemeral look and sound of the production; the *how* of the production, the method. Sometimes this is easy, as per the commonalities of everyone's research for *Visiting Edna*. This is particularly so with teams that have a long history of working together as they tend to have significant overlaps in the Venn diagram of their aesthetics. Sometimes it is more difficult, and it takes a lot of work, but it is nonetheless *absolutely essential*.

Finally, the fourth outcome of preproduction collaboration is for the designers to go to their studios and do the individual work on behalf of the joint artistic impulse. For the lighting designer, the goal of this period of the preproduction process is to make a light plot. For me, that is the physical manifestation—the infrastructure, if you will—of the box. I should clarify that this is a quasi-individual process. Quasi, because the lighting is in service of the joint artistic impulse. Individual, though, because the lighting designer—as both a craftsperson and an artist—will still have a personal style and aesthetic that will affect the final shape of the design. The meshing of the aesthetics of the creative team into a joint aesthetic is what makes that joint aesthetic unique, and that is one reason why we can see a 20 different productions of *Hamlet*, and none of them will be designed the same way.

Lists

The individual analysis and group creation of the meta-text eventually yields a list of conceptual and practical things—some specific, like time of day, and some abstract, like having a sense of confectionary color—the lighting needs to do. These processes will also begin to reveal ways that the lighting will work for the production. In the move from concept to execution, checklists become an essential part of my process, and as the design begins to take form, I collate my thoughts into two distinct lists: an "ideas list" and a "ways list." Creative names, I know.

Designing lighting is a complex task in a complex environment. The process of making the plot is a critical component and one that has a nontrivial amount of busy work that can be, well, boring (I remember Ming Cho Lee, in the days of hand drafting, used to say: "save the cross hatching for the end of the day"). Lists help keep me on track throughout the process. Surgeon and public health researcher Atul Gawande, in his book *The Checklist Manifesto*, writes:

> In a complex environment, experts are up against two main difficulties. The first is the fallibility of human memory and attention, especially when it comes to mundane, routine matters that are easily overlooked

under the strain of more pressing events ... Faulty memory and distraction are a particular danger in what engineers call all-or-none processes ... if you miss just one key thing, you might as well not have made the effort at all.[14]

If I have missed a step in the process of making a light plot it can cost the production a lot of time and money and/or make the design suffer. This is experience speaking. Gawande continues:

> A further difficulty, just as insidious, is that people can lull themselves into skipping steps even when the remember them. In complex processes, after all, certain steps don't *always* matter ... 'This has never been a problem before,' people say. Until one day it is.[15]

For example, skipping worksheets, i.e., the process of determining what the exact geometry of the shot of a fixture will be and, therefore, its efficacy on the plot, is a classic. Even after hundreds of light plots, "worksheet all systems" is still a step on my plot-making checklist. Those three words next to the check box keep my process honest and ensure that I will know what every single light is meant to do before I walk into the door of the theatre for focus.

Back to the ideas and ways lists: The ideas list is exactly what it sounds like—a list of ideas for the lighting design of the show. They precipitate from the processes described above. The very specific kind of night Shakespeare calls for in *Macbeth*, the sense of oppression and release in *Pass Over*, and the uncomfortable composition in *Visiting Edna* are ideas that would go on this list. Also, things like times of day, seasons, intensity, public or private, where the aesthetic sits on the spectrum of theatrical abstraction, etc. These are the ideas that the box needs to be capable of expressing.

Attendant to the ideas list, the ways list describes how light can get into, or exist within, the space. These can be design-based ways, like a window; architecture-based ways, like a front of house position; and, importantly, craft-based ways that are known to work, like cross light or particular color choices that have proven to be effective. The process of finding these ways begins with a robust examination of the physical environment for the show. This means a deep dive into exploring the set, costumes, and projections (if there are any), as well as the architecture of the venue. These ways are the "tools" with which the ideas will be expressed.

Set exploration

The next step in determining my ways list is what I call set exploration. This is a process of rigorously investigating what is possible within the physical environment. There are multiple methods of set exploration. The first is always "red-lining" the venue and set drawings. This means taking a red marker to the drawings and noting anything that could have any impact on the design: practical fixtures, apertures like doors and windows, ceilings, extant and possible positions, sight lines, scenic elements that move, masking, etc. This is an all-or-none item on the make-a-light-plot checklist because if one does not understand the space, how is one going to light it well?

Other methods include working with the model or model photos. There really is no substitute for sticking a flashlight in a model—it immediately reveals things that are possible in light that one might have not thought of. For example, during the design process for *Linda Vista,* I was very worried about carving out each of the rooms on the revolve. First, there was not enough real estate in the overhead positions. Second, there were not enough fixtures in the inventory to hang the multiple systems that would require. My preoccupation with those concerns kept me from seeing other possibilities for the design. However, one second with a flashlight and the model made me realize that the revolve of the set while being pseudo-realistic, where it was close to the actors, was also a sculptural object within a larger, very abstract surround. The single source of the flashlight allowed me to see that I could treat the architecture of the revolve as an object, and it unlocked a much more abstract design. The outcome was that large gestures of light made it onto the ways list.

In the absence of being able to play with the model, I find sketching over model photos or the set designer's storyboards to be a reasonable alternative. The one caveat to sketches of any sort is that they lie. Images that are produced in two dimensions are not always possible in the theatre; that light sweeping in through the window in the sketch might have to be on the other side of the stage wall and in the middle of 53rd street to make it sweep across the stage in such a manner. So, sketches need to be thoroughly reality checked, especially before showing them to the rest of the creative time. One does not want to write a check that the lighting design cannot cash.

The final step of set exploration for me, another all-or-none step, is doing exploratory worksheets to determine what shots are possible with the extant positions and where I might need to add positions to get the shots I want. While the exploratory worksheets may not be directly related to systems that will end up on the plot, they will dictate aspects of them. For example, with a wing and border set, exploratory worksheets might reveal that only three positions overhead are possible, and if I were to use backlight, it would have to come from the upstage two. This would mean that later on when I am laying out systems, there can only be backlight two rows deep. There are two important outcomes of exploratory worksheets. The first is that I have a good idea of what angles work and do not, which will have a direct bearing on the systems of lights that will end up on the light plot. For example, very tall walls might render the cross light too steep to be useful. The second is that I will have a very detailed drawing of the lighting positions available for the show and a list of physical ways light can get on the stage. I do this detailed drawing at this stage for several reasons: because it is easiest to do it while it is fresh in my mind, it will save me time later in the process, and I may need them to request changes to the set or masking. The carpenter, rigger, or electrician may also request a detailed drawing of the positions before the light plot deadline. Finally, it is always satisfying to complete a task: I can have the satisfaction of checking off "make positions drawings" on my light plot checklist.

My ways lists will almost always include systems of light that are, in a sense, "default." These include systems like cross light, front light, and backlight. In the section on accomplished craft, I wrote that an artist must learn the significance of certain recognized conventions to become a master at their craft and a thorough understanding of the techniques of a medium is the only way to master it. Part of that is understanding the utility of each angle of light. For example, I will always have some form of cross light because it is an extremely useful angle. Among other virtues, it is excellent for revealing figures in space, and it allows for significant foreground/background control. Also, actors usually face each other, so cross light goes directly to their faces. I did not figure this out on my own, it is a precedent handed down to me during my study of the craft. Where it becomes personal is in the minutia of what my eye prefers: the exact angle in elevation of the cross light, how much space each fixture covers, and the distribution of points of control. These minutia, multiplied across the choices that go into the crafting of the box are honed by repetition and become an expression of my style. While these systems are "default," I also ensure that they, as "ways," are mapped to ideas so that their iterations in *this* particular plot are meaningful to the overall design intent and not without a relationship to all the other ideas in the box.

Palette

One thing that makes itself apparent immediately during the initial part of the process is the palette for the show. For me, determining the palette is the result of a formal analysis of what is going on in the rest of the designs. If the costumes are varied and colorful, that argues for a fairly neutral palette in the lighting so that no particular hue is dampened by lighting hues leaning in the opposite direction. Likewise, a statement color within a largely neutral costume palette—Violetta in a purple dress amidst a chorus of black and white—argues for the inclusion of that color in the palette so that the light can echo the costume; when she enters a purple tint might paint the space, making it feel like the light is radiating off of her. Likewise, the palette of the set will directly inform the palette of the light. Cooler sets will favor cooler palettes and warmer sets will favor warmer palettes. Nothing looks worse than amber light on a blue floor. Ditto projections: if there is strong color content in a projection design, I will often choose my specific palette (or mix it during production) based directly on the projections. In this way, the palette for the show is unified and the edge between lighting and projections is blurred. Ultimately, the lighting palette is an expressive tool, but if it does not function well practically, then any expressive potential is lost.

After consideration of the palettes of the rest of the designs, I set the white point for the lighting. The white point is the whitest light in the show (this is a precedent, not my idea).[16] For a dominantly warm physical design, the white point for the light is likely to be clear but not too much warmer than that. For a dominantly cool physical design, the white point is likely to be some version of cool light. For sets with bold colors, I may want to echo that color in the light, which will make very specific demands of the light. To illustrate, a yellow tint of front light in a bright yellow set is a good way to echo the color of the walls. If I wanted to use the cross light for the white point, it would make clear appear slightly pink. So, I would drop the barest blush of green into the cross light to counter the pink and thus appear white. Sometimes shows will have palettes that run the gamut of color ranges, so multiple white points might be necessary.

After setting the white point, I determine what other specific color the production demands. Large blocks of saturated color in the set will have a direct impact on the hue and saturation of color in the lighting, whereas a sparse palette means that the show might be entirely no-color. Regardless of the technology available, it is critical to my process that I know the colors that I intend to use before settling the design. This takes discipline because the easy choice is to figure it out in the theatre, but that inevitably leads to a less structured palette. The whole point of the box is to constrain choices to those that are clearly thought out, and once the palette is set, those ideas get added to my ways list.

Mapping

Once the ideas and ways lists are developed, the next step is to map one to the other. Mapping is the process of determining what way(s) will be used to find an expressive form for each of the needs of the design in order to express ideas. For example, the lists may be:

Ways list	**Needs list**
Front of house truss	Day
Ceiling slot electrics	Night
Stage right window	Winter
Set walls	Spring
Living room lamp	Stark
Warm background	Oppressive
Cool background	Bright
Night background	Hot
Back light	Cold
Front light	Public
Big diagonal back over wall	Private
Cross light/cool white point	Saturate
Cross light/warm white point	Pseudo-realistic
Saccharine tints	Expressionistic
Saturate Blue	
Saturate Red	
Saturate Green	
Moving lights	

So, to map the ideas, I draw a line between a need and the way(s) that need will be expressed: lines connecting what I want the design to do to how I will do it. For example, for *Visiting Edna*, I mapped the idea of the Crewdson-esque sensibility to a wide range of colors on the background and in the bedroom. The fact that I needed multiple colors for this idea meant that each idea would require color changing ability, so I designed a system of color mixing lights for the upstage wall and alcove, and a hidden line of color changing LED tape in the header of the bedroom. If there are ideas that cannot be expressed in a way that has already been conceived, then a way needs to be determined. If there are ways that are not tied to an idea, it is likely those ideas will end up as nothing more than unnecessary decoration and must be cut. To reiterate an important point: this is true of "default" systems as well; they must be mapped to an idea to remain in the box. For me, fixtures without intent are analogous to Rams's idea of visual pollution and must be avoided at all costs.

Ultimately, each way becomes a single fixture or a system of lights, and the more systems that can do multiple things, the more efficient the plot will be, which is an argument for the efficacy of moving lights. Now, a note on moving lights: They are great, but for all of their functionality, they can also be a terrible crutch. In the same way that it is critical to know the colors I intend to use before tech, it is critical for me to know exactly why I am putting a moving light on the plot so that it is used specifically. An efficient light plot is a laudable goal—as an essentialist, I find that the more efficient the plot, the better the box, and the better the box, the better the resulting design—but moving lights are not always as efficient as they seem.

Magic sheet

Once the mapping is done, the next step in my design process is to lay out the largely conceptual "ways" into concrete systems of lights made up of individual fixtures. I do this by creating a working magic sheet. The magic sheet is a graphic representation of all the control channels for each light on a plot. It is a highly personalized tool, so every designer's is different. I arrange mine by system, with the channel numbers for each fixture roughly where it would be focused in plan view. The working copy is a rough version where I take each system and decide how I want to control it across the space. This is based on a largely formal analysis of the space combined with an idea of how I want to use the system in the show. Determining control also includes understanding how the system can be used to compose images using the vocabulary of design discussed in "On Design." While I am laying out the working magic sheet, I am always thinking compositionally, considering how each system will work together to give efficacy to the lighting design.

Once the working magic sheet has every idea I intend to put in the box, it is complete, and now becomes a checklist for the process of making the light plot. I either review the exploratory worksheets or create new worksheets for each system and plot them on the drawing as I go. Again, this is an iterative process influenced by feedback. There are many things to be considered: Does the inventory support the system? Is there enough real-estate overhead for all of the ideas? Are there enough dimmers? Sometimes systems get crossed out, combined, or split up. With experience comes the ability to look at the assets available for the lighting design and determine a rough scale that seems achievable. It is important to note that the biggest asset is *time*. Both with regards to the amount of time available for focus and the time available to write the cues. Limited focus argues for a small plot, whereas three weeks for tech argues for the possibility of a more complicated design.

Gravity redux

Ultimately, when all the lights are on the drawing, one has a light plot. But the light plot is not the only goal of this rigorous design process. The ultimate outcomes are to determine what is in the box, the intellectual, rational, and justified points of view, aesthetics, and metatextual intentions that are the outcome of individual work and collaboration, *and* how to effectively chart the box's path through the gravity wells it will encounter in the production. I have learned the necessity of the box to my process the hard way by walking into the first day of tech with an ill-considered, unjustified, plot, and no real plan of how to use it. Each time, the result—as you may imagine—was well-deserved mud all over my face. As I have said, the lighting designer is responsible for every second of stage time, so one *must* have ideas for the entirety of the production, even if those ideas do not make it to opening night. The conceptual construct of the box has become an indispensable process tool for me, one that is essential to making lighting designs that meet the criteria I set forth in my manifesto. Without the box, I might be able to illuminate a production of *Macbeth*, but with it, I will be confident that I can make a *good* lighting design of "fog and filthy air" where "fair is foul, foul is fair."[17]

Notes

1 Kenya Hara, *White*, trans. Jooyeon Rhee (Zurich: Lars Müller Publishers, 2012), 18–19.
2 David Brooks, "The Good Order," *New York Times*, September 26, 2014, A31.
3 *Macbeth*, by William Shakespeare, dir. Arin Arbus, set design by Julian Crouch, costume design by Anita Yavich, and composition and sound design by Sarah Pickett, Theatre for a New Audience, New York, US, 2011.
4 Arin Arbus, private correspondence with the author, November 10, 2010.
5 William Shakespeare, *Macbeth*, in *The Complete Works of Shakespeare*, ed. David Bevington, 4th ed. (New York: HarperCollins Publishers, 1992), 2.1.1–4.
6 Shakespeare, *Macbeth*, 2.2.2–4.
7 Shakespeare, 2.2.16.
8 Aristotle, *Poetics*, trans. S.H. Butcher, with an introduction by Francis Fergusson (New York: Hill and Wang, 1961), 62.
9 *Mary Page Marlowe*, by Tracy Letts, dir. Anna D. Shapiro, set design by Todd Rosenthal, costume design by Linda Roethke, sound design by Richard Woodbury, and original music by Diana Lawrence, Steppenwolf Theatre Company, Chicago, US, 2016.
10 Shakespeare, *Macbeth*, 2.3.54–61.
11 Edward Bond, "From Commentary on *The War Plays*," in *Twentieth Century Theatre: A Sourcebook*, ed. Richard Drain (London: Routledge, 1995), 144.
12 Antoinette Chinonye Nwandu, *Pass Over* (unpublished Broadway production script, 2021), 101, 105.
13 *Visiting Edna*, by David Rabe, dir. Anna D. Shapiro, set design by David Zinn, costume design by Linda Roethke, sound design by Rob Milburn, and original music by Michael Bodeen, Steppenwolf Theatre Company, Chicago, US, 2016.
14 Atul Gawande, *The Checklist Manifesto: How to Get Things Right* (London: Picador, 2009), 35–36.
15 Gawande, *The Checklist Manifesto*, 36.
16 This precedent is so ingrained in my process, I cannot remember who to credit for it.
17 Shakespeare, *Macbeth*, 1.1.11–12.

8   Praxis

Taking of Christ, 1602

Michelangelo Merisi da Caravaggio
Oil on canvas
52 5/8 × 66 3/4 in. (134.7 × 169.5 cm)
Society of Jesuits of Saint Ignatius, Dublin
Public domain, via Wikimedia Commons

DOI: 10.4324/9781003206460-9

Deadlines

Technical rehearsals are the forge in which a lighting designer's work is finally wrought. They are a particularly regimented process, where timing is dictated by finances, union rules, and the impending deadline of opening night. The lighting designer is required to be creative on demand. We sit down at such and such time in the afternoon and are consistently creative until dinner break, after which we return to the lighting table and continue to be creative until well into the evening hours. According to a maxim that is occasionally attributed to Leonard Bernstein but which was crafted and popularized by Elbert Hubbard, "to achieve great things, two things are needed: a plan, and not quite enough time."[1] I agree with this is sage wisdom. In fact, it is why the process of creating the box, described in "The Box," is so rigorous. It is the "plan." And technical rehearsals are "not quite enough time." Deadlines are a good thing, I think. They motivate, they are ruthless, and they make technical rehearsals a crucible. The stakes are always high.

Everything in the design process that precedes the praxis of technical rehearsals is in service of working thoughtfully and quickly. The adage is that the amount of time required to technically rehearse a show expands to the exact amount of time available is not true; I find that it expands to *just one more hour* than that. Time is money, after all, and as much as we are artists, we are also hired to light a show expertly, on time. That is why I maintain that an efficient lighting designer must always *and at once* make, look, evaluate, and adapt—turning lights on to articulate an idea, considering the result from multiple perspectives, determining whether the lighting idea has efficacy, often with collaborator input, and adjusting as necessary. These four seemingly distinct processes overlap, not only because it is inefficient for them to happen in a linear fashion (if there were enough time to try), but because together they create a feedback loop—where each iteration, informed by the last, is better. The make, look, evaluate, and adapt process of lighting a production is intellectual, logical, and structured and *simultaneously* instinctual, emotional, and chaotic.

Writing light cues

For me, the intellectual side of lighting a production is, first and foremost, the continuation of the process described in "The Box" through the process of writing light cues. This means that the beginning of the cueing process is simply *doing* what I have decided to do, often referencing the structure document. I want this scene to look like such and such, so I start turning those lights on. However, as I wrote in "On Design," anarchy soon takes over and my thinking starts to evolve beyond the studio ideas very quickly.

But, the rigor of the studio process—from the analysis and research phase to idea generation, through careful consideration of the ways the ideas will be expressed—means that the design concept, articulated in a light plot that is the physical manifestation of the box, is cohesive. Thus, any light that I choose to turn on will have a clear relationship to the production and its aesthetic and will be grounded in considered craft. This frees me to be instinctual in technical rehearsals, trusting that the choices I have made in the studio will still be rational and justified. The aesthetic, emotional, and individual foundations of the design that I predetermined will be present no matter what lights I use. I can work quickly within this framework and, better yet, be open to ideas as they make themselves apparent.

Regardless of the actual cue content—what the stage *looks* like—the predetermined structure of the lighting design remains, at least through the first iteration. This is because the intellectual framework of the design is sturdy enough to support content that may be radically different than I thought it would be in the studio. The cue may look like this or it may look like that, but since everything in the lighting design is interrelated by default (it is all from the same box), I trust that it will all come together. That is not to say that I throw lighting ideas at the stage pell-mell without considering them within the overall scope of the design. Quite the opposite. The iterative process of make, look, evaluate, and adapt does not only apply to specific states or transitions, it also applies to the design *as a whole*. I can always count on whatever work I have done on the first day of technical rehearsal not making it to opening night because it takes a while to figure out how the light is really working in process. The specifics of lighting vocabulary take time to develop in technical rehearsals, so sometimes an idea, say a lighting leitmotif for a character, does not become apparent until halfway through tech. While the content of the leitmotif can be the result of instinct, that it *is* a leitmotif is an intellectual construct, and as such, it must make sense within the overall design. Therefore, the intellectual process of determining what that means for the entirety of the design is the next step. I call this scoring an idea into the design.

When considering the rhythmic dimension of the box, I asserted that good lighting ebbs and flows through time in the same way that music does. As Appia says, "Light is to production what music is to the score."[2] To extend the metaphor, imagine that the vision for a lighting design is a tune. And like a composer orchestrates their tune for a symphony by writing a score, I orchestrate my lighting ideas across the plot by writing light cues. For the composer, one part of the tune might be best expressed with strings, others with horns, these with the full orchestra, and those with solos. Similarly, one part of the design might be best expressed with backlight, others with cross light, these with color, and those with contrast. But, what if I realize that a new idea has to be accounted for in the lighting, either because I have had a flash of inspiration or a colleague has come to me with a good idea? Whether it comes from me or someone else, the new idea is like someone walking over with a red crayon and scribbling in a new melody or a key change in the middle of the composer's carefully wrought score. It will not do to just leave the new idea there, alone, and move on. The lighting designer must evaluate and adapt, and score the new idea into the lighting. This means scrutinizing the new idea's relationship to its moment in the show, understanding the connective tissue between where that new idea sits and similar other parts of the production, and considering what choices need to be made to make the new idea *make sense* in the overall design. This means carrying the idea forward *and* backward through the lighting design in appropriate ways—distributing a newly developed leitmotif, for example—*and* considering the impact that idea has on other points of the design. This is the hard logical work of wrangling the chaos of instinct and it must happen quickly. This is yet another reason that all of the preparation that goes into making the box is essential: It is easier to make the synthetic connections required to score a new idea across a lighting design if one *really* understands the multiple dimensions of the production.

Situation awareness

So much of the technical rehearsal process has to do with conversations; those among the creative team, with the production staff, and with the performers. Some include the lighting designer, and many do not, but still may be of consequence. These are a lot of information streams to manage simultaneously. To do so effectively and make good use of time, I think it is critical to have a strong sense of situation awareness.

Situation awareness, according to human factors researcher Mica R. Endsley, is "the perception of the elements in the environment within a volume of time and space, the comprehension of their meaning, and the projection of their status in the near future."[3] This definition is categorized into three levels of situation awareness, which I here condense:

1 Perception of "the status, attributes, and dynamics of relevant elements in the environment."[4]
2 "Comprehension of the current situation based on a synthesis of [those disjointed elements] beyond simply being aware of the elements that are present to include an understanding of the significance of those elements."[5]
3 Projection of future status/actions of elements in the environment "through knowledge of the states and dynamics of the elements and comprehension of the situation."[6]

What this means for the lighting designer is that having a keen sense of what is going on in the room will, without a doubt, make them more efficient. This is why I try to maintain situational assessment of the multiple streams of communication happening in the room at any given time. Simply put, I keep one ear on the stage manager, one ear on the director (and playwright, composer, etc., should they be in the room), one eye on the stage, and one eye on the lighting table. From a level one perspective, always listening to the stage manager over the headset allows me to know exactly what is going on from a production standpoint. If we are in standby, what other design elements are doing, whether or not we are going to hold, etc. Always listening to the director allows me to keep track of their overall intent and focus. This can be as simple as having a direct conversation with them or listening in on their conversations with others. Some might call this eavesdropping, but I call it doing my job. If the director is talking to an actor on stage, it might change their blocking; if the director is talking to the sound designer, their conversation might affect a lighting choice; or the director may be having a big picture conversation with a producer, which might mean a large conceptual change. At the same time, keeping an eye on the stage gives me real-time information about what is going on because things change all the time in rehearsal. Keeping an eye on the table is a way of keeping up to date with what is going on in with the logistics of the design; the programming, follow spot tracking, etc. Finally, I keep a figurative finger on the 'temperature' of the room. Technical rehearsals *are* a crucible and when there is a room full of artists working together, sometimes tensions arise. It is good to be aware when it happens and of the cause, lest you fan any flames.

But, all of that info is *useless* without comprehending the *significance* of it, as in level two situation awareness. Of all the information streams I am monitoring, there may be only one significant bit of information in a given "volume of time and space," as Endsley would say.[7] For example, the relevant piece of information at level one could be that the stage manager told the fly-person that a cue is moved. That may not be relevant to anything the director is doing or what is afoot on stage or at the table in the moment. The significance, at level two, is that it could change the fly cue placement within a series of light cues. Level three situation awareness means realizing that the fly cue move will affect what the light cues are surrounding the move, which would lead me to call, "Hold please!" while we sort it all out. This is a simple example of how to go from levels one to three quickly because it is based on understanding very specific information about the dynamics of the situation. However, a more complex example might be hearing the director telling the stage manager that they are going to make a big change to the transition. This is not my first rodeo, so I comprehend the significance of this bit of information, but since I am not aware of exactly what the change is, I cannot gain level three situation awareness. A quick ask in the headset would give me that info, which would then allow me to begin to predict the future status of the transition and to think about what changes might be necessary. A keen sense of situation awareness might allow me to get pretty far along before the director has even made it to the lighting table to tell me what is going on. This is a skill that can be cultivated and I am spending so much time on it not only because it is important but because simply being *aware* of the idea of situation awareness is a good way to begin cultivating it.

OODA

Not all conversations are literal, though. Some are more metaphorical—the conversation one has with oneself and the conversation one has with the production as it is being wrought. The conversation one has with oneself is the essence of make, look, evaluate, adapt; the feedback loop that this process engenders *is* the conversation. My understanding of the efficacy of this feedback loop is informed by the "OODA Loop," a concept developed by U.S. Air Force Colonel John Boyd that was designed to ground thinking in confusing or chaotic situations.[8] He originally developed this idea by analyzing U.S. Air Force pilots during the Korean War. While it may seem odd to take lessons from air combat and apply them to making art, it works if one looks past the strictly martial aspect. OODA is an acronym for Observe, Orient, Decide, Act. The steps are summarized as follows:

1 Observe the situation, including circumstances, environment, outside information, etc.
2 Orient by recognizing how one's context affects how one observes.
3 Decide what the most appropriate course of action is, which may mean picking one of many options.
4 Act on the decision, and restart the loop.

The OODA Loop does not map perfectly onto my lighting mantra, but the linkages are essentially: "observe" corresponds with "look," "orient" and "decide" correspond with "evaluate," and "act" corresponds with "make" and "adapt." To be clear, my practice of cultivating situation awareness is a key component of what Boyd would file under observation. Boyd made several key clarifications about the complexity of the factors involved in the orientation step in a 1996 briefing called "The Essence of Winning and Losing" that are worth quoting in full:

> *Without our genetic heritage,*[9] *cultural traditions, and previous experiences,* we do not possess an *implicit* repertoire of psychophysical

skills shaped by environments and changes that have been previously experienced.

Without analyses and synthesis, across a variety of domains or across a variety of competing/independent channels of information, we cannot evolve new repertoires to deal with unfamiliar phenomena or unforeseen change.

Without a many-sided implicit cross-referencing process of projection, empathy, correlation, and *rejection*, (across these many different domains or channels of information), we cannot even do *analysis and synthesis* (italics replace bolding in original).[10]

Genetic heritage, cultural traditions, previous experiences, and analysis and synthesis are all interrelated components of the orientation or, in my case, evaluation process. These five things set up a personal context, as in "Beauty" and "Artist/Artwork," for the moment of orientation. In this regard, Boyd's steps one and two are direct corollaries of spectatorship, as I describe it in "The Spectator." Thus, observation and orientation are a process of meaning making. Boyd continues:

Without OODA loops, we can neither sense, hence observe, thereby collect a variety of information for the above processes, nor decide as well as implement actions in accord with those processes.

Or put another way:

Without OODA loops embracing all the above and *without the ability to get inside other OODA loops* (or other environments), we will find it impossible to comprehend, shape, adapt to, and in turn be shaped by an unfolding, evolving reality that is uncertain, ever changing, unpredictable (italics replace bold in the original).[11]

Boyd's conclusion illustrates that the OODA Loop is both a process of shaping events and being shaped by events. OODA Loops and my make, look, evaluate, and adapt—MLEA if you will—loops allow for multi-layered, high-level processing of information and decision-making in multiple directions of influence, which is a critical part of the lighting design process in technical rehearsal. Especially when there are multiple information streams happening at the same time. Because they are slightly different, each loop has a particular application in the design process: OODA Loops are useful for overall processing (including lighting specifically), whereas the MLEA Loop is specifically formulated for the process of lighting design. All of this seems pretty far away from "the artist as a mystic." It is not. The OODA Loop, MLEA Loop, and situation awareness make the mystic more efficient at expressing their vision. In this case, these techniques *are* part of the accomplished craft of the lighting designer.

Propositions with light

The conversation one has with the production through light is more difficult to describe. Trying to explain it reminds me of the S. Harris cartoon of two scientists looking at a chalkboard full of scientific formulae, where one is saying to the other, "I think you should be more explicit here in step two," while pointing at the words "Then a miracle occurs," because the world beyond rational objective understanding does not tend toward logic and order.[12] Making the lighting is the expression of the mystic's vision, so it is unique to the individual artist. For me, the best way to converse with the production is to make a proposition—an idea to try—by writing a light cue. One can use all the words one wants in discussion, but one never knows if a lighting idea has merit until it is on stage, interacting with the production.

That I need to see an idea articulated to judge its efficacy is true for me, whether it is self-generated or if it comes from a collaborator. Often ideas that come from collaborators are more disruptive, but they are also often more generative. Kentridge explains it well: "Collaborations work well when people from different fields cause provocations in each other's worlds...a mutual *heating of enthusiasms*, raising the temperature, which is essential for new ideas to come to the surface and bubble off. There are provocations that would never happen if I was working on my own, thinking on my own" (italics in original).[13] These "provocations" can sometimes be frustrating, but the lesson from Wagner of checking one's ego at the door is critical because that disrupting provocation could be the best idea for a given moment in a production. I often say—this is a bit glib, but hides a great truth—the best way to show a collaborator that their idea is terrible is to execute it perfectly. The hidden truth is that half of the time the idea is *not* terrible, and the other half of the time it *is*, but, in executing it, I will have learned something that feeds the next iteration (adapt). The discomfort could unlock a micro threshold concept that will feed further ideas. In that regard, it is a lot like a real-life gravity well: the provocation, whether successful or not, engenders forward movement and sets a new trajectory in the development of the design.

The final image of the Broadway production of *Pass Over* is a perfect example of how a collaborator's provocation can radically alter a design for the better. In early iterations of the show during technical rehearsals, we had decided not to use a giant light box in the shape of the sun in the final moments, something intended in the original set design. The image we had created of the promised land was minimal and clean without it, and, I thought, appropriate to the moment. However, the image was not as hopeful as director Danya Taymor wanted and after some convivial "heating of enthusiasms," the decision was made to try the sun light box. I was resistant because I felt that the state we had in place worked, but as it turns out, I was wrong. First added to the stage image as a dim, daylight-white orb, it then grew into an undulating magenta and purple disc (via a slow chase effect) which provided the logic for a much more expansive lighting state. The glowing disc as an expressionistic icon of the sun gave way to something that a more sweeping palette of surrounding color gestures could index to. The icon's presence in the image gave me permission to radically remake the final image into the lush, joyous, afrofuturistic dawn the production *really needed* by adding so much more color. In fact, I came to see that final lighting state as the cornerstone of the lighting design and the natural conclusion to the metatextual journey of the lighting for that version of *Pass Over*. Considering the lighting design as a component of the artwork that was the production, there are very clear lines of connection between that lighting state and the production-as-an-artwork. In formal construction, affective impact, and in counterpoint to the aggressive angles and icy palette of the rest of the show, the image was beautiful *and* it valorized the vision of the afrofuturistic utopia the production was advancing (cultural context, threshold concept, innovation). None of this would have happened without Taymor's provocation—without the sun, the color would not have made sense, and without the color, the image would not have been the right kind of beautiful for the moment.

Lighting choreographically

Working instinctually from within the box also allows me to light choreographically—taking the impetus for a composition based on where performers are on stage rather than from a purely intellectual idea—while knowing that it will all make sense within the larger design. The more abstract the production vocabulary is, the easier it is to do this, and it is a great point from which to start building a look.

The work of making sure that any given lighting idea will make sense in the space is taken care of in the studio, so the work in the theatre is to make each lighting idea make sense for the moment it is used. For example, I did not know going into technical rehearsals that I was going to use a diagonal slash of light for the dagger soliloquy in act two, scene one of the production of *Macbeth* I described in "The Box." Precedent dictates that a diagonal on a thrust is a strong staging line, as directors will stage actors following the line of the vom because they will not block audience sight lines to the rest of the stage. So, I included strong lighting ideas along the diagonals without knowing when I was going to use them because they had a specific compositional rationale, and I was confident that the right moment to use them would eventually reveal itself in rehearsal. This included strong, hard-edged diagonal back lanes of light from the grid, and opposing low angle, diagonal front lights (what I call diagonal head-highs) from the voms. When Arbus staged the titular character on the diagonal for this scene, instinct led me to turn on the backlight shaft running from upstage right to downstage left because this was the direction Macbeth was facing, and the gesture made sense within the overall design.

In performance, when Macbeth swiftly turned downstage looking for the imaginary knife, with a knife-blade-along-a-whet-stone sound, there was a half-second crossfade to the opposing light from the vom, keeping his face lit. Because the light change was 'hidden' in his turn—meaning that the timing of the crossfade was *exactly* the timing of his movement—the change was imperceptible yet subconsciously palpable. The effect was unsettling. It was as if Macbeth were being chased by searchlights, trapped from both sides in a dynamic slice of light that was the visual echo of both Shakespeare's words and the sharp sound cue. Not only that, but the idea worked conceptually as well: We wanted the shifts in the three worlds of this production—'reality,' what we called 'the poetic realm,' and 'Macbeth's mind'—to happen by beats, not by scenes. So, it was totally appropriate for the light to conform to our intentions by breaking with the diegetic and moving around like this in the context of 30 lines—showing the hand of the artist in the final composition on stage.

Instinct can also lead to realizations about the larger shape of the lighting design. For example, an earlier scene in the play, act one, scene five, begins with Lady Macbeth alone, reading a letter from her husband, where he describes his meeting with the "weird sisters." I had instinctively made the choice to light her reading the letter in a large, warm pool of light from four overhead fixtures arranged in the same square as the forestage, one down right, one down left, one up right, one up left, so it made sense to reuse it for Lady Macbeth in act two scene two, immediately after Macbeth's dagger soliloquy. As Lady Macbeth appeared from upstage left, instinct led me to turn on a similar low angle shaft to the one that had lit Macbeth, only from the opposite side, this time stage right. It lit Lady Macbeth on her diagonal move to center, where I met her with the same pool of light that she was previously in with the letter, only this time in modulated form, using just the upstage left fixture. The composition—low angle diagonal front met with a single high angle diagonal back pool from the opposite side—was just as dynamic as the previous scene and continued the emotion and energy forward, but this time composed of a different shape on the floor.

This simple example of two adjacent scenes is a perfect illustration of how my modern and postmodern influences coexist in praxis. On the modernist side, these shapes were in the box because they had a minimal, formal relationship to the space—they would work well within a less is more essentialist design—and they satisfied my need for order, precision, and minimalism. I also knew, based on precedent, that these lighting ideas, on this set, would allow me to create beautiful stage images, which, as you now know, is a necessary characteristic of all of my lighting. However, the reason for proposing those ideas for these scenes was based on play and instinct, which, as you also know, are firmly on the postmodern side of Hassan's schema.[14] I do not know precisely why I turned the pool on for Lady Macbeth in act one, scene five, but I will wager it was a combination of her position on stage and a felt sense of what was right for the moment. The design was already well into expressionistic territory, so I felt free to play with multiple options, leaving space for the unexpected. In the realm of mystic vision, the pool made sense. When I used it again for act two, scene two, it turned out that the pool was enough of a counterpoint to the slash to create a different space, but because the overall gestures—high diagonal backs with low diagonal fronts—were in harmony, there was a form to that segment of the production. It was only by pure chance that the pool became *such* an important gesture. It was beautiful, and it became a leitmotif for Lady Macbeth, returning again and again until her final "Out, dammed spot!"[15]

Imperfection

Sometimes, the unexpected is the only constant in a production process. In August of 2017, Hurricane Harvey devastated the gulf coasts of Texas and Louisiana, leaving an almost incomprehensible amount of damage in its wake. It flooded much of downtown Houston, including The Wortham Center, the home of Houston Grand Opera, where, in just a few short weeks, I was set to remount the production of *La Traviata* I have mentioned earlier. The opera company pivoted and set up a makeshift venue, christened "The Resilience Theatre," in Exhibit Hall A3 of the George R. Brown Convention Center, a space with all the aesthetic virtues of an airplane hangar, and we proceeded to plan for our production in that radically different venue. Set up as an end stage, the wing and border playing space alone was some 60 feet wide by some 80 feet deep, with a 110 feet long curved cyclorama. The *La Traviata* show deck and props would be used, with the orchestra in view, upstage of the action, all under a fairly standard repertory plot. *La Traviata* was meant to run in repertory with a remount of a production of *Giulio Cesare in Egitto*,[16] which was suddenly being entirely reconceptualized to fit the new space. As such, I was asked to light it as well. I cite this production of *Giulio Cesare* not because of the absolute chaos of designing it but because it turned out to be—in its imperfection—a design that exemplifies my notion of beauty.

The production conceit was simple: 1920s black and white film. Our production's Egypt consciously used the iconography of the movie studio; everything was meant to appear as a prop, boudoirs were played as

Heidi Stober, Anthony Roth Costanzo, and company in *Giulio Cesare in Egitto*

Houston Grand Opera, 2017
Photograph by Lynn Lane

dressing rooms, the mechanics of everything were exposed, the orchestra was onstage, and, of course, there were big Fresnels on rolling stands. In effect, the set design was a wonderfully curated collage of ideas existing in a postmodern space of here and now rather than an illusionistic version of 1920s Hollywood, and as such, there was no need for the lighting design to be pseudo-realistic. I was free to light the opera from an evocative, emotional perspective. I knew I would be using architectural ideas of light—pools, boxes, long shadows—in order to compositionally control the large space, but I wanted the design to be constrained to echo the idea of a black and white film. So, channeling Hara, I limited my palette to two color temperatures: the 3,200°K of clear incandescent, especially from the rolling Fresnels, and the 5,600°K of daylight white arc light, from an array of moving lights above and on the deck. Even within this tight palette, I find that there is an incredible difference between the two. The eye gets used to the subtlety and small differences become big differences.

Mind you, the quality of light of different kinds of emitters (e.g., arc light vs. fluorescent vs. incandescent vs. LED) at the same color temperature will be different because color temperature is a different measurement than the spectral output. Color temperature is a relative measure of the color of 'white' as compared to the corresponding temperature of an ideal black body radiator when heated to a particular temperature, whereas spectral output has to do with the amount of visible light at each wavelength across the entire spectrum. Meaning that multiple fixture types—including different kinds of LEDs and different manufacturers of arc lamps—can have the same color temperature but appear very different, especially in how they reveal color. I am hammering this point home because the difference between the same color temperature from a Vari-Lite and an Arri HMI is huge, and if one intends to create sophisticated meaning within narrow gradations, it will preempt a lot of handwringing at the lighting table if this difference is remembered in the studio.

My aesthetic leans toward precision, and, in practice, I prefer to control as many variables as possible. Controlling the palette for this *Giulio Cesare* in such strict measure was appropriate for the production, but it was also a way for me to minimize conceptual chaos from factors over which I had no control: the hastily designed rep plot, which was designed to accommodate the Houston Grand Opera's entire season; how the staging would *actually* work in such a vast space; and the very little time available to get the show on its feet. In the end, this process was about two things: determining the sufficient minimum version for the lighting design and embracing the wabi-sabi of it all.

As discussed in "Theatrical Abstraction" and "On Design," the sufficient minimum version has to do with both the required amount of abstraction for an idea to work *and* an essentialist aesthetic. Making the lighting states from an evocative, emotional perspective allowed me to free myself of any pseudo-realistic concerns. Under any circumstance, pseudo-realism would have been inappropriate for the production conceit and the form itself, and in this production, in this space, they would have been *absurd*. Reminding myself that "visual deception," as Appia says, "has no place in art" and therefore "demands a certain degree of refinement in us," I concentrated on using the tools at hand—pools, boxes, long shadows, and limited palette—to make lighting states that reinforced the emotions of the story: A box of light in relation to feeling trapped in a dressing room, a rolling Fresnel down dim to evoke a sense of artificial light in response to plaintive music, a lone 5k arc light all the way upstage right revealing the entire space in a single, broad gesture to support the feeling of being alone in a vast desert.[17]

However, it was all very messy, in a way that taught me a new lesson about beauty. Aesthetic philosopher Leonard Koren, in his book *Wabi-Sabi for Artists, Designers, Poets & Philosophers*, defines wabi-sabi as "a beauty of things imperfect, impermanent, and incomplete … It is a beauty of things unconventional."[18] Among other things enumerated by Koren, a wabi-sabi expression is variable, ostensibly crude, comfortable with ambiguity, and capable of embracing a lack of control over nature.[19] This has two edges: one if something can not by nature be perfect, why try to make it perfect? Two, the imperfections make it beautiful. However, making something imperfect is like trying to force punctum. Both, by their very definition, rely on factors outside the designer's control. The best one can do is to curate the circumstances for it and then decide whether to accept the imperfect, impermanent, and incomplete outcome. For me, this was a *very* unconventional approach—even given my penchant for chance and antiform—because by opening night, I tend to tidy the lighting up. But, that was not possible in this design because of the variables outlined above. For a specific example, a rolling Fresnel may be the key light for a scene, but since it is put there by a person, it is likely that it will not *exactly* hit its mark every night. The human fallibility makes the expression of the lighting idea variable—no two nights are the same—and thus, a little bit of chaos is always present. This was not my first time using a performer-driven fixture, but it was the first time I really understood the fact that sometimes it is the thing *over which I have no control* that makes the image beautiful.

I have carried this lesson of embracing the imperfect forward into other projects, including the 2019 Oregon Shakespeare Festival production of *Indecent*,[20] for example. This production made ample use of actor manipulated flood lights on the deck that were reconfigured to be footlights and shadow play lights at various moments, a rolling Fresnel, and a follow spot on a prop ladder. Flood lights are beautiful, but they are indiscriminate.

Using them as a major component of a design means that one has to accept the consequences of not being able to tightly control compositions. For this production, that was aesthetically appropriate because the set was made of rough-hewn, natural materials—curtains, props, etc.—that existed within the acknowledged space of the Angus Bowmer Theatre rather than an illusionistic, 'complete' space. Thus, the do-it-yourself aspect of actor manipulated fixtures and the resultant sense of imperfection made sense—dramaturgically, visually, and metatextually—within the overall aesthetic of the production.

Source, shadow, color

On the other hand, some designs call for precise control and a disciplined palette, with no room for wabi-sabi, as was the case with the 2021 production of *Tannhäuser*[21] that I designed for Los Angeles Opera. The set was an enormous, raked, glossy black triangle-shaped quadrilateral with two long walls of doors and windows that met at an upstage door. The downstage right and left sections of the walls were on turntables, allowing them to take different configurations. Each of the five scenes (over three acts) of this production was designed within very narrow parameters, each an iteration of the production's visual Big Idea: dominant color gestures on the floor of the set and in the costumes. For act one, scene one, in Venusberg, it was red silk on the floor and nude costumes. For act one, scene two, in the Valley below the Wartburg castle, it was a green astroturf floor with white costumes. For act two, scenes one and two, in the hallway and grand hall of Wartburg castle, it was a black floor and black and white costumes. Finally, for act three, it was a white cloth floor and a mix of green and white costumes. As such, the box for this production was conceptualized to meet each scene with an appropriate "source," "shadow," and saturate color response.

The terms source and shadow have to do with a precedent most firmly set in my mind by Tipton during my training: That there is *always* an implied source of light no matter how abstract the design, and the rest of the light in a lighting state functions in relation to that source. Either as some sort of "shadow" or reflected light. For instance, in the *Tannhäuser* design, Venusburg was a deep red back and side light "source," with purple "shadow," which cut through, from time to time, with clear footlights and follow spots. A stark version of that composition where the source is from stage left may not need any light from stage right to complete the lighting state, however, it may be necessary (compositionally or otherwise) to have light from that direction, so the light from stage right needs to function as "shadow" or as if it is bouncing off of a stage right surface. (This is not to say that it is not possible to have multiple sources in a composition, it only

Debra Lina Kreisberg, Kimberly Fitch, Christina Crowder, Anthony Heald, Aaron Galligan-Stierle, Linda Alper, Rebecca S'Manga Frank, and Benjamin Pelteson in *Indecent*

Oregon Shakespeare Festival, 2019
Photo by Jenny Graham

complicates matters slightly.) I have modulated this idea a bit to incorporate the term "echo," where some light in the composition is an echo of the source, to complete the image. For example, a strong gesture of light through a window stage left is a source and a reasonably low angle diagonal front from the stage left box boom at a similar apparent intensity is an echo—it echoes the key of the window and extends the gesture to fill the stage. What that shadow is, in terms of its technical execution, direction, etc., is entirely dependent on the source for the scene. For example, if the room is white and the source idea is clear, then the shadow could be stage right cross light and front light in a slightly cool color correction.

In this theoretical example, the set is dictating the source, and that is often the case. But with more abstracted designs, as in the *Macbeth* above and this *Tannhäuser*, the rationale for the source is likely to be extracted elsewhere. With *Macbeth*, it was a choreographic/emotional rationale, whereas with *Tannhäuser,* it was dictated by the principles of design and composition and a bit of science: red light on red silk makes a vibrant image. The purple that functioned as shadow was also a compositional choice, it was different enough to provide contrast to the composition but not so different as to wash out the dominant red gesture. In this instance, the saturate red implied a source, which is often the case for big color gestures (another lesson from Tipton). The deep red was also echoed on the surrounding cyclorama, which functioned as a conceptual 'sky,' if you will, and grounded the red source on the performers. In other words, at a visceral level, if the sky is red, it makes sense that the light on the people is too. This idea of echoing the color in a scene on the sky carried forward in the production.

A few key points on color: the color wheels for pigment and light are not the same. In pigment, the primary colors are red, yellow, and blue, and white is the *absence* of all color. In light, the primary colors are red, *green*, and blue, and white is the *presence* of all color (all wavelengths of light in the visible spectrum). Ergo, color mixes, analogous colors (colors that are adjacent to each other on the color wheel), and complementary colors (colors that are opposite to each other on the color wheel) are different for each medium.[22] In lighting, all primaries and complementary colors will, in theory, mix to white. This has important ramifications in understanding both additive and subtractive mixing. The relationship between primaries in pigment is just as important for two big reasons: First, as I often say, light is nothing without that which it reveals, and, as such, you get what you give. Color in pigment works by absorbing some wavelengths hitting it and bouncing back the others. So, green astroturf basically absorbs all colors of light hitting it, except for green, which it returns to the eye. Therefore, light without any green in it (primary red, for example) will render astroturf colorless. Second, color relationships in pigment are important when treating foreground, middle ground, and background as planes of color. Take, for example, treating a set that with a neutral floor and a neutral backing as an opportunity to create two distinct color planes: While the rules of mixing light apply if one were using multiple fixtures to light one plane—three cell cyclorama lights for example—the rules governing the juxtaposition of colors between the planes are those of pigment since planes are essentially being 'painted' with light. This is important because understanding the difference has everything to do with understanding how to use color as "paint."

When color in lighting is not employed as a source—for example, in the second scene of this *Tannhäuser*, the one with the green floor—it can be used to "paint" the space. The source for this scene was a strong gesture of daylight white from stage right, with a slightly cooler shadow from stage left. I then lit the floor with a green backlight to get it to vibrate, in effect painting the space independent of a source and shadow idea. I also lit the cyclorama with the same color intensity as the floor to continue the paint idea into the background. (Had I chosen a different color for the surround, I would have considered the color relationships of pigment rather than in light when choosing.) In this instance, the green cyclorama was not intended to evoke sky, per se, but rather a sense of being surrounded by nature. The green was an expressionistic articulation of the power of nature in an opera where the story has to do with a man being torn between natural, human impulses and the constricting morals of Catholic culture.

Act two, where the dominance of those morals reached their apogee, with the eventual banishment of Tannhäuser to Rome to seek absolution, was lit in stark whites. First, in arc white, to reveal the black and white costumes in as monochromatic a way as possible. Then, in the second half of the act, in the grand hall itself, there was warmer, diffuse white, with the light being indexed by the warm chandeliers. The cyclorama was an almost imperceptible deep indigo, first, to evoke a sense of night beyond the windows, and second, as a compositional necessity; the color outside acted as a counterpoint and made the light inside, while very warm, still feel monochromatic. Without the indigo, the composition felt too "dry," which was not appropriate for the first half of the scene. As the scene progressed, and as Tannhäuser's fate became clear, the lighting state very slowly crossfaded away from the diffuse incandescence to a strong, high contrast, arc white architectural gesture from downstage right that threw shadows on the starkly lit stage left wall. The indigo went away, which was appropriate for this later look. In this instance, the rationale for altering the source from something that was pseudo-realistic to completely expressionistic had everything to do with Wagner's music. Modern European culture scholar Krisztina Lajosi explains that in Wagner, "the separate artistic media—*music,* text, dance, painting, architecture," and light, I might add, "can only fulfill their original function if the interact in perfect harmony with each other" (italics mine.)[23] The emotion and intensity expressed by the soaring orchestrations, director Louisa Muller's architectural staging of the massive, accusatory chorus, and the sheer scale of the room demanded a Big Idea in the lighting to complete the Gesamtkunstwerk.

Pseudo-realism *and* expressionism

Sometimes a lighting design needs to function at the pseudo-realistic and expressionistic ends of the spectrum of theatrical abstraction at the same time. A prime example of this is the storm in the TFANA production of *King Lear,* first mentioned in "Theatrical Abstraction." Dramaturgically, the storm is expressionistic in that it is evocative of the cracking of Lear's psyche, for he refers to the "tempest in my mind," yet, it is also an actual storm that the characters experience.[24] The Earl of Kent marvels:

> Such sheets of fire, such bursts of horrid thunder,
> Such groans of roaring wind and rain I never,
> Remember to have heard.[25]

Kent, Lear, and others are experiencing this storm as a storm, and as such, a pseudo-realistic storm is a lighting requirement for this part of the play. So, what is the storm? And what does that mean for what comes before and what comes after? These were essential questions to be explored in the process of creating the lighting for this *King Lear.*[26]

The character of Lear is a singularity. He is extraordinarily powerful and very seductive. His energy, through the course of the play, expands, and expands, and expands—until it collapses in on itself. Lear's world at the top of the play is one of primal masculine power, a brutal, man-made, military world. Arbus described it in her director's notes as "sexy."[27] It needed to encompass the full spectrum of theatrical abstraction: on the pseudo-realistic side, I wanted it to be mercurial and shadowy, as though lit by torches and other artificial sources; on the expressionistic side, I wanted the lighting to be in dialog with the unstable nature of this world. The play is about the simultaneous fracturing of the state, the family, and self, and I wanted the light to fracture in the same way—starting out warm, incandescent, and jewel-like at first, then becoming more and more elemental as the play progresses so that by the final scene, it is broken into asymmetrical, arc-lit compositions. The arc of the lighting was divided into three movements: the opening through Lear's exit onto the heath, the storm through the plucking of Gloucester's eyes, and the calm after the storm through the battle. I felt it critical that the lighting design be expressive of that structure as it progressed.

Issachah Savage, Yulia Matochkina, and the company of *Tannhäuser*
Los Angeles Opera, 2021
Photograph courtesy of Cory Weaver

The first movement and certain scenes in the second movement (the interior of Gloucester's castle and then the hovel) were dominated by Caravaggio-esque lighting. His *The Taking of Christ* was the defining research for this idea, with its well-defined foreground, looming darkness, and foreboding energy, which are all strangely seductive. I did this by creating patches of warmth and suggesting artificial sources with uplights and low angles, subdominating the background. The primary color of the light was clear incandescent, which has a warmth to it and becomes more fire-like the dimmer it gets. I was very rigorous about maintaining that palette, even to the extent of prioritizing that over more diegetic concerns such as time of day. Also, this kind of light looked very, very sexy with the costumes and against the color of the set. Rhythmically, the light would transition from scene to scene with the actors and end up in static states for each scene up until act two, scene four. That scene, Lear's confrontation with Regan and Goneril and his subsequent exit to the heath, was the first point in the production where the light changed within the course of a scene: As Lear became more and more frustrated, the warm incandescence was slowly broken by a shaft of icy white arc-source light cascading over the corner of the looming upstage wall, the harbinger of the storm. After his exit, while Regan, Goneril, and Cornwall were looking downstage, the light dropped to its most unnatural angle thus far—a direct icy-white front light that would be echoed in the storm.

So then, how does one put an authentic storm on stage?

One does not.

In a preproduction workshop, a space was rigged up with natural elements: water, fans, strobes, and leaves to test what vocabulary could be useful in the theatre, and the result was that it was all pretty lame. The rain was just a little water, the strobes looked like a bad disco, and the wind was too loud. Nothing drew close to the cataclysmic tempest that Lear was experiencing internally. Which was great, both because it freed us as the creative team to move beyond the pseudo-realistic toward an expressionistic state that might actually meet the intensity of Lear's experience and because it proved Craig's point in "Theatrical Abstraction," that "actuality, accuracy of detail, is useless upon the stage."[28] Still, I felt that the elements of a "real" storm were critical to the telling of the story because the characters are talking about it and are experiencing it. The storm needed to be scary and dangerous and really feel real, even in its abstraction. This meant taking the naturally occurring phenomena of a storm—bright light, deep darkness, and cacophonic rhythm—and arranging them expressionistically.

So, the second movement of the design—Lear on the heath through the blinding of Gloucester—began with the storm: imperceptible light, barely illuminating Lear and the others, interspersed with moments of blinding

Timothy D. Stickney, Jacob Fishel, Jake Horowitz, and Michael Pennington in *King Lear*

Theatre for a New Audience, 2013
Photograph © Carol Rosegg

intensity, shifts of perspective and focus, in constant motion with unpredictable rhythm, all in merciless arc white, the same color temperature as lightning. Of course, all of this would be meaningless if it was not specifically curated with the text, so we were very careful about that as we scored the sequence. For example, when Lear says "*Singe* my white head! And *thou*, all-shaking thunder,/Strike flat the thick rotundity o' the *world!*" (my italics), the events were thus: Lear was in a dim single spot cutting through a thick blanket of haze in the air.[29] On '*Singe*' an extremely bright flash illuminated the entire space from an unnaturally low angle in front for one second, fading in two, leaving Lear in silhouette from a dim single spot from behind. On '*thou*' the spot sharply crossfaded to another from the diagonal front, which then slowly grew larger in size. On '*world*' lighting strobes cracked around high up in the flies over the following line "Crack nature's molds, all germens spill at once/That makes ingrateful man!" before finally resolving back to a single, dim spot.[30] For the duration of the storm, the space continued to expand and contract, cut through by columns of light from unpredictable sources, and rapidly plunged into darkness, evoking both nature and the relentless confusion in Lear's mind.

Trust

As I bring this book to a close, I reflect on a very recent production of *The Merchant of Venice*, which I designed after almost the entirety of this book was drafted.[31] It was an exciting proof-of-concept for all of the ideas I have advanced in these pages and a lesson in trusting the process and my collaborators. It was the best possible scenario: Another Shakespeare directed by Arbus at TFANA (that subsequently transferred to Shakespeare Theatre Company) with a creative team and many actors with whom I have a rich history. So much of the work of collaboration—getting to know each other, developing a common vocabulary and aesthetic, etc.—was already done, honed over previous productions, before we even started on the play.

The production was predicated on the Venice of this play as a duplicitous, ugly place. A dystopian world where every relationship is transactional and every character is complicit, somehow, in the governing capitalist, misogynistic, homophobic, and racist power structures. This is not restricted to Venice, however. Belmont, which is often characterized as an oasis, is equally as seedy. The viciousness that rules the people of Venice, rules the people of Belmont. It is, as Portia says, a "naughty"—meaning wicked—"world."[32] Riccardo Hernández's set capitalized on this, drawing inspiration from the raw concrete and monumental scale of the mid-century brutalism architectural movement. It was a minimal but grand gesture, consisting of a full width staircase broken by three landings and a massive upstage wall made from concrete slabs.

Yonatan Gebeyehu, John Douglas Thompson, Graham Winton, Isabel Arraiza, Alfredo Narciso, Shirine Babb, Nate Miller, Maurice Jones, Sanjit De Silva, Varín Ayala, and Haynes Thigpen in *The Merchant of Venice*

Theatre for a New Audience and Shakespeare Theatre Company, 2022
Photograph by the author

The metaphor of the entire play happening in the headlights kept asserting itself in my imagination. I was intrigued by the question of what would a brutalist lighting state look like and remembered an article where the journalist and writer Owen Hatherly described brutalism as "an architecture that was heavy, uncompromising and rather photogenic."[33] For me, this translated into expansive architectural gestures of light, states that would encompass the entirety of the space (which I knew would be necessary from a formal perspective because it is hard to make a large concrete wall "go away"), which were also beautiful. I also wanted the world of this play to seethe more and more as the play went on, so I resolved to use a palette that began with color corrected white that would then slowly evolve into tints of acid green to introduce a little anarchy to the proceedings.

While I knew what the long form shape of the design wanted to be, I did not know *exactly* how I would deploy the box to light each scene. However, I trusted my process and took the chance that I would be able to express what I was seeing in my mind's eye that was just beyond rational objective understanding through the lighting design. So, the palette, the heavy, uncompromising, and rather photogenic aspects of brutalism, and the architecture of the set (especially the rhythm of the seams in the concrete) became the inspiration for my design. Every element in the box for this production was related to these ideas. Elements in the box included large gestures of cool white cross light, backlight, head high side light, and long gestures of starkly directional light on the back wall. The acid green manifested itself in the design via systems of shin busters and lights from the downstage right and left corners that starkly lit the wall. There was also a row of fixtures that were abstractions of headlights from about hip high on the booms (mids) and skimming along the surface of the wall in acid green. There was a row of color changing LED tape as footlights and an array of framing profile moving lights overhead.

I relied on the shapes on the floor to create space by making boxes with the backlight in various configurations along the seams in the set and making them more or less dominant depending on how constrictive I wanted the scene to feel. For instance, the room where the caskets in which Portia's father held her fate were located was a sharp rectangle of light on the second landing. The downstage landing had a separate sharp rectangle, where Portia was often staged, trapping her in a similar, constrained space. Another trope was using the same downstage sharp rectangle to box out only the downstage landing for the various street and hall scenes, with the rest of the stage dark. Specificity through light for each locale was irrelevant because the content of the scenes makes that clear. This allowed me to repeat the composition, which had the benefits of making the design even that more minimal *and* allowing the light to quickly slide between scenes, effecting transitions that did not take a lot of time or visual space. All of this allowed the palette to progress through each scene, articulating the long form of the design even though the shapes of the states were relatively the same.

Ultimately, my studio idea for the progression of the palette proved not wicked enough. First off, the color was not quite right, so after some trial and error, I landed on a combination of fluorescent and plus green correction, which were surprisingly more saturated colors than I had expected in the studio. Second, after seeing the first preview—which is the first time I feel like I really see the show as a unified whole—I realized that the world of this *Merchant* needed to be ugly from the get-go, so I ended up scoring in subtle hints of the acid green in from the top, which made the progression more subtle, but logically correct.

The first ten scenes of the play are basically continuous time from midday to night, so the gestures became more directional and higher contrast until the masquer's scene (act two, scene six), which was lit only with a few lights from a downstage corner. That scene marked a complete transition from the pseudo-realistic conceits of the first part of the play to the pure expressionism that dominated the design from there on out. The remaining states were influenced by the architectural (where people were staged) and affective (how I wanted the audience to feel) needs of each scene, with only a casual relationship to the text. The streets were compressed, the trial was heavy, and the ultimate scene—a night described by Portia as "… but the daylight sick … a day/Such as the day is when the sun is hid"—was lit exclusively with shin busters, floating the bodies from the floor.[34] All of these states were articulated with as few fixtures as possible. The end result was a design that was precise, minimal, unobtrusive, and rather beautiful.

Philosophy redux

My hope is that by examining my concrete choices in various productions and showing how they are based on the theoretical underpinnings of my aesthetic point of view, I have been able to illustrate how my practice is my theory and my theory is my practice. It has been a linear, logical investigation, but the truth is, all art making is chaotic to a certain extent. After all, we mystics traffic in the unknowns of the world beyond rational understanding. In practice, the ideas contained in this book live entwined—objective and subjective, determinate and indeterminate, efferent and aesthetic, logical and emotional, modern and postmodern, pseudo-realistic and expressionistic, formal, contextual, affective, compositional, visual, musical, etc.—as if all the pages were smashed up together at once, comingling, informing one another, and breathing vibrancy and meaning into a lighting design. I believe it is the job of the lighting designer to consider as many of these dimensions as possible when designing a production and to bring those conceptual findings in the form of the box, along with their best artist selves, to the heat of collaboration. In parallel, we must also engage in considered introspection of our own artistic impulses and aesthetic tendencies, and we must scrutinize our work. Considering each production as an opportunity to push, pull, and wrestle with the work at hand *and* with the form itself is how we will grow as artists and designers in our pursuit of good lighting for the stage.

Notes

1. Garson O'Toole [pseud.], "Two Necessities in Doing a Great and Important Work: A Definite Plan and Limited Time," Quote Investigator, August 19, 2020, https://quoteinvestigator.com/2020/08/19/plan-time/.
2. Adolphe Appia, "Music and the Art of the Theatre," *Adolph Appia: Texts on Theatre*, ed. Richard Beacham (London: Routledge, 1993), 51.
3. M.R. Endsley, "Toward a Theory of Situation Awareness in Dynamic Systems," *Human Factors* 27, no. 1 (March 1, 1995): 36, https://doi.org/10.1518/001872095779049543.
4. Endsley, "Situation Awareness," 36.
5. Endsley, 37.
6. Endsley, 37.
7. Endsley, 36.
8. "The OODA Loop: How Fighter Pilots Make Fast and Accurate Decisions," Farnam Street Blog, accessed March 31, 2021, https://fs.blog/ooda-loop/.
9. Having to do with genetic predispositions. For example, being a visual learner.
10. John R. Boyd, "The Essence of Winning and Losing," ed. Chet Richards and Chuck Spinney, produced and designed by Ginger Richards (June 28, 2995; September 2012), accessed November 28, 2021, https://fasttransients.files.wordpress.com/2010/03/essence_of_winning_losing.pdf, 1. This version includes the following note: "This edition of 'The Essence of Winning and Losing' is a PDF of an Apple Keynote rendering of the version that appeared for years in HTML on the now-defunct website belisarius.com. Boyd's first edition carried the date '28 June 1995,' and the last appeared sometime in January 1996, a little over a year before Colonel Boyd died. This was the only one of Boyd's briefings that was originally created in PowerPoint and it was later published on the web as an HTML frameset."
11. Boyd, "Essence," 1.
12. Sydney Harris, "Then a Miracle Occurs," n.d., cartoon, Science Cartoons Plus, http://www.sciencecartoonsplus.com/pages/gallery.php.
13. William Kentridge and Jane Taylor, "In Dialog," *Handspring Puppet Company*, ed. Jane Taylor (Johannesburg, ZA: David Krut, 2009), 205.
14. Ihab Hassan, "Toward a Concept of Postmodernism," *The Postmodern Turn: Essays in Postmodern Theory and Culture* (Columbus: Ohio State University Press, 1987), 91.
15. William Shakespeare, *Macbeth*, in *The Complete Works of Shakespeare*, ed. David Bevington, 4th ed. (New York: HarperCollins Publishers, 1992), 5.1.33.
16. *Giulio Cesare in Egitto*, composed by George Frideric Handel with libretto by Nicola Francesco Haym, dir. James Robinson, original set design by Christine Jones and costume design by James Schuette, Houston Grand Opera, Houston, US, 2017.
17. Adolphe Appia, "Music and the Art of the Theatre," *Adolph Appia: Texts on Theatre*, ed. Richard Beacham (London: Routledge, 1993), 39.
18. Leonard Koren, *Wabi-Sabi for Artists, Designers, Poets & Philosophers* (Point Reyes, CA: Imperfect Publishing, 1994), 7.
19. Koren, *Wabi-Sabi*, 25–29.

20 *Indecent*, by Paula Vogel, dir. by Shana Cooper, set design by Sibyl Wickersheimer, costume design by Deborah M. Dryden, projection design by Rasean Davonte Johnson, and sound design by Paul James Prendergast, Oregon Shakespeare Festival, Ashland, US, 2019.
21 *Tannhäuser*, by Richard Wagner, dir. Louisa Muller, set and costume design by Gottfried Pilz, and additional costumes by Misty Ayres. Los Angeles Opera, Los Angeles, US, 2021.
22 For lighting, the most effective color wheel is the CIE (Commission Internationale de l'Éclairage) Chromaticity Diagram, where the edges define the deepest saturation of color and where the center is white. For more information on color relationships, *Interaction of Color*, by Josef Albers, is a good start.
23 Krisztina Lajosi, "Wagner and the (Re)mediation of Art: Gesamtkunstwerk and Nineteenth-Century Theories of Media," *Frame* 23, no. 2 (November 2010): 44.
24 William Shakespeare, *King Lear*, in *The Complete Works of Shakespeare*, ed. David Bevington, 4th ed. (New York: HarperCollins Publishers, 1992), 3.4.12.
25 Shakespeare, *King Lear*, 3.2.46–48.
26 An earlier version of this discussion of my lighting for *King Lear* appeared in Michael Pennington's excellent book, *Lear in Brooklyn* (London: Oberon Books, 2016).
27 Arin Arbus, private correspondence with the author, 2014.
28 Edward Gordon Craig, "From the Artists of the Theatre of the Future," in *Twentieth Century Theatre: A Sourcebook*, ed. Richard Drain (London: Routledge, 1995), 241.
29 Shakespeare, *King Lear*, 3.2.6–7.
30 Shakespeare, 3.2.8–9.
31 *The Merchant of Venice*, by William Shakespeare, dir. Arin Arbus, set design by Riccardo Hernández, costume design by Emily Rebholz, and original music and sound design by Justin Ellington, Theatre for a New Audience, New York, US, and Shakespeare Theatre Company, Washington DC, US, 2022.
32 William Shakespeare, *The Merchant of Venice*, in *The Complete Works of Shakespeare*, ed. David Bevington, 4th ed. (New York: HarperCollins Publishers, 1992), 5.1.91.
33 Owen Hatherly, "Strange, Angry Objects," London Review of Books 38, no. 22 (2016), December 10, 2021, https://www.lrb.co.uk/the-paper/v38/n22/owen-hatherley/strange-angry-objects.
34 Shakespeare, *Merchant*, 5.1.124–126.

Coda: So, Now What?

A mural by the artist Banksy covers a wall in the West Bank village of Beit Sahour, June 18, 2014

Ryan Rodrick Beiler/Alamy Stock Photo

DOI: 10.4324/9781003206460-10

In writing this book and considering the thinkers and artists who have shaped both my aesthetic and my process, as well as the work I have designed, I see a preponderance of white, Eurocentric and male points of view, which, in many regards is worrisome. However, I am also glad that I intersected with each and every one of them. I would not be who I am without these influences, regardless of who they are. An idea that I have returned to many times in this book is that my cultural context informs my aesthetic and, as such, I believe that what I bring to my interactions with these ideas—and my contribution to the productions I design—acts as a change agent to bring an expanded perspective to the form.

Much change is required and, right now, society urgently needs theatre that is more equitable and representative. While addressing casting is one of many steps required to foster this vision of the performing arts, it must be done in concert with deliberate, well-funded action to not only change the make-up of who is on stage to one that is more equitable and representational, but to also do the same with the material they are performing and who is behind the scenes, on the creative team, and in the audience. All this should take place alongside developing vocabulary and techniques with which to analyze and criticize the work on its own terms.

My hope is that we can be kind to each other as we do so. That even in our iconoclasm, we will throw flowers instead of grenades. Collaboration is hard and it is to be expected that passions will arise—it would be strange if they did not given that our work traffics in high emotion and conflict—but we must take care of ourselves if we are to take care of the form. I remember attending a Theatre Communications Group conference in the early 2000s when many theatres were wrestling with increasing economic pressures. In a group discussion, I was making a case for theatres to protect the artists that actually make the work as they contemplated budget cuts. I evoked the metaphor of crossing a desert: The further one goes, the more one divests oneself of the things one is carrying in order to lighten the load so one can actually make it to the other side. The only problem is that by the time one gets to the other side, all one has is what one has kept. I argued that it was vital for the theatres to keep the artists, and I think it is equally vital now—existential even—in the context of our current syndemic of COVID-19, social justice crises, and threats to democracy. We are carrying ourselves, and we owe it to each other to keep holding on to one another as we chart a path into an uncertain future. There is much work to be done, and I am hopeful that it will involve some non-trivial amount of negentropy, which will lead to innovation. After all, every production is a chance to start anew, to make, look, evaluate, and adapt.

Onwards!

Index

Page numbers followed by "n" indicate a note on the corresponding page.

4:48 Psychosis 65
1867 Das Kapital 98

Abboud, Carole 107
abstract form lighting 5, 94
abstraction *see* theatrical abstraction
Adams, Gabrielle S. 136n5
Adams, John 67
Adjepong, Oberon K.A. 53
aesthetics view 2, 4; aesthetic negentropy 52; aesthetic trait 13; aesthetic virtue 6–7, 89–90
affective critique 21–24
Alien movie 12
Alleman, Austin Reed 113
Allen, Rick 127
Alper, Linda 175
Anderson, Kevin 103
Angelou, Maya 139
Angels in America 43
angle 19, 104, 114–115, 130, 148, 155, 168–169, 176, 180, 182; for day scenes 110; disjointed angles 114; low angle 114, 168–169, 176, 180, 182; quoting pre-naturalistic theatre 112; unnatural angle 108, 180; utility of 155
Antoine, André 99
Appia, Adolphe 72, 78–79, 92n10, 96–97, 112, 116n9–10, 162, 173, 186n2, 17
apples and hats 124–126
applied art 2, 80, 119–120, 136
Arbus, Arin 5, 43, 56n35, 57n59–60, 116n8, 117n43, 120, 125, 139, 159n3–4, 169, 178, 182, 187n27, 187n31
aria 133
Arison, Amir 135
Aristotle 142–143, 159n8
Arnheim, Rudolf 66, 71n20

Aronson, Arnold 126, 129, 137n17, 137n22, 137n23
Arraiza, Isabel 183
Artaud, Antonin 84, 92n24, 125, 137n15
Articulation 70, 102, 120, 125, 128–129, 130, 132–133, 177
artist/artwork 29–54; accomplished craft 34–36; aesthetic negentropy 52; applied innovation 49; beyond objectness 36–40; bounded threshold 43–44; conceptual innovation 50–51; craft object 38–39; craft object and artwork, overlap between 39–40; cultural borrowing 51–54; form forward 48–54; integrative threshold 43; irreversible threshold 42; medium, techniques and materials of 35; mystic 30–31; non-aesthetic negentropy 52; point of view and need 31–34; (re)definitions 30; signs in semiotics 35–36; transformative threshold 42; troublesome knowledge 40–44; troublesome threshold 44; urge to innovate 44–48; utility 54
art movement -isms 94–96
Art-Work of the Future, The 33, 55n13, 71n6, 92n11
artwork redux 85–86
Auden, W.H. 139
Ayala, Varín 183

Babb, Shirine 183
balance, and visual composition 131
Baldick, Chris 117n37
Barford, Ian 75, 151
Barthes, Roland 22, 28n32–34
Bass, Eric 125, 137n16
Battista, Leon 49
Bausch, Pina 32, 44, 56n40

Beacham, Richard 72, 92n10, 116n9, 186n2, 186n17
beauty 8, 10–27, 44, 50, 60, 66, 84, 95, 166; aesthetic trait 13; culture and context 13–16; efficacy of 11–13; Gordian Knot 11; intentional beauty 25–27; non-aesthetic trait 13
Berg, Alban 49
Berger, John 86–87, 92n27–28, 33
Bernard, Claude 98
Bernstein, Leonard 161
Betrayal 73
Bhabha, Satya 135
Billington, Michael 116n7
Birch, Thomas 62
Black Lives Matter 47
Black Power Movement 46
Black Watch 85
Bond, Edward 146, 159n11
Booker, Christopher 74, 91n2
Boretz, Benjamin 33, 55n11
bounded threshold 43–44
the box 138–159; analysis 142–143; boundaries 140; character 143; diction 143; dimensions 144–148; dramaturgical dimension 144–148; dramaturgical research 149; gravity 139–142; gravity redux 158–159; lists 152–153; magic sheet 158; mapping 156–158; metatextual dimension 146; needs list 157; outcomes 150–152; overlap 148; palette 155–156; physical dimension 145; plot 143; research 149–150; roadmap 142; set exploration 153–155; song 143; spectacle 143; thought 143; visual research 149; ways list 157
Boyd, John R. 165–166, 186n10–11
Braque, Georges 43, 51
Brecht, Bertolt 84, 92n25, 100, 111, 117n25, 120, 136n4
Brooks, David 139, 159n2
Brown, Jason Robert 73
Brunelleschi, Filippo 49
Buell, Bill 135
Burke, Edmund 11, 27n6
Butler, Andrew R. 113

Cabaret 86
Cage, John 32
Camera Lucida: Reflections on Photography 22, 28n32
Campbell, Joseph 31, 54n3–4, 55n3–4, 6–8, 74, 91n3

Caravaggio-esque lighting 180
categories, art 16–18; contra-standard 16–17; standard 16; variable 16
"Categories of Art," essay 16, 28n16–17, 24, 56n53, 71n21
Caught in a Gale 62
character 49, 112, 115, 125, 133, 143, 169, 182; archetypical 74; expressionism and 108–109; lighting leitmotif for 162; in *Linda Vista* 102; at the pinnacle of theatre 83–84
Charles, Jencks 128, 137n21
Checklist Manifesto, The 152, 159n14–15
Chekov, Anton 99
choices, in theatrical abstraction 115–116
Chorus Line, A 86
chroma 131
Cincinnati Contemporary Arts Center 15
Civil Rights Movement 46
coexistence 128–130
Collingwood, R.G. 7, 9n6, 38–39, 55n24–26
color 131, 152, 174–178; in applied innovation 49; architectural gesture using 106; in cultural borrowing 51; dominant interior color 112; emotional content expressed using 62; in Gregory Crewdson's work 110, 149; LED tape 184; modernism in 95; multiple colors 157; in *Pass Over* 148, 168; in pigment works 124, 176; primary color of the light 180; saturated color 150, 156, 185; temperature 131, 172
competency 65, 66, 71n16
contextual critique 19–21, 24
contrast 19, 129, 131, 134, 176–177, 185
contra-standard category of art 16–17
Costanzo, Anthony Roth 171
Cousin, Glynis 41–42, 56n33
craft object 30, 38–39, 119, 150
Craig, Edward Gordon 15, 31, 55n9, 96–97, 112, 116n11, 125, 136n3, 187n28
creative team 73, 80, 91, 100, 125, 163, 180, 182; choices in 115; definition 9; essentialism and 120; evaluating 70; importance 78; lighting designers and 109; main outcomes for 150–152; in *Pass Over* 147
Crewdson, Gregory 110, 138, 149, 157
Crowder, Christina 175
Cultural Appropriation and the Arts, 27n9, 34, 55n20
culture and context 13–16; macro-cultures 14; micro-culture 14
curation 100

da Caravaggio, Michelangelo Merisi 160
Dahlström, Carl E. W.L. 98, 116n15–16
Darger, Henry 34
Darwin, Charles 98
Davis, Tracy C. 111, 117n40
De Silva, Sanjit 183
deadlines 155, 161
depth 33, 41, 131–132
Der Kaiser Von Atlantis 23, 24, 28n35
design 118–136; apples and hats 124–126; applied art 119–120; coexistence 128–130; essentialism 120–122; idealized perspective 129; legacies 122–124; MTV 126–128; vocabulary 130–136
diction 143
dimensions 104, 142, 144–148, 148, 150, 154, 163, 185; dramaturgical 144–145; of lighting for the stage 5; metatextual 146; overlapping of 148; physical 145; rhythmic 148; of space 78, 140; time as 136; visual 146
Doll's House, A 96, 99, 105, 109, 116n8
dominant lights 35, 114, 131, 148
Donahoe, Emily 135
Douglas, Emory 32
Dramatic Imagination, The 77, 91n9, 116n12
dramaturgical dimension 144–145
dramaturgical research 149
Dream Play, A 50, 105
Drew, Richard 10, 12, 19–22

Edgerton, Samuel Y. 56n54
education of the spectator 65–67
Eisenberg, Ned 45
Elektra 84, 92n22, 92n23, 109
Elich, Michael 53
Elliott, Joe 71n3, 91n8, 127
'emancipated' spectator 63
emitters, light 172
emotional engagement 83–84
empathetic connection 74
Endsley, M.R. 163–164, 186n3–7
energy 15, 34–35, 51, 59, 95, 134, 139, 169, 180
ephemeral form lighting 5
Epstein, Fred 113
Eskine, Kendall J. 27n7–8
essentialism 120–122, 136n6
Essentialism: The Disciplined Pursuit of Less 122, 136n6
Eurocentric theatrical design 95
expectation 101, 134
expressionism 94, 108–111, 114, 117n37, 178–182

Exter, Aleksandra 43, 51, 57n63
extrinsic interest 62

Farago, Jason 56n27
Farber, Eric 113
Father, The 50, 96, 99, 116n8
feedback loop 60, 73, 77, 81, 84–85, 90, 161, 165
Fishel, Jacob 181
Fitch, Kimberly 175
flow 134; between the artist and the spectator 62–63, 73; rhythmic dimension of 148, 162; *The Skin of Our Teeth* 112
form(s) 44–48, 132, 134; abstract form 94, 111; advancement of 79; of applied art 119; art forms 2, 41, 78, 87, 90, 99; of craft object 38; of cultural borrowing 51–52; of emotional engagement 83; graphic designer in 124; importance of 123; of Lighting for the stage 5; pushed forward 48–54; temporal form 90, 134
form forward 2, 36, 48–54, 85; applied innovation 49; conceptual innovation 50–51; cultural borrowing 51–54
formalism 18–19, 28n22, 66, 71n18
Frank, Rebecca S'Manga 175
French, Arthur 22, 62, 65, 68, 84, 113
Freud, Sigmund 98

Galligan-Stierle, Aaron 175
Ganizate, Eva 37
Gardon, Mathieu 37
Gawande, Atul 152–153, 159n14–15
Gebeyehu, Yonatan 183
Géricault, Théodore 25–26
Giulio Cesare in Egitto 170–171, 186n16
Godfrey, Tony 95, 116n4
Gombrich, Ernst H. 105, 117n34–35
The Goodman Theatre 81, 82, 92n19, 121, 136n7
Gordon, Max 113
graveyard shift 81–83, 92n19, 128–130, 136
gravity 139–142, 159, 167
gravity redux 158–159
Great Reckonings in Little Rooms 100, 116n23
Greenberg, Clement 47, 56n48, 87, 92n30–32, 95, 116n1, 127
Guys and Dolls 86

Hair 86
Hall, Lucas 45
Hamilton 86
Hamlet 90, 152
Hammerstein, Oscar 42, 56n32

Handspring Puppet Company 80, 92n17, 186n13
Hara, Kenya 47, 56n49, 95, 116n2, 124, 137n12, 139, 159n1, 172
Haring-Smith, Tori 69, 71n25, 101, 117n26
Harris, Sydney 167, 186n12
Harris Theatre 77
Hassan, Ihab 95, 116n3, 116n5, 126–127, 137n18–20, 186n14
Hatherly, Owen 184, 187n33
Heald, Anthony 175
Hekkert, Paul 66, 71n17, 71n19
Hernández, Riccardo 57n59, 57n60, 116n8, 182, 187n31
Hesse, Eva 49
Hickey, Dave 5, 11, 15–16, 19, 25, 27n1–2, 28n13, 28n15, 28n22, 54n5, 60, 66, 71n18, 76, 86–87, 91n5, 92n29
Hidden Fortress, The 52
hierarchy 27, 38–39, 78, 128–129, 131
Hill, Jon Michael 147
Hirsch, E. D. Jr. 65, 71n15, 71n23
Hitler, Adolph 79
Hopper, Edward 58–59
Horowitz, Jake 70, 181
Horowitz, Jeffrey 43, 44, 120
Hubbard, Elbert 161
hue 131–132, 156
Hume, David 21–22, 28n29, 28n30, 28n31
Hysteria 127

Ibsen, Henrik 96, 99, 116n8, 116n17
'idealized' spectator 129
Indecent 173–175, 187n20
inertia 134
Innes, Christopher 98–99, 116n13, 116n20–22
innovation 13, 15, 44–48, 85, 189; applied 49; conceptual 50–51; macro-structure 50; micro-structure 50; urge to 44–48
integrative threshold 43
intensity 110, 131–132, 153, 176–177, 178, 180, 182
intent 8, 12, 18, 39, 85, 97, 134, 164; artist's 62–63; as basis of criticism 18, 20; compositional 144; dramatic 5, 100–102, 109
intentional beauty 25–27
interest 60–62; extrinsic 62; intrinsic 62
Interpretation of Dreams, The 98
intrinsic interest 62
irreversible threshold 42
Ismail, Abdalrhman 69–70
-isms 94–97, 105; design and 96–97; interrogating 94–96

Jencks, Charles 128, 137n21
Jim and Tom, Sausalito 1977, 45
Jiménez, Gizel 53
Jones, Maurice 79, 101, 183
Jones, Robert Edmund 77, 91n9, 96, 102, 116n12
Jung, Carl Gustav 30, 54n1
Junod, Tom 28n23

Kandinsky, Wassily 44–46, 56n41–42
Kane, Sarah 65
Kapoor, Anish 49
Karate Kid Part III, The, 1989 1
Keller, Ramona 53
Kelsey, Quinn 61
Kennedy, A.L. 27, 28n40
Kentridge, William 80, 92n17, 119, 167, 186n13
Khmer aesthetic 6, 15, 51–52
Kidd, Chip 124–125, 137n13–14
King Lear 9, 51, 57n59, 97, 149, 178, 181, 187n24, 187n25, 187n26, 187n29
Koren, Leonard 173, 186n18–19
Kovalenk, Georgii 57n63
Kreisberg, Debra Lina 175
Krohg, Christian 93, 96
Kurosawa, Akira 52
Kushner, Tony 43

La Cage aux Folles 86
La Traviata 51, 57n60, 60–61, 170
Lajosi, Krisztina 92n13, 177, 187n23
Land, Ray 41, 56n28–29, 56n30–31, 56n34, 56n39
Langdon Lloyd, Robert 45, 113
LaRusso, Daniel 2
Last Five Years, The 73
Lauren, Liz 82, 121
Lee, Ming Cho 79, 110
legacies 122–124, 128
Les Mamelles de Tirésias 36–37, 55n23
Letts, Tracy 57n61, 109, 144, 159n9
LeWitt, Sol 30, 54n2, 56n52
light choreography 168–170; arc white 177; Arri HMI 172; Caravaggio-esque lighting 180; color in pigment works 176; color temperature 172; cyclorama 177; different kinds of emitters 172; propositions 167–168; Vari-Lite 172
light plot 9, 38–39, 102, 104, 110, 122, 124, 126, 142, 145, 146, 152–155, 158, 162; angles for 155; as a craft object 38–39; moving lights 158; not-so-natural angles in 104; as physical manifestation of the box

142, 162; physical structure determining 145; process of making 152–153; worksheet for 153–154, 158
lighting designers 5, 64, 78, 140, 185; aesthetic virtue and market value, understanding by 89; applied innovation by 49; as artist 109, 120; as craftsperson 38; essentialism in 122; methodologies 18; modes/periods to 96; production style of 90–91; responsibility of 142, 145, 159, 163; situation awareness of 163–164; technical rehearsal 124, 161
lighting for the stage; as abstract form 5, 94; as applied art 119; coexistence between two aesthetic movements 128; ephemeral and temporal form 5; essentialism in 120; good lighting 5, 129; in understanding story 73; vocabulary and grammar of stage design in 130
liminal space 84
Linda Vista 51, 57n61, 74–75, 101–102, 104, 109, 144, 154
line, and visual composition 131
Lion King, The 47, 86
Lives of Giants, The 15, 27n11
Livingston Christopher 53
Lloyd, Robert Langdon 45, 113
Lost Boys, The 19
Lovell, Sophie 123–124, 136n10–11
Lucas, George 52

Macbeth 139–141, 144, 145, 146, 153, 159n3, 159n5–6, 159n10, 159n17, 168–170, 176, 186n15
Macchio, Ralph 1
macro-cultures 14
Madison, Soyini D. 2, 9n2
magic sheet 126, 158
make, look, evaluate, and adapt (MLEA) 5, 25, 54, 65, 70, 161–162, 166, 189
manifestos 4–5, 8, 83, 94, 120, 123, 152, 159, 159n14–15
mapping 156–158
Mapplethorpe, Robert 15–16, 41, 44
market value 86–89
Marshall, Kerry James 19
Marx, Karl 98
Mary Page Marlowe 144, 159n9
Matochkina, Yulia 179
McKeown, Greg 122, 136n6
meaning-making of spectator 68–70, 73
Measure for Measure 105, 121–122, 136n7
Meditations on a Hobby Horse or the Roots of Artistic Form 105, 117n34

Merchant of Venice, The 182–183, 185, 187n31, 187n32
methodologies 12, 18–24, 25, 50, 60; affective critique 21–24; contextual critique 19–21; critical methodologies 50; formal critique 18–19; in the search for beauty 25
Meyer, Jan 41, 56n28–31, 56n34, 56n39, 84
Meyerhold, Vsevolod 11, 27n3, 46, 56n47, 111
micro-cultures 14
Mielziner, Jo 79
Miller, Nate 183
Mimesis as Make-Believe 74, 91n4
Miss Julie 50, 57n55, 56
Moayed, Arian 135
modernism 8, 87, 95, 96, 126–128
Moholy-Nagy, László 19
Monk, Debra 151
Morales, Sam 113
Morazin, Nathalie 37
Moscow Art Theatre 99
movement 125, 132–133; aesthetic 128; of arc of the lighting 178–182; artistic 6, 15, 50; avant-garde 105, 108; -isms 94–96; modernist art 87; naturalism as 97–99; revolutionary movements as catalysts 46; rhythmic 148
Muller, Louisa 92n16, 178, 187n21
Murphy, Sally 151
musical composition 130, 132–136
Muti, Riccardo 67
mystic and artist 30–31

Narciso, Alfredo 183
National Theatre of Scotland 85
naturalism 79, 94, 96, 97–100, 101, 104–105, 108, 116n15, 116n18
navigational markers 96
Necessity of Theatre, The 60, 71n1, 91n7, 117n39
needs list 157
negentropy 15, 44–46, 52, 189
Neher, Caspar 120
Newcomb, James 121
A 19 19
non-aesthetic negentropy 52
non-aesthetic trait 13, 15–16, 19, 24
Nwandu, Antoinette Chinonye 55n18, 159n12

Oklahoma! 86
Omran, Amal 107
OODA (Observe, Orient, Decide, Act) 165–166, 186n8
Opera, Seattle 84, 89, 92n23, 170, 186n16
Orfeo ed Euridice 72
On the Origen of Species 98

On the Question of Form 44, 56
Othello 43–44, 56n35, 56n36, 56n37, 120, 122
O'Toole, Garson 186n1
overlap 15, 95, 140, 148; between craft object and artwork 38–40; in cycle of innovation 48; of methodologies 18

palette 24, 35, 129–130, 155–156, 168, 174; color temperatures 172; electric lighting needs and 149; limiting 124, 173; maintaining 180; multi-attribute lights 49; self-styled Afrofuturistic palette 146
Palmer, Alex 28n14
Parks, Suzan-Lori 89, 92n34, 123, 136n8
Party People 33, 51–53, 55n17
Pascal, Romain 37
Pass Over 33, 55n18, 146–148, 153, 159n12, 167–168
pattern 19, 132, 133, 139
pedagogy 3–4
Pelteson, Benjamin 175
Pennington, Michael 181, 187n26
Perez, Jesse J. 53s
Phantom of the Opera, The 16, 86
Philosophical Enquiry into the Origin of Our Ideas of the Sublime and Beautiful, A 11–12, 27n6
philosophy redux 185–186
philosophy role 2
photographs, components 22, 32, 41, 110
physical dimension 144, 145
Picasso, Pablo 43, 51, 95
Pinter, Harold 73
plot (story) 73–74, 83–84, 89, 108–109, 142; Aristotle's Six Parts defining 143; George Lucas's borrowing of 52; *La Traviata* 170; of *Thérèse Raquin* 98; see also light plot
Poetics 142, 159n9
Postlewait, Thomas 111, 117n40
Prampolini, Enrico 105, 117n33
praxis 8, 160–186; deadlines 161; imperfection 170–174; light, propositions with 167–168; lighting choreographically 168–170; make, look, evaluate, and adapt (MLEA) 166; OODA (Observe, Orient, Decide, Act) 165–166; philosophy redux 185–186; pseudo-realism *and* expressionism 178–182; situation awareness 163–165; source, shadow, color 174–178; trust 182–185; writing light cues 161–163
Principles of Art, The 7, 9n6, 55n24, 55n25
privilege issue 67–68
production style 90–91, 97, 104
progression 95, 110, 128, 132, 185

proportion 132
pseudo-realism 94, 101, 173, 178–182

Queens Boulevard (The Musical) 133, 135, 137n24

Raft of the Medusa, The 25–26, 68
Ramos, Sophia 53
Rams, Dieter 5, 118–119, 123, 136n2, 136n9
Rancière, Jacques 62–64, 71n3–5, 71n14, 77, 84, 91n8
realism (Blergh) 100–104; artistic merit 100; curation 100; dramatic intent and stage-worthiness 100; naturalism and 104; *pseudo*-realistic 101, 109, 114
realism in theatrical design 15, 80, 95, 111, 119
(re)definitions 30
Régy, Claude 65
Rent 86
repetition 76, 132, 155
Requiem 67
research, dramaturgical 146–149
rhythmic dimension 144, 148, 162
Rockwell, Norman 87–89
Rodriguez, Robynn 53
Rogers, Horace V. 42, 53
Rome 24, 84, 177
Rooms by the Sea 58–59
Rorschach tests 69
Rosato, Mary Lou 113
Rosenblatt, Louise M. 64, 71n9–11, 71n14
Rosenthal, Todd 87, 102, 159n9
Ross, Alex 79, 92n14–15
Rothko, Mark 62
Rouse, Elizabeth Meadows 45
Rudnitsky, Konstantin 56n45
Ruiz, William 53
Ruiz-Sapp, Mildren 53
Russian Great October Socialist Revolution 46

San, Daniel 102, 130
Sapp, Steven 53
saturation 132, 156, 187n22
Savage, Issachah 179
Savage, Rick 127
Schaefer, Donovan O. 21, 28n26
Schneider, Jon Norman 135
Schoenberg, Arnold 27, 28n38, 49
Scott, Ridley 12
Scribe, Eugène 98
semiotics 35; index 35; signs in 35–36
set exploration 153–155

Seurat, George 51
Seven Basic Plots, The 74, 91n2
Shakespeare, William 44, 55n17, 56n35–38, 57n59, 76, 85, 90, 125, 136n7, 140, 144, 148, 153, 159n3, 159n5–7, 159n10, 159n17, 169, 173, 175, 182–183, 186n15, 187n20, 187n24–25, 187n29–32, 187n34
shape/form 132
Shapiro, Anna D. 81, 159n9
Shaw, George Bernard 99
Shelton, Jessie 113
Shepard, Sam 104, 110, 117n30–32
Sherman, Zachary Ray 103
Show Boat 85
Shrigley, David 29
situation awareness 163–165, 166, 186n3, 186n4
Siurina, Ekaterina 61
Skin of Our Teeth, The 76, 112–113, 115, 117n43
Smallwood, Namir 147
social revolutions and theatre 47
Solga, Kim 99, 116n19
song 17, 39, 42, 114, 143
Sourcebook on Naturalist Theatre, A 98, 116n13
Sovronsky, Alexander 45
space 43, 74, 76, 97, 104, 132, 144, 150, 169–172; bound in three dimensions 140; of coexistence between two aesthetic movements 128; dimensions of 78; in ideas list 153–155; large volumes of light in 109; liminal space 84; in musical composition 132; painting the space, in *Tannhäuser* 177; pseudo-realistic domestic space 150; shapes on the floor and 184; theatre as a space of collaboration 3; time and 163–164
Speaker's Progress, The 106–107, 117n36
spectacle 59, 89, 143
spectator 24, 36; aesthetic string theory of 83; aesthetic virtue and 89; affective stylistics 63; artist and 7; artwork and, transaction between 68, 129; in artwork investigation 17; basic competencies of 66–67; competency 65; conceptual shift of 42; in contextual critique 19–21; design elements to attract 106; education 65–67; efficacy of theatre and 90–91; 'emancipated' 63; evaluating 70; expressionistic 108; feedback loop between the artwork and 73; good audience member 80; integrative 43; interest of 60–62; in meaning-making of the artwork 7, 68–70; operator and 22; privilege 67–68; response and criticism 18; response to aesthetic and non-aesthetic properties 27; spectare 59; spotlight 70; threshold concepts altering the perceptions of 44; transaction 62–65; view from a different culture 33
spectrum 94, 131; of aesthetic virtue 6–7; between pseudo-realistic and purely expressionistic 5; competency in 65; of criticism 63; good art side of 87; primary witnessing end of 81; pseudo-realistic side of 109, 178; of theatrical abstraction 102, 104–105, 115, 145, 153, 178
Spiderman: Turn Off the Dark 86
spotlight 60, 70, 112, 114
standard category of art 16
Stanislavski, Konstantin 99
Star Wars movie 14, 52
Starlight Express 86
Starry Night, The 18
States, Bert O. 100, 116n23, 117n24
Stickney, Timothy D. 181
Still, Clyfford 67, 70
Stober, Heidi 171
story 63, 73–76, 85, 114; analysis 142–143; beats tying 115; in dramaturgical dimension 144; form as integral part of 123, 134; lighting echoing 129, 136, 140; *Linda Vista* 109; stage design in telling 100; telling a 91
Stradivari, Antonio 49
Strauss, Richard 84, 92n22–23
Stravinsky, Igor 49
Strindberg, August 50, 57n55–56, 93, 96, 99, 105, 116n8, 116n15
structuralist lens 50
Study of Perspective 32
Sunset Boulevard 86
surface phenomena 50

Taking of Christ 160, 180
Tannhäuser 79, 92n12, 174–179, 187n21
Tantsits, Peter 23
Taymor, Danya 55n18, 92n19, 167, 168
temporal composition 5, 134–136
texture 33, 95, 132, 148
Thanksgiving: Girl Praying 87, 88
theatre 52; as abstract form 94; abstraction importance in 105; aesthetic virtue 89–90; aim of 24; architecture of 145; Artaud on 125; artist to creative team 73; artwork redux 85–86; artwork to production 73; choices in 115; complexity of 16; definition 8, 73; efficacy of theatre 90; Eurocentric theatre 66, 105; experiencing emotion 83–84; expressionism in 94; intentional

beauty presented 26; lighting choreography in 2, 168; liminal space 84; manifestations of 4, 8; market value 86–89; naturalism in 98–99; near-constant 35; need for 189; people 77–80; production style 90–91; evolutionary movements as catalysts for artistic change 46; self-referential aesthetic of theatre-making 111; sign system of 112; as a space of collaboration 3–4; spectator to audience 73; story 73–76; storytelling 136; time and place 76–77; in the United States 47; to witness 80–83
Theatre for a New Audience (TFANA) 43–44, 51, 56n35, 57n59, 76, 96, 112–113, 116n8, 117n43, 120, 141, 146, 149, 159n3, 178, 182, 182–183, 187n31
Theatre Libre 99
theatrical abstraction 8, 93–116, 120, 143, 145, 153, 172, 178, 180; choices 115–116; expressionistic 108–111; importance of 105; interrogating -isms 94–96; lighting designers, modes/periods for 96; modernism 95; naturalism 97–100; navigational markers 96; realism in 95; spectrum 94; see also realism (Blergh)
theatrical/theatricality 5, 94, 104, 111–112, 139, 143; design process 119; from lighting design perspective 17; production 84; spectrum of 145, 153, 178; works of art 123
Theory for Theatre Studies: Space 99, 116n19
Thérèse Raquin 98, 116n14
Thigpen, Haynes 183
Thomas, Storm 113
Thompson, John Douglas 45, 141, 183
thought 3, 125, 143; abstract 13; mood and 21; rational 87; synthetic 3
Thuy, Chantal 75
time, as dimension of composition 9, 44, 73, 76–77, 90, 140, 144, 161
tint 132, 156
Tipton, Jennifer 5, 142, 174, 176
Tolstoy, Leo 33–34, 55n12, 55n19, 55n21
Tosca 85, 108, 117n38
Toward a Concept of Postmodernism 95, 116n3, 126, 137n18, 186n14
transaction 60, 62–65, 69, 71n11–14, 89, 129
transactional reader-response theory 64
transformative threshold 41–42
troublesome threshold 44
True West 101, 103–104, 109–110, 117n30–32, 145, 150
trust 162, 182–185
Tucker, Jeffrey 23
Tyson, Lois 5, 13, 18, 27n10, 28n21, 35, 50, 55n21, 55n22, 57n57–58, 63, 64, 71n7–8, 71n12, 71n16

Ugelstad, Janike Sverdrup 116n6

Vakhtangov, Yevgeny 42, 46, 56n46, 111, 117n41
value: aesthetic 120; market 86–89; of spectators 63; virtue and, relationship 90; visual composition and 132
van der Rohe, Mies 51
Van Wieringen, Pier 66, 71n19
variable category of art 16–17, 41, 66, 78, 173
variety/unity 132
Verdi, Giuseppe 57n60, 67
Visiting Edna 149–152, 149–153, 157, 159n13
visual composition 130–133, 134, 146
visual dimension 146
visual dramaturgy 125, 137n16
visual research 149
vocabulary: angle 130; aria 133; articulation 132; balance 131; chroma 131; color 131; color temperature 131; contrast 131; depth 131; dissonant 133; dominant/recessive 131; dynamics 133; emphasis 133; energy 134; expectation 134; flow 134; form 134; harmony 133; hierarchy 131; hue 131; inertia 134; intensity 131; intent 134; leitmotif 133; line 131; movement 132; musical composition 132–136; pattern 132; progression 132; proportion 132; repetition 132; rhythm 133; saturation 132; shape/form 132; space 132; temporal composition 134–136; texture 132; time 136; tint 132; value 132; variety/unity 132; visual composition 130–132

Wabi-Sabi for Artists, Designers, Poets & Philosophers 173, 186n18
Wagner, Richard 33, 55n13–14, 71n6, 78–80, 92n11–13, 108, 133, 167, 177, 187n21
Wagnerian hyperbole 78
Wake, Caroline 81, 92n18
Walton, Kendall L. 16–17, 20, 28n16–20, 28n24–25, 29–31, 48, 56n53, 66, 71n21, 74, 91n4
Way of Art, The 31
ways list 152–157
Ways of Seeing 59, 86, 92n27, 92n28, 92n33, 129

Webern, Anton 49
West Side Story 86
What Is Art? essay 33, 55n12, 55n19
Where Elephants Weep 33, 51–52, 55n16
Wicked 86, 182, 185
Wilder, Thornton 76, 90, 91n6, 117n43
Wilson, August 46, 56n43–44
Wilson, Robert 32
Winton, Graham 183
Witkiewicz, StanisławIgnacy 32–33, 55n10, 55n15

Woodruff, Paul 60, 69, 71n1–2, 71n24, 77, 83, 85, 91n7, 92n20, 92n21, 92n26, 108, 117n39
Woolf, Virginia 11, 27n4

Yabroff, Jennie 9n5
Young, James O. 13, 27n9, 34–35, 48, 51–52, 55n20, 56n51, 57n62, 57n64–65

Zeffirelli, Franco 89
Zinn, David 149, 159n13
Zola, Emile 98–99, 116n14, 116n18

For Product Safety Concerns and Information please contact our EU
representative GPSR@taylorandfrancis.com
Taylor & Francis Verlag GmbH, Kaufingerstraße 24, 80331 München, Germany

www.ingramcontent.com/pod-product-compliance
Lightning Source LLC
Chambersburg PA
CBHW070608300426
44113CB00010B/1457